Brainard's Hotel Register Boulder, Colorado

1880

An Annotated Index

Compiled by Dina C. Carson

Brainard's Hotel Register
Boulder, Colorado
1880

An Annotated Index

Compiled by Dina C. Carson

Published by:

Iron Gate Publishing
P.O. Box 999
Niwot, CO 80544

Copyright © 2015 by Dina C. Carson, Iron Gate Publishing

Printed in the United States of America

ISBN   1-879579-86-3   ISBN 13   978-1-879579-86-6

Introduction

Brainard's Hotel was built in 1874 by Anthony Arnett, a leading merchant in early Boulder, Colorado. Originally the hotel was named the Sherman House, then the National House before it became Brainard's Hotel. The hotel was one of Boulder's elite hotels. It was a two-story brick building located at 1025-1027 Pearl Street. Thomas Corwin Brainard was the proprietor from 1877 until 1884.

Some of the more notable occurances in the register are:

- June 11 1880, Friday night, Fay Templeton, Star Alliance Opera Company at Boettcher's Hall
- June 12 1880, Saturday night, the Two Headed Lady Combination appearing at Union Hall Saturday Evening, along with J Ruth, Champion Rifle, Mrs D Ruth, Pistol Shots of the World, and Christine Millie and Blanche Brook, the two-headed lady.
- July 19, 1880 and September 19, 1880, Plunkett Troupe, consisting of Charles, Blanche, Carra and Sue Plunkett.
- Aug 1-3, 1880, P. T. Barnum's Show.
- August 21, 1880, Brainard's Hotel hosted a dinner for former President Ulysses S. Grant and his wife. More than 100 people attended the ten course dinner along with cocktails and desserts while they were entertained by the Cremona Park Brass Band of Denver.
- September 23, 1880, the Longmont Coronet Band was in town.

Some of the more notable signatures in the register are those of Philadelphia financier Charles Yerkes, Herman and Charles Boettcher, and Colorado Governor John L Routt.

The register begins on the 6th of March 1880 and ends on the 18th of December 1880. There are no page numbers in the book, so none are given in the index. The date of registry is given instead.

In this index, the names and locations are spelled as they were in the register, including the obvious misspellings, except for 11Worth, Kansas which was a common shorthand for Leavenworth, Kansas. The shorthand has been spelled out as Leavenworth. The word "City" was often used to indicate Boulder.

Most of the time, patrons signed the book for themselves, although there are places where a clerk has signed on behalf of the patron.

Each page has a column for the patron's name, place of residence, time and rooms. The abbreviations B, D, S, and L are given in the column for time. Based upon the order in which these abbreviations were used, it is likely that they stood for breakfast, dinner, supper and late arrivals.

Printed at the top of each page is:
Brainard's Hotel

For good livery inquire at the office
Guests without baggage please pay in advance.

All Moneys, Jewels, Coats, Valises and other valuables, must be left at the Office, and checks received for them otherwise the Proprietor wil not be responsible for any loss.

Boulder, Col.
T. C. Brainard, Proprietor

The top of the blotter page reads:
Established 1864, James T Hair, Publisher, 69 Dearborn St, Chicago
Leading Business Houses of Central City, Col.
Advertising ... Register Books ... April 16th, 18..

The register has sign-in sheets separated by blotter pages that are covered with the advertisements of businesses, including:
- Faribanks Scales, John Ray, Agent. No. 393 Blake St, Cor. Sixteenth. Denver, Col.
- Charles Weitfle, Portrait and Landscape Photographer, Main Street, Headquarters for Stereoscopic Views
- Dr. D M Daley, Surgeon Mechanical Dentist, Office over Union Bank, Central City, Officer hours ... All Work Warranted.
- The First National Bank, Officers, J A Thatcher, Pres, Otto Sauer Vice Pres, Frank C Young, Cash. Capital Paid in-$50,000, Surplus-$20,000, Deposits-$250,000.
- Wm McLaughlin, dealer in Harness, Saddlery Hardward, Bridles, Collas, etc. Eureka Street.
- Best's Pharmacy. Headquarters. Drugs, Mill Chemicals, Etc. Opposite Teller House.
- Dentfcher Advocat. Avocat Francais. J. F. Frueauff. Attorney & Counselor at Law. Rooms 11, 12 & 13, McCLintock Block, P.O. Box 1957 Denver, Col. Have had nineteen years practice at

the Bar; Offer my services for the purpose of examining Land and Mining Titles; Make collections in any part of the State of Colorado.

- Sam V Newell. L S Newell, Jr. Newell Bros. Hay, Grain and Coal. Lawrence Street.
- Otto Sauer, Wholesale and Retail Dealer in Groceries, Provisions, Confectionery & Crockery. Wines, Liquors, Tobacco, Cigars, Etc. Agent for Laflin & Rand Powder Co. Also, Dealers in Flour and Feed. Main Street.
- Gilbert Hubbard & Co. 209 to 208 S Water Street, Chicago. Dealers in Cotton Goods, Tents, Awnings, Waterproof Covers, Twines & Cordage, Flags & Banners, Wire Rope.
- City Book Store. Chandler Freeman. Books, Stationery, Cutlery, Gold Pens, Wall Paper, Toys, Fancy Goods, Picture Frames, Mountain Views, Musical Instruments, etc. News Depot. Main Street.
- M.E. Pace & Co. Wholesale Confectioners. Confectionsers' Supplies and Tools. 211 & 213 Lake St. Chicago.
- Central Clothing House. Fine Clothing and Furnishing Goods. Hats and Caps. Trenoweth & Polglase, Proprietors.
- H. J. Hawley, dealer in Staple and Fancy Groceries, Crockery, Glassware, Furniture, Powder & Fuse. Hay and Grain. Main Street.
- Ensminger & Davis, Manufacturers of Mining Machinery, Furnace Castings, Water Jackets, Engines, Boilers, Saw Mills and Hoisting Machines, Denver, Colorado.
- J. A. Smith, Undertaker and Dealer in New and Second-Hand Furniture and Brass-Furnishing Goods of all kinds. Head of Main Street.
- Manufacturers of Street Cars Omnibuses, Business, Freight and Circus Wagons, Cages, &c. Andrew Wight Co. 2300 Broadway. St. Louis.
- H. Boettcher & Co. Hardware, Stoves and Tinware. Dry Goods, Clothing, Boots, Shoes & Groceries. Leadville & Boulder, Colorado.
- Novelty MFG Company, Manufacturers of Improved Hotel and House Annunciators, Burglar and Thero Alarms, Electro-Medical Apparatus, Telegraph Supplies, Seals, Stencils, Rubber Stamps, etc. 284 Sixteenth St, Denver, Col.

- W. W. Goodrich, M.A.; C. E., Architect & Sanitary Engineer. Office over First National Bank, Denver, Col.
- W. T. Newell Lumber. Yard & Office, Gregory Street.
- Johnson & Co., Plumbers, Gas and Steam Fitters, 299 Fifteenth Street, P.O. Box 1741, Denver, Col.
- C Cove & Sons, Denver Armory Man'frs & Wholesale & Retail Dealers in Guns, Fishing Tackle and all kinds of Sporting Goods. 340 1-2 Blake St, Denver, Col.
- For Guide to over 1,000 HOtels, together with their Rates per Day: Also the Estimated Population of Cities and Towns, where they are Located, See Inside Front Cover of this Book.
- Annex 47 (Central City, Col) 9-4-'79-260

The original *Brainard's Hotel Register, Boulder, Colorado 1880* is held by the Boulder Historical Society and is on display in its museum. The *Register* is not generally available for research. Many thanks to the museum staff for allowing the Boulder Pioneers Project to photograph the book in order to create this index.

A

Abbott, S C
Des Moines; 1880 Oct 2; Saturday; L; room 2

Abernathy, __nd Sr (Mrs)
& Children; Leavenworth; 1880 June 18; Friday; S; room 44

Able, Geo
Bod & Daniels; 1880 Mar 24; Wednesday; D

Abshire, J H
Chillicothe, Mo; 1880 Aug 5; Thursday; S; room 5

Acheson, David
City; 1880 Sept 21; Tuesday; L; rm 10

Acheson, Geo B
Fairfield; 1880 Sept 1; Wednesday; S; room 11

Acheson, George
Fairfield, Iowa; 1880 Sept 21; Tuesday; S; room 10

Acheson, M W
& Wife; Pittsburgh; 1880 Sept 21; Tuesday; S; room 21

Acky, Frank
1880 Aug 3; Tuesday; D

Aclains, H W
Denver; 1880 Aug 21; Saturday; D

Adams, Mrs
Davenport, Ia; 1880 Aug 11; Wednesday; D; room 3

Adams, Mrs
Denver; 1880 Aug 18; Wednesday; S; room 8

Adams, Mrs
Absent after Bkfst; 1880 Sept 1; Wednesday

Adams, W D
Chicago; 1880 Aug 3; Tuesday; D; room 2
Chicago; 1880 Nov 12; Friday; S; room 1

Adler, Chas E
San Francisco; 1880 July 19; Monday; D; room 1

Akin, James
City with T H W; 1880 Sept 17; Friday; S

Albert, Man__
San Francisco; 1880 Apr 1; Thursday; S; room 16

Albert, W W H
Philada; 1880 Mar 26; Friday; S; rm 6

Aldman, M D
Cheyenne, Wy; 1880 Nov 6; Saturday; L; room 1

Aldner, R (Mrs) & Son
Denver; 1880 Sept 8; Wednesday; D

Alexander, D
Denver; 1880 July 27; Tuesday; S; room 5

Alexander, L
Denver; 1880 Apr 1; Thursday; S; room 6
Denver; 1880 Apr 3; Saturday; S; room 33
Denver; 1880 May 3; Monday; S; room 12
Denver; 1880 May 4; Tuesday; S; room 3
Denver; 1880 May 6; Thursday; D; room 6
Denver; 1880 June 10; Thursday; D
Denver; 1880 June 7; Monday; S; room 11
Denver; 1880 June 8; Tuesday

Alexander, L (cont.)
Denver; 1880 July 29; Thursday; D; room 8
Denver; 1880 July 30; Friday; S; rm 5

Allen, Ed
Jamestown, Col; 1880 July 5; Mon; D

Allen, H C
St Louis; 1880 Nov 22; Monday; S; room 3

Allen, H F
Denver; 1880 Mar 24; Wednesday; S; room 1
Denver; 1880 May 14; Friday; S; rm 1

Allen, H T
Denver; 1880 Dec 13; Monday; L; room 3

Allen, J R
Agt Tag Tanpeldon [?] N York; 1880 June 8; Tuesday; D; room 10

Allen, R (Mrs)
Leadville, Colo; 1880 Dec 18; Saturday; D; room 3

Allen, R H
Denver; 1880 May 22; Saturday; S; room 25

Allenton, Thomas
Louisville; 1880 Nov 27; Saturday; D

Allie, Martha A
Boulder; 1880 Apr 3; Saturday; S; room 15

Allison, Chas E
Wilmington, Del; 1880 Oct 29; Friday; S

Allison, Sam'l
Tenica, Ohio; 1880 July 21; Wednesday; S; room 6

Allison, Sam'l M
Henice, Ind; 1880 July 22; Thursday

Allison, Sam'l M
Xenia, O; 1880 July 29; Thursday; S; room 12

Allman, Charles
Ward; 1880 July 3; Saturday; S; rm 34
Wood, O; 1880 Nov 18; Thursday; S; room 26
City; 1880 Nov 20; Saturday; S; rm 25

Allsebrook, G S
Salina; 1880 Nov 22; Monday; D

Alpin, F A
Chicago; 1880 Sept 7; Tuesday; S; room 11
Chicago; 1880 Dec 9; Thursday; S; room 2

Altenstein, A
New York; 1880 Mar 8; Monday; S; room 2

Altman, M D
Cheyenne; 1880 May 28; Friday; S; room 1

Alvord, C C
Denver; 1880 May 17; Monday; D
Denver; 1880 May 27; Thursday; D
Denver; 1880 Aug 11; Wednesday; D
Denver, Col; 1880 Aug 14; Saturday; S

Alvord, C C
1880 Aug 15; Sunday; S
1880 Aug 4; Wednesday; S; room 5
1880 July 12; Monday; S; room 12
1880 July 2; Friday; S; room 10
1880 July 26; Monday; D
1880 Sept 20; Monday; S; room 12

Alvord, Samuel
1880 Apr 6; Tuesday; L; room 28
Denver; 1880 Aug 14; Saturday; D
Denver; 1880 Oct 13; Wednesday; S; room 1

Alwood, W J
Gothic City; 1880 Mar 21; Sunday; B with ALW; Longmont; 1880 Mar 27; Saturday; B

Ambrook (Dr)
& Wife; 1880 Aug 21; Saturday; D

Ames, D P
New Orleans, La; 1880 July 9; Friday; S; room 12

Anderson, C W
County Court Jury; 1880 Mar 11; Thursday; S

Anderson, Finley
New York; 1880 Mar 15; Sunday; S; room 4

Anderson, H Y
Denver; 1880 Aug 30; Monday; L; room 11

Anderson, Hattie (Miss)
Denver; 1880 May 15; Saturday; S; room 5

Anderson, J W
Denver; 1880 June 30; Wednesday; D; room 19

Anderson, Jos (Dr)
Golden; 1880 May 15; Saturday; S

Anderson, R Y
Alma, Col; 1880 Mar 17; Wednesday; S; room 6

Anderson, W C
Nobles Company, New York; 1880 Oct 23; Saturday; D; room 14

Andres, Wm
Black Hawk; 1880 May 15; Sat; D

Andress, W
Black Hawk; 1880 May 16; Sunday; S; room 25

Andrews, A E
City; 1880 Dec 17; Friday; S

Andrews, C
City; 1880 Oct 29; Friday; S
City; 1880 Nov 12; Friday; B

Andrews, Chas
City; 1880 Aug 22; Sunday; B

Angelo, A C
Ward; 1880 July 8; Thursday; L; rm 20

Anguotus, Ellen (Miss)
Spring Dale; 1880 Aug 3; Tuesday; D

Aniser, C T
St Joe; 1880 July 3; Saturday; S; rm 1

Anstee, Alderman
Denver; 1880 Aug 2; Monday; S

Anstee, George
Denver; 1880 Aug 21; Saturday; S

Anster, George
Unreadable; 1880 Mar 30; Tues

Aplin, F A
Chicago; 1880 Mar 15; Sunday; D; room 15
Chicago; 1880 Apr 20; Tuesday; S; room 2
Chicago; 1880 May 27; Thursday; S; room 6
Chicago; 1880 July 15; Thursday; D; room 1
Chicago; 1880 Oct 22; Friday; D; room 3

Arbuthnot, Mrs
1880 Aug 26; Thursday; D

Armington, E Howard
Leadville, Col; 1880 May 28; Friday; D; room 34

Armstrong, F W
New York; 1880 Aug 28; Saturday; D; room 1
New York; 1880 Aug 30; Monday; D; room 2
New York; 1880 Sept 6; Monday; S; room 6

Armstrong, Scott J
Denver; 1880 May 19; Wednesday; D

Arnold, Ed P
St Vrains; 1880 May 19; Wed; D

Atchison, David
Kansas; 1880 Aug 15; Sunday; B

Aufet, S M
Pool, Ind; 1880 June 14; Monday; S; room 3

Auiser, C T
St Joe; 1880 Apr 12; Monday; D; rm 6

Austen, Geo
Denver; 1880 Oct 18; Monday; S

Auster, Geo
Denver; 1880 July 8; Thursday; S

Austin, F C
Kansas City; 1880 Aug 19; Thursday; L; room 2
Kansas City; 1880 Aug 20; Friday; L; room 2

Austin, Geo
Denver; 1880 Aug 22; Sunday; S

Austin, J M
St Louis; 1880 May 24; Monday; D; room 2

Austin, Jas A
1880 Mar 16; Tuesday; S; room 12

Averill, A M
St Louis; 1880 Aug 14; Saturday; L; room 2

Avery, F C
Fort Collins; 1880 Sept 12; Sunday; B

Avery, S P
Breckenridge; 1880 Dec 1; Wednesday; L; room 11

Avery, Wm H
Lamar, MO; 1880 June 20; Sunday; S; room 35

Lamar, MO; 1880 June 21; Monday; S; room 29

B

Babcock, W N
Denver; 1880 Apr 12; Monday; D
Denver; 1880 Apr 21; Wednesday; S

Babcock, Wm
With Jones 6; 1880 June 4; Friday; D

Backus, F A
Nederland; 1880 Apr 13; Tuesday; D

Backus, Fred A
Melburn, IL; 1880 Apr 2; Friday; S; room 13

Bacon, A R
Longmont; 1880 July 5; Monday; D

Bacon, Ward S
Denver, Col; 1880 Sept 9; Thursday; S

Bagby, M A
Spring Dale; 1880 Sept 11; Sat; D

Bagg, C L
& Wife; Barnums Show; 1880 Aug 1; Sunday; L; room 10

Bagley, H F
Seltzeybons Spring Dale, Colo; 1880 Aug 3; Tuesday; D

Bagnall, E J
Albion; 1880 Sept 25; Saturday; L; room C

Bailey, A R
San Jose; 1880 Oct 28; Thursday; S; room 12

Bailey, G F
Manager, Breakfast only; 1880 Aug 3; Tuesday; B

Baker, A T
Longmont; 1880 Aug 3; Tuesday; D

Baker, J A
Golden; 1880 May 15; Saturday; S

Baker, John A
Denver; 1880 Apr 26; Monday; D

Baldof, C S
St Louis; 1880 Mar 11; Thursday; S; room 2
St Louis; 1880 May 15; Saturday; D; room 1

Baldorf, C S
St Louis; 1880 Sept 22; Wednesday; D; room 1

Baldwin, C G
Longmont, guest LPS; 1880 Sept 11; Saturday; S
Longmont; 1880 Sept 22; Wednesday
Longmont; 1880 Sept 24; Friday; D

Baldwin, F W
Denver; 1880 Dec 7; Tuesday; S; rm 6

Baldwin, H L
Agt Bryants History; Denver; 1880 Apr 21; Wednesday; D; room 26
Denver; 1880 July 5; Mon; L; rm 28

Baldwin, H W
Denver; 1880 Mar 31; Wednesday; D

Ball, C
Chicago; 1880 Apr 27; Tuesday; L; room 35

Ball, C A
Ward; 1880 Dec 1; Wednesday; S; room 27

Ball, J J
Denver, Col; 1880 Aug 21; Saturday; D

Ball, J W
St Louis; 1880 Apr 27; Tuesday; D
St Louis; 1880 Nov 15; Monday; S; room 1
St Louis; 1880 Nov 16; Tuesday; D; room 1

Ball, Richard
Jamestown; 1880 July 5; Monday; L; room 25

Ballard, Helen (Miss)
Springfield, Ohio; 1880 Aug 2; Monday; D; room 8

Ballard, Susie (Miss)
Springfield, Ohio; 1880 Aug 2; Monday; D; room 8

Ballard, W W
Springfield, O; 1880 Apr 30; Friday; S; room 44

Bander, A
Juniata, NE; 1880 Apr 9; Friday; S; room 26

Bangs, Mark
Chicago; 1880 July 12; Monday; S
Chicago, IL; 1880 Mar 9; Tuesday; S; room 15

Baniger, L S
Omaha; 1880 June 9; Wednesday; S; room 15

Banks, F B
Sugar Loaf; 1880 Oct 15; Friday; D

Barber, Matthew
Louisville; 1880 July 26; Monday; room 28

Barclay, J C
Longmont; 1880 Aug 3; Tuesday; D

Bard, Irvin
Sugar Loaf; 1880 June 2; Wednesday; L; room 34

Barker, C T
Union City; 1880 Mar 30; Tuesday; L; room 27

Barker, E J
Valmont; 1880 May 14; Friday; D
Valmont; 1880 May 17; Monday; D

Barker, Geo L
Erie, Col; 1880 Apr 7; Wednesday; L; room 28

Barnard, F A
Denver; 1880 Aug 21; Saturday; D
Denver; 1880 Oct 19; Tuesday; D; room 2
Denver; 1880 Oct 30; Saturday; D

Barnes, F J
Chicago; 1880 July 26; Monday; S; room 44
Chicago; 1880 Nov 9; Tuesday; S; room 11
Chicago; 1880 Dec 8; Wednesday; D; room 1

Barnes, F J
& Wife; Chicago; 1880 June 25; Friday; D; room 16

Barnes, Milton H
New York; 1880 May 20; Thursday; D; room 6

Barnes, Mrs
Mountains; 1880 Aug 26; Thursday; D; room 3

Barnett, James
& Wife; Sommerville; 1880 Aug 3; Tuesday; S; room 8
with J H S; 1880 Oct 21; Thursday; D; room 35

Barney, Geo
Louisville; 1880 Apr 2; Friday; D

Barney, John Y
Express; New York City; 1880 May 25; Tuesday; S; room 2

Barney, N D
Denver; 1880 Nov 13; Saturday; D

Barnum, Geo W
& Wife; 1880 Oct 23; Saturday; D; room 33

Barnum, J E
Denver; 1880 Sept 30; Thursday; D; room 3

Barnum, Mrs
Grand Rapids, MI; 1880 May 14; Friday; D; room 16

Baron
Denver; 1880 Apr 24; Saturday; L; room 12

Baron, N D
Denver; 1880 Nov 17; Wednesday; L; room 33
Denver; 1880 Dec 11; Saturday; D

Baron, Nicholas D
Paris; 1880 Oct 19; Tuesday; D

Barr, Ivan
Gold Hill; 1880 Mar 26; Friday; L; room 28
Gold Hill; 1880 Mar 28; Sunday; L; room 35
Gold Hill; 1880 May 8; Saturday; S; room 12
Gold Hill; 1880 May 9; Sunday; S; room 5
Gold Hill; 1880 May 14; Friday; L; room 32
Gold Hill; 1880 May 15; Saturday; S; room 32
Gold Hill; 1880 July 1; Thursday; S; room 14

Barr, J N
Golden, Colo; 1880 Aug 26; Thursday; L; room 33

Barrowman, Chas
Erie, guest of Brown; 1880 June 5; Saturday; D

Barrows, E S
Chicago; 1880 Nov 20; Saturday; S; room 12

Barry, A D
1880 Aug 10; Tuesday; S; room 28

Bartell, H
Providence; 1880 Mar 22; Monday; L; room 28
Providence; 1880 Mar 23; Tues
Providence; 1880 Mar 25; Thursday; L; room 27
Providence; 1880 Apr 20; Tuesday; L; room 27

Bartels, H
Jamestown; 1880 June 21; Monday; L; room 29
Jamestown; 1880 June 23; Wednesday; L; room 28
Jamestown; 1880 July 10; Saturday; L; room 33
Jamestown; 1880 July 10; Saturday; S; room 29

Barter, John
South Boulder; 1880 May 11; Tuesday; D

Bartholoma, Geo
Dan Castello & Co Circus; 1880 May 23; Sunday; L

Basam, John
Wife & Daughter; Madison, Wis; 1880 July 24; Saturday; S; room 19 & 20

Bash, C A
Denver; 1880 Oct 17; Sun; S; rm 28

Bashor, M E
Left Hand; 1880 Aug 3; Tuesday; D

Bassett, Fred
Agent; 1880 May 11; Tues; S; rm 27

Bassett, G M
Denver, Col; 1880 July 10; Saturday; D; room 17

Bassett, J M
& Wife; Denver, Col; 1880 Aug 14; Saturday; D; room 16

Batchelder & Sebastian
1880 Aug 3; Tuesday; B

Batchelder, Hattie (Miss)
Left Hand; 1880 Aug 3; Tuesday; D

Batchelder, W W
NiWot; 1880 Aug 3; Tuesday; D

Batchelor, J D
Leavenworth, Ks; 1880 Nov 5; Friday; L; room 2

Batchelor, J P
Leavenworth, Ks; 1880 June 30; Wednesday; S; room 3
Leavenworth, Ks; 1880 Dec 15; Wednesday; D; room 1

Batchelor, Jas P
Leavenworth, KS; 1880 Apr 19; Monday; L; room 1

Bates, J E
Denver; 1880 Oct 8; Friday; S

Baton, M
Greeley; 1880 Apr 1; Thursday; D; room 26

Batterburg, Thomas R
Wilmington, Del; 1880 Oct 29; Friday; S

Batterbury, Thomas
With J A R; 1880 Sept 13; Monday; D

Baucroft, Q A L
Chicago; 1880 Aug 12; Thursday; L; room 12

Baxter, E K
Central; 1880 July 28; Wednesday; D; room 5

Bayler, B N
Denver; 1880 July 10; Saturday; D

Beach, C H
Denver; 1880 Sept 6; Monday; D; room 1

Beach, C H (cont.)
Denver; 1880 Oct 6; Wednesday; L; room 10
Denver; 1880 Dec 2; Thursday; L; room 35

Bean, D V
with Donner; 1880 Oct 20; Wednesday; D

Bearce, H B
Denver; 1880 Nov 11; Thursday; S; room 2
Denver; 1880 Nov 13; Saturday; S
Denver; 1880 Dec 10; Friday; D; rm B

Beason, J A (K P)
Denver; 1880 Aug 16; Monday; S; room 3

Beason, J H
Denver; 1880 Dec 13; Monday; S; room 11

Beaumont, Lathe (Miss)
1880 Apr 22; Thursday; D; room 8

Becher, Charles
Kiowa; 1880 July 27; Tues; S; rm 29

Beck, W E
Denver; 1880 July 30; Friday; D

Beck, Wm E
Boulder ; 1880 May 8; Saturday; D
Denver; 1880 June 2; Wednesday; D; room 16
Denver; 1880 July 9; Friday; D; rm 16 & Wife; Denver; 1880 Nov 20; Saturday; S; room 16
Denver; 1880 Oct 26; Tuesday; D

Beckwith, W C
Denver; 1880 Mar 6; Saturday; D
Denver; 1880 Mar 24; Wednesday; D
City; 1880 Sept 8; Wednesday; S
Boulder; 1880 Sept 9; Thursday; L; room 29
Denver; 1880 May 2; Sunday; S

Beckwith, W C (cont.)
City; 1880 Oct 27; Wednesday; L; room 5

Bedal, J J
Sunshine; 1880 Sept 22; Wed; D

Bedson, D H
Denver; 1880 Sept 11; Saturday; B

Beecher, J H
New York City; 1880 Aug 17; Tuesday; S; room 2

Beecher, P H
New York; 1880 May 27; Thursday; D; room 14

Beem, D N
Ottawa, Neb; 1880 Aug 19; Thursday; S; room 1

Beer, Max
Denver; 1880 Dec 15; Wednesday; S

Beggs, Johnson
Saint Louis; 1880 July 26; Monday; D

Belcher, J W
Golden; 1880 May 15; Saturday; S; room 14

Belford, James B
1880 Oct 16; Saturday; S; room 16

Bell, Charles
unreadable; 1880 Oct 3; Sunday; L; room 29

Bemis, H G
Longmont Cornet Band; 1880 Sept 23; Thursday; S; room 3

Benedict, F M
Chicago; 1880 Nov 12; Friday; D
Lawrence, Ks; 1880 Oct 23; Sat; D

Benedict, H S
Osage Mission, Ks; 1880 July 15; Thursday; S; room 3

Benjamin, M
Chicago; 1880 Oct 6; Wednesday; S; room 3

Bennett, John
Sugar Loaf; 1880 Apr 10; Saturday; L; room 26

Bennett, Thomas
Wickes, Montana; 1880 Apr 5; Monday; S; room 3

Benson, C
Philadelphia; 1880 May 23; Sunday; S; room 15

Benson, I
Ward Dist; 1880 Mar 25; Thursday; S; room 28
Ward; 1880 Apr 13; Tuesday; D; rm 27
Ward; 1880 May 24; Monday; D
Ward Dist; 1880 June 2; Wed; D
& Wife; Ward; 1880 Aug 3; Tuesday; D; room 33

Bentley, T D
Denver; 1880 Dec 1; Wednesday; S; room 10
Denver; 1880 Dec 4; Saturday; L; room 12
Denver; 1880 Dec 5; Sunday; L; rm 3
Denver; 1880 Dec 14; Tuesday; D

Berger, Frank
Longmont Cornet Band; 1880 Sept 23; Thursday; S

Berin, L M
Denver; 1880 Nov 3; Wednesday; S

Berkley, Junius
City; 1880 Dec 14; Tuesday; S
Guest of Blake; 1880 Oct 2; Sat; D

Berlin, I
Wife & Daughter; City; 1880 May 11; Tuesday; D

Berlin, Isaac
Returned to Denver; 1880 Nov 23; Tuesday; D
Wife & Daughter; City; 1880 Sept 3; Friday; S

Bert, Earl
St Jo; 1880 June 29; Tuesday; D

Bertwick, Geo
Omaha; 1880 Oct 26; Tuesday; L; room 1

Besony, J R
St Louis; 1880 Apr 26; Monday; S; room 16

Bettis, Mrs
Holden, Mo; 1880 Aug 17; Tuesday; D

Birdsell, D H
San Francisco, Cal; 1880 Oct 26; Tuesday; D

Birney, A M
Michigan; 1880 Aug 8; Sunday; D; room 6

Birney, A M
Estes Park, Col; 1880 July 25; Sunday; L; room 6

Bishet, Aaron
1880 Aug 21; Saturday; D

Bissell, G F
Chicago; 1880 Aug 6; Friday; D

Black, A R
Lincoln, Neb; 1880 Mar 22; Monday; S; room 12
Lincoln, Neb; 1880 Mar 27; Sat; D

Black, John A
Chicago, Ills; 1880 Oct 28; Thursday; D; room 3
Chicago, Ills; 1880 Dec 10; Friday; L; room 2

Blackburn, John W
Rosita; 1880 Apr 26; Monday; D;
room 3
Rosita, Col; 1880 Nov 6; Saturday; D;
room 8

Blair, Chas H
New York; 1880 Sept 23; Thursday; S

Blake, Frank O
City; 1880 Apr 6; Tuesday; B
City; 1880 May 10; Monday; B
City; 1880 Sept 30; Thursday; S

Blake, H (Mrs)
Boulder; 1880 July 5; Monday; D

Blake, Jennie (Miss)
Boulder; 1880 July 5; Monday; D

Blake, M M
Boulder; 1880 July 5; Monday; D

Blake, Orris
with FOB; 1880 Sept 30; Thursday; S
guest of FOB; 1880 Sept 30; Thur; D

Blakeney, Joseph
Denver; 1880 June 5; Saturday; D

Blamey, Samuel
Erie, Colo; 1880 Dec 3; Friday; D

Blanche, Brook Miss
Two headed Lady; 1880 June 12; Saturday; D; room 6

Blanche, Miss
Plunkett Troupe; 1880 Sept 19; Sunday; S; room 17

Blavener, A S
Chicago; 1880 Aug 5; Thursday; S; room 21

Bleyer, T T
St Louis; 1880 Apr 20; Tuesday; S; room 1

Blinn, Cora
Longmont; 1880 Apr 3; Saturday; D

Blore, M P
Thompson; 1880 Mar 13; Saturday; L; room 28

Bodine, John
1880 Aug 26; Thursday; D

Boettcher, C
Leadville; 1880 Apr 19; Monday; S
Leadville; 1880 June 15; Tuesday; S; room 6
& Wife; Leadville; 1880 Oct 2; Saturday; D
Leadville; 1880 Nov 25; Thursday, Thanksgiving; S; room 17

Boettcher, C (Mrs)
& Son; Leadville; 1880 June 26; Saturday; S

Boettcher, H
& Children; 1880 May 11; Tuesday; L; room 25
City; 1880 May 19; Wednesday; D; room 25
Boulder; 1880 Nov 19; Friday; D; room 17

Bohun, Paul
NY; 1880 May 28; Friday; S; room 2

Bonner, T F
Central City; 1880 Aug 12; Thursday; L; room 25

Bonuct, J N
NY; 1880 Sept 30; Thursday; S; room 1

Boot, Wm H
Denver; 1880 June 8; Tuesday; D

Bordman, C G
Chicago; 1880 Sept 21; Tuesday; L; room 6

Bore, [unreadable]
1880 Apr 29; Thursday; S; room 21

Boserton, S W
& Wife; 1880 Aug 11; Wednesday; L; room 16

Bostwick, J W
Central City; 1880 Nov 9; Tuesday; L; room 10

Boulke, A
Denver; 1880 May 16; Sunday; S; room 15

Bourne, C
Wife & Daughter; Longmont; 1880 Aug 3; Tuesday; D

Bowman, H F
Omaha; 1880 Sept 29; Wednesday; D; room 2

Bowman, John
Black Hawk, Colo; 1880 Nov 8; Monday; D; room 29

Bowman, W E
City; 1880 June 27; Sunday; D

Boyd, E
& Wife; Elyria, OH; 1880 Apr 20; Tuesday; D; room 16

Brace, C C
1880 July 21; Wednesday; L

Brace, C C (Dr)
With Miss Annie Ellet; 1880 Aug 21; Saturday; D

Brace, Frank
Cremona Park Brass Band, Denver; 1880 Aug 21; Saturday

Brackett, F W
Denver; 1880 May 27; Thursday; D

Bradford, Web
1880 Mar 16; Tuesday; L; room 35

Bradley, H N
City; 1880 Mar 28; Sunday; D
Absent after B; 1880 July 8; Thursday

Bradley, H N (cont.)
Absent after S; 1880 Oct 20; Wednesday
Boulder; 1880 Oct 25; Monday; D

Bradley, V U
City; 1880 Sept 23; Thursday; D

Brahn, John
1880 Sept 1; Wednesday; B

Brainard, Belle
Ward; 1880 Oct 23; Saturday; L; rm 6

Brainard, Imiy
Ward; 1880 Oct 23; Saturday; L; rm 6

Brainard, T C
New York; 1880 Mar 31; Wednesday; S; room 18

Brainard, Thos C
Poland, Ohio; 1880 Oct 19; Tuesday

Brainard, Wesley (see Brainerd)
Ward; 1880 Apr 3; Saturday; D; rm 6
Ward; 1880 May 2; Sunday; D
Ward; 1880 May 5; Wednesday; D; room 15
& Wife; Ward; 1880 Sept 29; Wednesday; D; room 16
& Wife; Ward; 1880 Oct 7; Thursday; D; room 16
Wife & servant; Ward; 1880 Oct 23; Saturday; L; room 18
Ward; 1880 Dec 18; Saturday; D

Brainard, Wesley (Col)
Boss friends; Ward; 1880 Mar 7; Sunday; S; room 12

Brainerd, I G
Ward; 1880 Oct 16; Saturday; S; rm 5

Brainerd, Irving G
Ward Boulder; 1880 Aug 13; Fri; D
Ward; 1880 Sept 20; Monday; S; rm 14

Brainerd, Wesley (see Brainard)
 Ward; 1880 May 28; Friday; S; room 3
 Ward; 1880 June 13; Sunday; S; rm 6
 & Wife; Ward; 1880 July 13; Tuesday;
  S; room 4
 Ward; 1880 July 28; Wednesday; S;
  room 12
 & Wife; Ward; 1880 Sept 27; Monday;
  S; room 1

Branch, C A (Mrs)
 Denver; 1880 Apr 5; Mon; S; rm 16

Branch, Geo
 Central; 1880 May 15; Saturday; S;
  room 27

Branson, Thos
 Cheyenne, Wy; 1880 Nov 18; Thursday; L; room 12

Braor, J P
 & Mrs; New York; 1880 Aug 4;
  Wednesday; D; room 16

Braun, A
 Denver, Col; 1880 Nov 11; Thursday;
  S; room 6

Breath, S M
 Nederland; 1880 Aug 15; Sunday; B

Bredin, E M
 Marshall; 1880 May 15; Saturday; D
 Marshall; 1880 May 21; Friday; D

Bredin, E M Jr
 Marshall; 1880 May 12; Wednesday; S

Bredin, J M
 Marshall; 1880 May 11; Tuesday; D

Bredin, Jno P
 Marshall; 1880 Mar 13; Saturday; L;
  room 5
 Marshall; 1880 Mar 17; Wednesday; L;
  room 35
 Marshall; 1880 Apr 3; Saturday; L;
  room 13

Bredin, Jno P (cont.)
 Marshall; 1880 Apr 6; Tuesday; S;
  room 27
 Marshall; 1880 Apr 16; Friday; S
 Marshall; 1880 Apr 18; Sunday; D
 Marshall; 1880 Apr 21; Wednesday; S
 Marshall; 1880 Apr 21; Wednesday; B
 Marshall Mine; 1880 Apr 26; Monday;
  L; room 2
 Marshall; 1880 Apr 29; Thursday; S
 Marshall; 1880 May 1; Saturday; S
 Marshall; 1880 May 9; Sunday; S;
  room 12
 Marshall; 1880 May 12; Wednesday; D
 Marshall; 1880 May 12; Wednesday; S
 Marshall; 1880 May 13; Thursday; S;
  room 12
 Marshall; 1880 May 14; Friday; S
 Marshall; 1880 May 16; Sunday; S
 Marshall; 1880 May 18; Tuesday; S
 Marshall; 1880 May 22; Saturday; L;
  room 25
 Marshall; 1880 May 27; Thursday; L;
  room 13
 Marshall; 1880 May 29; Saturday; S;
  room 14
 Butler, Pa; 1880 June 1; Tuesday; S;
  room 20
 Marshall; 1880 June 3; Thursday; L;
  room 13
 Marshall; 1880 June 5; Saturday; L;
  room 13
 Ouray; 1880 July 3; Saturday; S; rm 13
 City; 1880 July 5; Monday; L
 Denver; 1880 July 27; Tuesday; S;
  room 12
 Marshall; 1880 July 28; Wednesday; S
 City; 1880 Aug 8; Sunday; B
 Marshall; 1880 Aug 14; Saturday; D;
  room 12
 guest of E M Styles; 1880 Sept 17;
  Friday; B
 Marshall; 1880 Sept 17; Friday; S

Bredin, John P
Marshall; 1880 May 8; Saturday; L;
room 6

Bredin, O M
Butler, PA; 1880 Apr 21; Wed; S

Bretton, A N
Chicago; 1880 Apr 27; Tuesday; D;
room 2

Brewster, Robt
Louisiana; 1880 June 8; Tuesday; D

Bridge, Charles H
Wilmington, Del; 1880 Dec 1;
Wednesday; B

Briggs, David
Erie; 1880 Mar 16; Tuesday; D

Briggs, H
Erie; 1880 Apr 20; Tuesday; D
& Wife; Erie; 1880 Aug 3; Tuesday; S;
room 17

Bringham, R W
Denver; 1880 Aug 2; Monday; L;
room 2

Brink, Leander
Middletown, NY; 1880 May 15; Saturday; D; room 12

Brinker, Geo
Denver; 1880 Mar 22; Monday; S;
room 16

Brinkman, A
New York; 1880 Aug 11; Wed; D

Briston, H C
New York; 1880 June 15; Tuesday

Brittan, A N
Chicago; 1880 Apr 28; Wednesday; L;
room 10
Chicago; 1880 July 27; Tuesday; D;
room 1
Chicago; 1880 Nov 20; Saturday; D;
room 2

Broadwell, H C
1880 May 9; Sunday

Brokate, D C
& Wife; Denver; 1880 Sept 22;
Wednesday; S; room 6

Bromler, H C
Mining Revino; 1880 Sept 3; Friday; S

Bronson, A E
Chicago; 1880 June 22; Tuesday; S;
room 16

Brook, Jno
Milwaukee; 1880 Sept 30; Thursday; S;
room 12

Brookfield, Mrs
Guest of Miss Luce; City; 1880 May
29; Saturday; D

Brooks, L S
Denver; 1880 Oct 25; Monday; S;
room 5

Brooks, Thos M
Wilmette, Ills; 1880 Sept 16; Thursday; S
Chicago; 1880 Dec 2; Thursday; S;
room 2

Broubaugh, J T
Chicago; 1880 Mar 17; Wednesday; D

Brown
Findley O; 1880 Apr 9; Friday; D

Brown, B
Left Hand; 1880 Apr 17; Saturday; L;
room 25
Left Hand; 1880 Apr 18; Sunday; D;
room 26
Gold Hill; 1880 July 4; Sunday; S;
room 27
Gold Hill; 1880 July 8; Thursday; D
Gold Hill; 1880 July 14; Wednesday;
S; room 28
Gold Hill; 1880 Aug 3; Tuesday; S;
room 27

Brown, B (cont.)
Gold Hill; 1880 Aug 8; Sunday; S; room 27
Gold Hill; 1880 Sept 18; Saturday; S; room 29
Gold Hill; 1880 Sept 22; Wed; D

Brown, Bruce
Gold Hill; 1880 July 1; Thursday; S; room 27

Brown, C H
Denver; 1880 Dec 13; Monday; S; room 13

Brown, C M
Sugar Loaf; 1880 Aug 25; Wednesday; L; room 29

Brown, C W
City; 1880 June 28; Monday; L; rm 26

Brown, F M
Leadville; 1880 Dec 1; Wednesday; S; room 8
Leadville; 1880 Nov 29; Monday; S; room 3

Brown, Francis M
City; 1880 Mar 18; Thursday; D
Boulder; 1880 June 5; Saturday; D
City; 1880 Dec 17; Friday; D

Brown, G R
Sugar Loaf; 1880 May 5; Wed; D

Brown, G T
NY; 1880 May 12; Wednesday; room 3

Brown, H J
Phila; 1880 May 4; Tuesday; D

Brown, H M (Mrs)
Fort Collins; 1880 July 9; Friday; S; room 21
Ft Collins; 1880 July 14; Wednesday; S; room 8 & 9

Brown, H P
Veeley; 1880 Mar 6; Sat; L; rm 28

Brown, Ira
Maysville, MO; 1880 Mar 22; Monday; S; room 12

Brown, J B
Golden; 1880 Aug 31; Tuesday; D; room 13

Brown, J G
Denver; 1880 Nov 4; Thursday; L; room 20

Brown, J L
1880 Apr 12; Monday; S; room 44
Denver; 1880 Aug 22; Sunday; L; room 12
Denver; 1880 Aug 23; Monday; D

Brown, M (Miss)
Denver; 1880 Sept 19; Sunday; D; room 11

Brown, M T
& Family; Denver; 1880 May 25; Tuesday; S; room 1

Brown, Mrs
Guest of Mrs E Smith; Nederland; 1880 May 27; Thursday; D

Brown, N
Denver; 1880 Apr 20; Tuesday; D

Brown, N D
Denver; 1880 Nov 27; Saturday; S; room 5

Brown, N F
1880 Oct 5; Tuesday; S

Brown, Richard
Jamestown; 1880 May 10; Monday; S

Brown, S E
Denver; 1880 Mar 8; Monday; D; room 12

Brown, T T
Philadelphia; 1880 July 29; Thursday; D; room 8

Brown, W H
Chicago; 1880 July 11; Sunday; D;
room 1

Brown, W K
Albany; 1880 Apr 21; Wednesday; S;
room 1

Brown, W T
& Family; Denver; 1880 May 13;
Thursday; S; room 15

Brown, Wm H
Chicago; 1880 July 5; Monday; S

Brown, Y M
K City; 1880 Mar 17; Wednesday; L;
room 12

Browne, J
1880 July 2; Friday; S; room 11

Browne, John C P
Nederland; 1880 Dec 4; Saturday; S;
room 35

Brunswick, S
St Louis; 1880 June 23; Wednesday; S;
room 3
St Louis; 1880 Sept 16; Thursday; S

Bruster, B C
Gold Hill; 1880 Aug 10; Tuesday; D

Bryan, Kenneth
St Louis; 1880 May 11; Tuesday; S;
room 8

Bryan, Mrs
& Daughter; Leadville; 1880 Aug 31;
Tuesday; S; room 33

Bryant, Carrie (Miss)
1880 Aug 21; Saturday; D

Bryant, F L
Agt, Renner Hervine Colorado
Springs; 1880 July 23; Friday; S
Colo Springs; 1880 Nov 8; Monday; S

Bryant, Wm
Nederland; 1880 Nov 9; Tuesday; D
Nederland; 1880 Oct 20; Wednesday;
L; room 27

Buchanan, James
Cheyenne, WY; 1880 Apr 22; Thursday; S; room 27

Buchanan, Jules
Denver; 1880 Dec 2; Thursday; B

Bucherdee, F C
Jamestown; 1880 Dec 10; Friday; S;
room 6
Jamestown; 1880 Nov 9; Tuesday; S

Buckingham, Geo H
Louisville; 1880 Mar 16; Tuesday; L;
room 35
Louisville; 1880 Mar 16; Tuesday; D

Buckley, Harry
Star Alliance Opera Co; 1880 June 11;
Friday; D; room 12

Buckley, J A
Longmont; 1880 May 6; Thursday; D
Wife & 2 children; Longmont; 1880
July 5; Monday; S; room 19-20

Buckley, Jno A
Longmont Cornet Band; 1880 Sept
23; Thursday; S

Bud, Henry
In jail; 1880 May 8; Saturday; S

Buecking, Geo H
Kansas City; 1880 Dec 2; Thursday; S;
room 6

Buelman, Jno M
Denver; 1880 Oct 12; Tuesday; S;
room 35

Buford, E J
Denver; 1880 June 8; Tuesday; S;
room 13
Denver; 1880 June 9; Wednesday; S;
room 19

Bulin, Hatta (Miss)
California; 1880 July 13; Tuesday; S; room 34

Bullard, Frank D
Denver; 1880 Mar 23; Tuesday; S; room 33

Bullock, F W
Chicago; 1880 Apr 16; Fri; S; rm 15
Chicago; 1880 Nov 4; Thursday; D ; 8

Bullven, F W
Chicago; 1880 July 28; Wednesday; S; room 1

Burgen, L
Chicago; 1880 Sept 29; Wednesday; D; room 3

Burger, Henry
Caribou; 1880 Nov 1; Monday; D

Burgman, Miss
New York; 1880 Oct 8; Friday; L; room 8

Burke, Carl W
Boulder; 1880 July 1; Thursday; D

Burke, Frank R
Boulder; 1880 July 1; Thursday; D

Burnell, C F
Denver; 1880 Aug 21; Saturday; D

Burnham, R W
Denver, Col; 1880 July 27; Tuesday; S; room 6

Burns, J E;
with Halbert; 1880 Mar 28; Sunday; S

Burns, Jus J
1880 Apr 1; Thursday; D

Burr, A
Chicago; 1880 Mar 11; Thursday; S

Burr, D
Chicago; 1880 Sept 7; Tuesday; S; room 10

Burrows, Jas
Salt Lake; 1880 May 2; Sunday; D

Burt, Fanny (Miss)
Nobles Company, New York; 1880 Oct 23; Saturday; D; room 20

Bush, Harvey
Chicago; 1880 July 24; Saturday; D; room 1

Bush, J J
Fort Collins; 1880 Dec 10; Friday; S
Ft Collins; 1880 Nov 29; Monday; S

Bush, J P
Ft Collins; 1880 Nov 22; Monday; D

Bush, Jno J
Ft Collins; 1880 Dec 7; Tuesday; L; room 34
Ft Collins; 1880 Dec 8; Wednesday; D
Ft Collins; 1880 Dec 8; Wednesday; L; room 34

Busick, S A
NY; 1880 Aug 10; Tuesday; S; room 6

Busle, J C
Chambers Lake; 1880 Oct 21; Thursday; D; room 3

Busput, J Even
1880 Oct 18; Monday; L; room 6

Butler, F J (Mrs)
Denver; 1880 Aug 21; Saturday; D

Butler, Grade (Miss)
Denver; 1880 Aug 21; Saturday; D

Butler, Hugh
Denver; 1880 May 13; Thursday; S; room 16
Denver; 1880 Nov 10; Wednesday; S; room 3

Butler, Ida (Miss)
Denver; 1880 Aug 21; Saturday; D

Butler, Jos K
Denver, Colo; 1880 Nov 26; Friday; D

Butler, Thomas
Longmont; 1880 Aug 14; Saturday; D

Butler, Thos
Longmont Cornet Band; 1880 Sept 23; Thursday; S; room 3

Butler, Wm
Longmont Cornet Band; 1880 Sept 23; Thursday; S

Butsch, Miss
Boulder; 1880 July 5; Monday; D

Butter, George
Longmont; 1880 May 10; Monday; S

Buttler, J F
& Family; Denver; 1880 May 8; Saturday; S; room 9

Byers, J M
Sunshine; 1880 Oct 13; Wednesday; D

Byers, Jas J
Sunshine; 1880 Mar 6; Saturday; D
Sunshine; 1880 Apr 9; Friday; D
Sunshine; 1880 Apr 11; Sunday; D
Sunshine; 1880 May 2; Sunday; D
Sunshine; 1880 Oct 1; Friday; S; rm 27

C

Cabb, G W
Davenport, Ia; 1880 Sept 21; Tuesday; S

Cadwalader, E B
Denver, Col; 1880 Aug 30; Monday; D

Cafron, J D (see Capron)
St Louis; 1880 Sept 16; Thursday; L; room 10
Denver; 1880 Nov 30; Tuesday; S; room 8

Caldwell, A H
Wife & 3 children; Loveland, Colo; 1880 July 22; Thursday; S; room 1

Calkins, W H
Denver; 1880 May 18; Tuesday; S; room 6
Denver; 1880 May 19; Wednesday; S; room 6

Came, Ed
Denver; 1880 Apr 20; Tuesday; D

Came, V M
Chi Ma N W Ry [Chicago and North Western Railway]; 1880 Apr 21; Wednesday; S

Cameron, J S
Denver; 1880 May 11; Tuesday; S; room 6
& Wife; Denver; 1880 July 7; Wednesday; S; room 21
Denver; 1880 Sept 1; Wednesday; S
Denver; 1880 Sept 30; Thursday; S; room 17

Cameron, R A
Denver; 1880 Aug 25; Wednesday; S

Camp, H A
Leadville; 1880 Dec 16; Thursday; D

Campbell, Chas
Denver; 1880 Apr 9; Friday; S; rm 21

Campbell, D C
Ward; 1880 Oct 13; Wednesday; D; room 28
Ward; 1880 Nov 16; Tuesday; S; rm 28
Ward; 1880 Dec 17; Friday; D; rm 28

Campbell, Jacob
Fonda's Pharmacy ; 1880 July 13; Tuesday; L; room 28

Campbell, O F
Gold Hill; 1880 Apr 3; Saturday; D

Campbell, R C
Agt MacAllister; 1880 July 21; Wednesday; D
Agt MacAllister; 1880 July 23; Fri; S

Campbell, W L (Gen)
Denver; 1880 Mar 15; Sunday; S; room 4

Campbell, Wm L
Denver; 1880 Apr 11; Sunday; D; room 16
Denver; 1880 Aug 9; Monday; D
Denver; 1880 July 19; Monday; S; room 4
Denver; 1880 Sept 2; Thursday; D

Capper, Hugh
Agent Plunkett Troupe; 1880 July 19; Monday; L; room 28

Capron, J D (see Cafron)
St Louis; 1880 May 25; Tuesday; D; room 6

Capt Jack Combination
1880 Apr 22; Thursday; D

Car, Geo F
Absent after B; 1880 May 24; Monday

Caramu, Wm
Leadville; 1880 Oct 21; Thursday; D

Carey, James A
Saginaw, Mich; 1880 Aug 20; Friday; S

Carey, M
Silver City, Utah; 1880 Aug 13; Friday; S; room 25
Blue Bird [Mine]; 1880 Aug 27; Friday; S
Blue Bird; 1880 Aug 28; Saturday; S; room 20
Blue Bird; 1880 Sept 11; Saturday; S; room 11

Carhart, Th P
_asefork; 1880 June 2; Wednesday; S

Carhart, Thomas P
New York; 1880 June 21; Monday; S; room 6

Carmany, W A
Fort Scott, Ks; 1880 July 2; Friday; S; room 3

Carnahan, Jane
1880 Sept 24; Friday; S

Carnahan, Josie
1880 Sept 24; Friday; S

Carnell, Jno R
Wife & 2 children; Troy, NY; 1880 June 8; Tuesday; D; room 12

Carr, B L
Longmont; 1880 Mar 8; Monday; S; room 6
Longmont; 1880 Mar 10; Wednesday; S; room 15
Longmont; 1880 May 4; Tuesday; D
Longmont; 1880 May 10; Monday; S
Longmont; 1880 May 12; Wednesday; S; room 34
Longmont; 1880 May 21; Friday; S; room 14
Wife & Children; Longmont; 1880 Aug 3; Tuesday; D; room 3
Longmont; 1880 Aug 4; Wednesday; L; room 21
Longmont; 1880 Aug 14; Saturday; D
Longmont; 1880 Aug 18; Wednesday
Longmont; 1880 Aug 19; Thursday; S
Longmont; 1880 June 7; Monday; L; room 20
Longmont; 1880 June 13; Sunday; L
Longmont; 1880 July 19; Monday; D
Longmont Cornet Band; 1880 Sept 23; Thursday; S; room 3
Longmont; 1880 Oct 16; Saturday; L; room 20
Longmont; 1880 Nov 9; Tuesday; L; room 26

Carr, B L (cont.)
Longmont; 1880 Nov 11; Thursday; S; room 29
Longmont; 1880 Nov 16; Tuesday; D; room 13
Longmont; 1880 Nov 23; Tuesday; D
Longmont; 1880 Dec 6; Monday; S; room 12
Longmont; 1880 Dec 9; Thursday; D; room 12

Carr, B L (Col)
Longmont; 1880 July 21; Wed; D
Longmont, Col; 1880 Oct 15; Friday; L; room 2
Longmont; 1880 Nov 15; Monday; L; room 12

Carr, S H
& Daughter; Boulder Creek; 1880 Mar 30; Tuesday; D; room 12

Carrie, Miss
Plunkett Troupe; 1880 Sept 19; Sunday; S; room 17

Carson, H B W
& Wife [crossed out]; Central; 1880 Aug 12; Thursday; D; room 8

Carter, M S (Mrs)
1880 June 28; Monday; S; room 14

Carter, Mrs
Colo Springs; 1880 Oct 28; Thursday; S; room 5

Carter, Thom C
Nederland; 1880 June 3; Thursday; L; room 25

Case, Alliene (see Case, J Alliene)
Blue Bird Mine; 1880 Aug 10; Tuesday; room 5
Nederland; 1880 Sept 14; Tuesday; S; room 19

Case, C C
Black Hawk; 1880 May 15; Saturday; S; room 17

Case, E H
Nederland; 1880 Sept 22; Wed; D

Case, Harlow
Buffalo; 1880 Oct 6; Wednesday; S

Case, J A
Blue Bird Mine; 1880 June 13; Sunday; S; room 12
Blue Bird Mine; 1880 June 21; Monday; S; room 20
& Son; Blue Bird Mine; 1880 Aug 3; Tuesday; S; room 6
Nederland; 1880 Aug 14; Saturday; D; room 21
Blue Bird; 1880 Sept 1; Wednesday; S; room 10
Nederland; 1880 Oct 11; Monday; S; room 5
Nederland; 1880 Oct 18; Monday; S; room 5
Nederland; 1880 Oct 20; Wed; S
Nederland; 1880 Oct 23; Saturday; S; room 35
Nederland; 1880 Oct 30; Saturday; S; room 14
Nederland; 1880 Sept 22; Wednesday; L; room 5

Case, J Alleine (see Case, J Alliene)
Blue Bird Mine; 1880 May 5; Wednesday; D; room 27
Blue Bird Mine; 1880 May 6; Thursday; S; room 17
Blue Bird Mine; 1880 July 20; Tuesday; L; room 29

Case, J Alliene (see Case, J Alleine)
Blue Bird Mine; 1880 Mar 8; Monday; S; room 1
Blue Bird Mine; 1880 Mar 13; Saturday; S; room 12

Case, J Alliene (see Case, J Alleine) (cont.)

Blue Bird Mine; 1880 Mar 19; Friday; S; room 5

Blue Bird Mine; 1880 Mar 27; Saturday; S; room 44

Blue Bird Mine; 1880 Apr 2; Friday; S; room 6

Blue Bird Mine; 1880 Apr 7; Wednesday; S; room 5

Blue Bird Mine; 1880 July 22; Thursday; D; room 17

Blue Bird Mine; 1880 July 25; Sunday; S; room 17

Nederland; 1880 Aug 13; Friday; S; room 6

Nederland; 1880 Sept 10; Friday; D; room 35

Nederland; 1880 Sept 17; Friday; S; room 13

Nederland; 1880 Sept 20; Monday; S; room 33

Denver; 1880 Nov 12; Friday; S; rm 5

Case, M G

Blue Bird; 1880 Mar 12; Friday; S; room 12

Blue Bird Mine; 1880 Apr 19; Monday; D

Blue Bird Mine; 1880 Apr 2; Friday; S; room 6

Blue Bird Mine; 1880 Apr 28; Wednesday; S

Blue Bird; 1880 May 3; Monday; D 1880 Oct 12; Tuesday; S; room 14

Blue Bird Mine; 1880 May 12; Wednesday; S; room 17

Blue Bird; 1880 May 28; Friday; S; room 11

Blue Bird Mine; 1880 Aug 1; Sunday; D; room 3

Blue Bird Mine; 1880 Aug 3; Tuesday; S; room 6

Case, M G (cont.)

Blue Bird Mine; 1880 June 6; Sunday; S; room 6

Blue Bird; 1880 June 15; Tuesday; S; room 12

Blue Bird; 1880 Sept 4; Saturday; S; room 2

Blue Bird Mine; 1880 Sept 7; Tuesday; D; room 12

Blue Bird; 1880 Sept 17; Friday; L; room 12

Denver; 1880 Oct 9; Saturday; D; room 5

Denver; 1880 Oct 18; Monday; S; room 12

Case, W G

Blue Bird Mine; 1880 Mar 31; Wednesday; S; room 12

Santa La Loria, Mex; 1880 Apr 14; Wednesday; S; room 17

Blue Bird [Mine]; 1880 Apr 20; Tuesday; S; room 17

Blue Bird Mine; 1880 May 23; Sunday; S; room 3

Blue Bird Mine; 1880 June 21; Monday; S; room 17

Blue Bird Mine; 1880 June 24; Thursday; S; room 21

Blue Bird Mine; 1880 July 1; Thursday; S; room 17

Blue Bird; 1880 July 10; Saturday; D; room 20

Blue Bird Mine; 1880 July 22; Thursday; S

Blue Bird; 1880 Aug 27; Friday; S

Blue Bird; 1880 Aug 28; Saturday; S; room 19

Blue Bird; 1880 Sept 3; Friday; S; room 6

Blue Bird; 1880 Sept 1; Wednesday; S; room 6

Boulder; 1880 Sept 19; Sunday; L; room 11

Case, W G (Mrs)
Denver; 1880 Mar 16; Tuesday; S; room 8

Case, W L
Denver; 1880 May 18; Tuesday; S; room 6
Denver; 1880 May 19; Wednesday; S; room 6

Case, W Y
Blue Bird; 1880 Sept 11; Saturday; S; room 10

Case, Wm G
Blue Bird Mine; 1880 Apr 7; Wednesday; S; room 6

Castello & Day
Dan Castello & Co Circus; 1880 May 23; Sunday; L; room 6

Caster, W G
Ward, Col; 1880 Oct 9; Saturday; S

Cates, Wm Jr
D&Ry RR; 1880 Sept 3; Friday; S

Catt, Wm J
Marshall; 1880 May 13; Thursday; S

Cecil, John
Memphis, Mo; 1880 Aug 20; Friday; S

Chabronou, Thos
Wife & Daughter; Chicago; 1880 July 14; Wednesday; S; room 4 & 44

Chadbourn, H
Loveland; 1880 Nov 20; Saturday; L; room 13

Chamberlain, A H
Wizard Co; 1880 July 25; Sunday; D; room 33

Chamberlin, C H
St Louis; 1880 July 19; Monday; S; room 3

Chamberlin, J W
Denver; 1880 Apr 10; Saturday; D

Chamberlin, M H
Springfield, Ill; 1880 May 24; Monday; S; room 6
Springfield, Ill; 1880 May 26; Wednesday; D; room 6

Chambers, Geo W
1880 June 3; Thursday; D

Chambers, Jas K
Denver; 1880 June 27; Sunday; S

Chaney, J H
Louisville; 1880 Apr 29; Thursday; D; room 3
Louisville, Ky; 1880 Sept 6; Mon; D

Chapman, Chas R
Hartford; 1880 Apr 21; Wednesday; S; room 16
Hartford, Conn; 1880 Aug 23; Monday; S; room 16
Hartford; 1880 May 1; Saturday; S; room 16

Chapman, Geo B
1880 May 16; Sunday; S; room 14

Chapman, J W
Guest with Kirk; 1880 May 9; Sun; D

Chapman, John C
Boston; 1880 May 21; Friday; S; rm 3

Chapman, Thos R
Dayton O; 1880 Apr 12; Monday; S; room 16

Chapperton, Wm
England; 1880 May 28; Friday; S; room 25

Charannes, N Burlson
Nederland; 1880 Apr 12; Monday; D

Charley & Jack
Denver; 1880 Sept 19; Sunday; D

Charlton, Wm
Phila; 1880 June 28; Monday
Philadelphia, PA; 1880 June 29; Tuesday; D; room 15

Chase, A Q
Louisville; 1880 July 21; Wednesday; S

Chase, Byron E
Guest of E M Styles; 1880 Sept 12;
Sunday; D

Chase, F A
& Family; Independence, Mo; 1880
Nov 5; Friday; L; room 10

Chase, G H
Golden; 1880 May 4; Tuesday; D

Chase, John
Cremona Park Brass Band, Denver;
1880 Aug 21; Saturday

Chase, Mr
& Wife; 1880 Aug 21; Saturday; D

Chedsey, Mr
With Miss F Erhardt; 1880 Aug 21;
Saturday; D

Chedsey, N L
Left after B; 1880 Apr 6; Tuesday; B
Home again; 1880 Apr 7; Wednesday;
D; room 45
Left after D; 1880 July 22; Thursday
Boulder, Col; 1880 Aug 19; Thur; S

Cheney, L K
Westminster, Mass; 1880 Oct 2; Saturday; L; room 3
Longmont; 1880 Nov 2; Tuesday; S;
room 3
Longmont; 1880 Nov 6; Saturday; L;
room 3

Cheney, Louis K C
Longmont; 1880 Dec 15; Wednesday;
S; room 3

Cheny, J A
Denver; 1880 Aug 29; Sunday; D;
room 16

Cherry, J A
Denver; 1880 July 1; Thursday; S;
room 6

Chimney, G A
Westfield, Mass; 1880 Sept 7; Tues; S

Chittenden, H W
Burlington, Ia; 1880 July 31; Saturday;
S; room 12

Chittenden, N H
Burlington; 1880 Apr 17; Saturday; S;
room 15

Chittenden, N W
Burlington; 1880 Apr 20; Tuesday; S;
room 15

Christine, Millie
Two headed Lady; 1880 June 12; Saturday; D; room 6

Chuck, J M S
Denver; 1880 Oct 21; Thursday; L;
room 6

Church, Gus
Denver; 1880 Oct 4; Monday; S; rm 3

Church, J L
Boulder; 1880 Aug 6; Friday; room 28

Church, Jno B
Wife & Child; 1880 Oct 20; Wednesday; S; room 19&20
Wife & Child; Denver; 1880 Oct 21;
Thursday; S; room 19&20

Churchill, C W (Mrs)
Gold Hill; 1880 Oct 6; Wednesday; D

Churnasbro, I T
Chicago; 1880 June 15; Tuesday; S

Ci__ton, Q C
[illegible]; 1880 May 4; Tuesday; S;
room 27

Clark, _ O
Black Hawk; 1880 May 15; Saturday; S

Clark, A K
Denver; 1880 Dec 8; Wednesday; L; room 12

Clark, A L
& Wife; Denver; 1880 Aug 2; Monday; L; room 10

Clark, C V
Jamestown; 1880 June 6; Sunday; D

Clark, Daniel
Georgetown, Col; 1880 Aug 7; Saturday; S; room 35

Clark, H W
Left Hand, Col; 1880 Mar 29; Monday; S; room 35
Left Hand; 1880 Apr 21; Wednesday; L; room 35
Left Hand; 1880 Apr 28; Wednesday; L; room 35
City; 1880 May 4; Tuesday; D; rm 35
Returned; 1880 May 9; Sunday; L; room 35
Absent after dinner; 1880 May 22; Saturday
Returned; 1880 June 7; Monday; S; room 35
Absent after B; 1880 June 13; Sunday
Returned; 1880 June 14; Monday; L; room 35
Absent after dinner; 1880 June 19; Saturday; D
Ret'd for S; 1880 June 21; Monday; S; room 25
Absent after breakfast; 1880 June 27; Sunday
Ret'd for Supper; 1880 June 28; Monday; S; room 35
Absent after dinner; 1880 July 3; Saturday
Returned; 1880 July 5; Monday; L; room 35

Clark, H W (cont.)
Left after breakfast; 1880 July 7; Wednesday; D
Longmont; 1880 July 8; Thursday; L; room 25
Longmont, Col; 1880 July 10; Saturday; D; room 35
Absent after breakfast; 1880 July 10; Saturday
Absent after breakfast; 1880 July 11; Sunday
Lefthand; 1880 Nov 22; Monday; S; room 5

Clark, H W (Mrs)
1880 June 19; Saturday; D
Modock; 1880 May 15; Saturday; S; room 25

Clark, J T
Salina; 1880 May 17; Monday; D

Clark, L J
Detroit, Mich; 1880 Oct 16; Saturday; S; room 12

Clark, Len J
Denver; 1880 Nov 11; Thursday; S; room 2
Detroit, Mich; 1880 Nov 13; Sat; D
Detroit, M; 1880 Nov 22; Monday; S; room 12

Clark, M J
St Louis; 1880 May 27; Thursday; S
St Louis; 1880 July 24; Saturday; S
Golden; 1880 July 31; Saturday; D

Clark, Mrs
Returned; 1880 Aug 25; Wednesday; D; room 15

Clark, Orill
Longmont; 1880 July 5; Monday; D

Clark, R N
Col Springs; 1880 Nov 17; Wednesday; S; room 6

Clark, S A
D; 1880 Mar 29; Monday; S; room 6

Clark, W G
Denver; 1880 Oct 26; Tuesday; S; room 8

Clark, Wm
Absent after supper; 1880 Aug 16; Monday

Clark, Wm B (Mrs)
Kalamazoo, Mich; 1880 July 2; Friday; S; room 15

Clarke, C H
Denver; 1880 Sept 24; Friday; D; room 6

Clarke, K H
Chicago; 1880 Sept 15; Wednesday; L; room 12
Chicago; 1880 Sept 16; Thursday; L; room 12

Clarke, Mrs
Rollinsville; 1880 Sept 30; Thur; D
Denver; 1880 Nov 17; Wednesday; L; room 1

Clifford, Alfred
St Louis; 1880 Aug 2; Monday; S; room 16

Clifford, M F
So Ulster, NY; 1880 Aug 4; Wednesday; S; room 12
So Ulster, NY; 1880 Aug 7; Saturday; S; room 5

Clifford, R H
NY; 1880 Nov 17; Wednesday; L; room 13

Clifton, A J
Sunshine; 1880 Sept 7; Tuesday; D

Clifton, J D
Plunkett Troupe; 1880 Sept 19; Sunday; S; room 15

Clifton, J D (Mrs)
Plunkett Troupe; 1880 Sept 19; Sunday; S; room 15

Cline, George P
1880 Aug 19; Thursday; D

Cliven, T R
Absent after B; 1880 May 7; Friday; D

Cloflin, C C
Chicago; 1880 Sept 30; Thursday; L; room 2

Coan, A
Hagudia; 1880 Mar 8; Monday; D
Hagudia; 1880 Mar 9; Tuesday; D; room 25
Wife & Child; Magnolia; 1880 Mar 18; Thursday; D
Magnolia; 1880 Mar 24; Wed; D
Magnolia; 1880 Mar 27; Saturday; D
& Wife; Magnolia; 1880 Mar 28; Sunday; D; room 15
Magnolia; 1880 Apr 10; Saturday; D
Magnolia; 1880 Apr 12; Monday; D
Magnolia; 1880 Apr 20; Tuesday; D
Magnolia; 1880 Apr 26; Monday; D
Magnolia; 1880 Apr 28; Wed; D
Magnolia; 1880 Apr 30; Friday; D
Magnolia; 1880 Apr 5; Monday; D; room 49
Magnolia; 1880 May 17; Monday; D
Magnolia; 1880 Oct 4; Monday; D

Coan, A (Mrs)
& Daughter; Magnolia; 1880 Apr 12; Monday; D; room 4

Cochran, J L
Lima, O; 1880 Aug 10; Tuesday; D

Coffin, C F
City; 1880 June 2; Wednesday; rm 13

Coffin, Chas F
Manchester, NH; 1880 June 1; Tuesday; L; room 32

Coffin, Chas F (cont.)
News & Courier; 1880 Oct 17; Sunday; S; room 32

Coffin, Gertrude
Longmont; 1880 Apr 3; Saturday; D

Coffin, H
& Guest; 1880 July 8; Thursday; D

Coffin, James B
Vermont; 1880 Nov 2; Tuesday; D

Coggins, Jas
City Hotel; 1880 Apr 21; Wed; D

Cole, J M
Denver; 1880 Apr 30; Friday; D

Cole, Miss
New York; 1880 Oct 8; Friday; L; room 8

Cole, Q I
Paris, LA; 1880 June 29; Tuesday; D; room 33

Coleman, Thomas
Wife & Son; Lafayette, Ind; 1880 June 13; Sunday; S; room 19-20

Colley, Jonas
City; 1880 May 24; Monday; S; rm 34

Collie
Four Mile; 1880 Apr 23; Friday; D

Collie, J
Sugar Loaf; 1880 June 23; Wed; D
Sugar Loaf; 1880 July 17; Saturday; D; room 29
Sugar Loaf; 1880 July 22; Thursday; L; room 27
Crisman, Colo; 1880 Dec 3; Friday; D

Collie, Jas
Sugar Loaf; 1880 Sept 9; Thursday; S

Collie, Joe
Four Mile; 1880 May 17; Monday; D
Sugar Loaf; 1880 Sept 11; Saturday; D
Sugar Loaf; 1880 Oct 3; Sunday; D

Collier, John Z
Black Hawk; 1880 June 21; Monday; S; room 33
Black Hawk; 1880 July 5; Monday; D
Black Hawk; 1880 Oct 29; Friday; L; room 17

Collier, Wm
& Wife; Longmont; 1880 July 5; Monday; D

Collins, Benj J
Denver, Col; 1880 July 27; Tuesday; S; room 35

Collins, W M
Kansas City; 1880 Sept 14; Tuesday; D; room 1

Colm, Herman
Las Vegas, NM; 1880 June 12; Saturday; D

Colorado Youth
1880 May 28; Friday; L; room 46

Colson, Chas
Roaring Ford; 1880 Sept 8; Wednesday; S

Colvin, C K
County Court Jury; 1880 Mar 11; Thursday; S

Comstock, A
Boston, Mass; 1880 May 27; Thursday; D; room 1

Comstock, H G
Blue Bird Mine; 1880 May 29; Saturday; D
Blue Bird; 1880 June 13; Sunday; S; room 12
Blue Bird Mine; 1880 June 21; Monday; S; room 19
Blue Bird Mine; 1880 June 24; Thursday; S; room 15
Blue Bird Mine; 1880 July 16; Friday; D; room 12

31

Comstock, H G (cont.)
Blue Bird Mine; 1880 July 19; Monday; S; room 44
Blue Bird Mine; 1880 Aug 3; Tuesday; S; room 6
Blue Bird; 1880 Aug 31; Tuesday; D
Blue Bird Mine; 1880 Sept 2; Thursday; D
Ohio; 1880 Sept 17; Friday; S; rm 12
Columbus, Ohio; 1880 Sept 21; Tuesday; B
Nederland; 1880 Oct 4; Monday; D
Ohio; 1880 Sept 30; Thursday; S

Comstock, H S
Ohio; 1880 Apr 22; Thursday; S

Condan, John
Unreadable; 1880 Oct 3; Sunday; L; room 29

Confell, C A
Crisman, Colo; 1880 Sept 11; Saturday; D

Congdon, G S
Chicago; 1880 Apr 26; Monday; L; room 10

Conker, G J
Valmont; 1880 Apr 24; Saturday; D

Conkin, Samuel
NY; 1880 Aug 18; Wednesday; D

Conklin, J D
Middletown, NY; 1880 July 5; Monday; S; room 17
1880 Sept 28; Tuesday; D; room 35
Nederland; 1880 Oct 1; Friday; S; room 17
1880 Oct 21; Thursday; D; room 13
Nederland; 1880 Nov 3; Wednesday; D; room 33

Conklin, Samuel
NY; 1880 Aug 19; Thursday; S; rm 12

Conkling, Henry M
Rockford, IL; 1880 Mar 19; Fri

Connell, Chas T
Boulder; 1880 Sept 14; Tuesday; D

Connell, H C M
Chicago; 1880 Oct 30; Saturday; D; room 3

Connerford, M J
Livingston, MN; 1880 Mar 18; Thursday; D
Livingston, MN; 1880 Mar 6; Saturday; D

Connerly, R
Illinois; 1880 July 23; Friday; S; rm 10

Conners, C A C
Toledo, Ohio; 1880 Sept 23; Thur; S

Connor, John P
Boston; 1880 July 9; Friday; D

Connor, William, Jr
Guest of Wm Connor; 1880 Sept 26; Sunday; D

Connor, Wm
Lake City; 1880 Sept 25; Saturday; S; room 6

Connors, J C
Lafayette, Ind; 1880 Apr 22; Thursday; D; room 25

Connors, John
Loveland; 1880 Oct 19; Tuesday; S; room 29

Connors, John T
Loveland, Col; 1880 June 9; Wednesday; D

Conrad, Prof
Phila, Pa; 1880 Oct 26; Tuesday

Conrad, V L (Prof)
Philadelphia; 1880 Oct 22; Friday; S; room 6

Conradt, Geo
Boulder; 1880 Sept 9; Thursday; D

Conradt, Geo W
Guest of FOB; 1880 Oct 6; Wednesday; D

Conway, Harry
Denver; 1880 May 13; Thursday; S

Cook, Albert
NY; 1880 Apr 26; Monday; D

Cook, Chas A
Langrisha, Co; 1880 Aug 9; Mon; D
& Wife; 1880 Aug 10; Tuesday; D; room 17

Cook, H T
Burlington, Ia; 1880 Aug 29; Sunday; L; room 1

Cook, H W
Returned; 1880 May 23; Sunday; L; room 35
Absent after breakfast; 1880 May 29; Saturday

Cook, N H
Oumar, guest of J Cloper; 1880 Aug 24; Tuesday; D

Cook, Nellie (Miss)
Nederland; 1880 Aug 3; Tuesday; D; room 14

Cook, W H
Crisman; 1880 Mar 21; Sunday; S; room 17
Wife and child; Crisman; 1880 May 15; Saturday; S
Wife & Child; Orodelfan, Colo; 1880 Oct 21; Thursday; S

Cooke, Chas M
Nederland; 1880 Nov 26; Friday; S; room 26

Cooke, H M
London; 1880 June 16; Wednesday; D; room 11

Cooke, Nellie
Nederland; 1880 July 24; Saturday; L; room 21
Nederland; 1880 July 25; Sunday; D

Cooke, Percival
Leeds, Eng; 1880 June 16; Wednesday; D; room 10

Cooper, Chas
The only trombone; Cremona Park Brass Band, Denver; 1880 Aug 21; Saturday

Cooper, J C
Brooklyn, NY; 1880 Mar 20; Saturday; S; room 3
New York; 1880 Apr 29; Thursday; D
Brooklyn; 1880 May 5; Wednesday; D
Brooklyn; 1880 May 6; Thursday; D; room 12
Crisman, Col; 1880 Aug 12; Thursday; B; room 1
Orodelfan; 1880 Sept 14; Tuesday; L; room 14
Orodelfan; 1880 Sept 15; Wednesday; L; room 13
Orodelfan; 1880 Sept 16; Thursday; L; room 14
Orodelfan; 1880 Sept 17; Friday; L; room 14
Orodelfan; 1880 Sept 18; Saturday; L; room 11
Orodelfan; 1880 Sept 21; Tuesday; S; room 13
Orodelfan; 1880 Sept 22; Wednesday; L; room 27
Orodelfan; 1880 Sept 23; Thursday; S; room 11
Orodelfan; 1880 Sept 29; Wednesday; S; room 13
Orodelfan, with Denny; 1880 Oct 22; Friday; D; room 35
1880 Oct 24; Sunday; L; room 19
1880 Oct 27; Wednesday; D; room 13

Cooper, J C (cont.)
Orodelfan; 1880 Nov 23; Tuesday; L; room 35
Orodelfan; 1880 Nov 27; Saturday; L; room 35
Orodelfan; 1880 Dec 6; Monday; S; room 35

Cooper, J H
Boulder; 1880 Dec 4; Saturday; S; room 35

Cooper, Joseph C
Orodelfan; 1880 Dec 4; Saturday; D

Cooper, R K
St Joe; 1880 Apr 12; Monday; D; rm 6

Coper, Jos
& Wife; Boulder; 1880 Aug 10; Tuesday; S

Corbaley, Robt C
San Francisco; 1880 Nov 20; Saturday; D; room 6

Corcoran, John
Denver; 1880 Sept 25; Saturday; B

Corey, C A
Denver; 1880 Sept 25; Saturday; D; room 29

Cornelius, Will
Denver; 1880 June 19; Saturday; S; room 11

Cornell, C W
1880 Sept 24; Friday; S

Cornell, Chas T
Boulder; 1880 Sept 24; Friday; S

Cornell, H C M
Chicago; 1880 Apr 27; Tuesday; D; room 3

Cornell, L S
& Wife; 1880 Aug 21; Saturday; D

Corria, James
Galena; 1880 July 5; Monday; L; rm 2

Corube, Charles
St Louis; 1880 Oct 2; Saturday; L; room 15

Corydon, G S
Chicago; 1880 June 3; Thursday; D; room 6

Coryell, C A
Denver; 1880 July 21; Wednesday; S
Madison, Wis; 1880 Aug 21; Sat; D
Crisman, Colo; 1880 Oct 16; Saturday; D
Crisman, Colo; 1880 Dec 3; Friday; D

Cosarone, F A
Boss friends; Chicago; 1880 Mar 7; Sunday; S; room 12

Cosgrove, W L
Chicago; 1880 Oct 15; Friday; D

Costurtunas, Capt
Breakfast only; 1880 Aug 3; Tues; B

Couer, A
Magnolia; 1880 Sept 14; Tuesday; D

Covert, D S
Chicago Tribune; 1880 Nov 26; Friday; S; room 8

Covey, Joel
Colo Springs; 1880 Sept 22; Wednesday; S; room 12

Cowie, James
Nederland; 1880 Nov 23; Tuesday; D; room 13
Nederland; 1880 Sept 5; Sunday; D; room 21

Cox, Wm
Alexander's guest; Marshall; 1880 June 8; Tuesday; S

Coy, John
Great Show; 1880 May 11; Tuesday; S; room 27

Coyle, Jas F
St Louis; 1880 July 26; Monday; D

Crabb, J H (Mrs)
Denver; 1880 Oct 14; Thursday; S;
room 35

Craig, R P
unreadable; 1880 June 17; Thursday;
D; room 12
Milwaukee, Wis; 1880 Sept 19; Sunday; D; room 6
Milwaukee; 1880 Nov 12; Friday; S;
room 3

Crammer, John J
1880 Mar 13; Saturday; L; room 27

Crampton, H
Kansas City; 1880 Mar 10; Wednesday; S; room 3

Crandall, C W
Omaha; 1880 Sept 22; Wednesday; D

Crandell, H E
Chicago; 1880 July 2; Friday; S; rm 44

Crane, Cora
Star Alliance Opera Co; 1880 June 11;
Friday; D; room 11

Crane, F A
Longmont; 1880 Mar 9; Tuesday; S
Longmont; 1880 Apr 5; Monday; S;
room 5
& Wife; Longmont; 1880 May 7;
Friday; S
Longmont; 1880 May 25; Tuesday; S
Longmont; 1880 May 27; Thursday; S
Longmont; 1880 July 15; Thursday; D
Longmont; 1880 July 24; Saturday; S
Longmont; 1880 Aug 13; Friday; B
Longmont; 1880 Aug 25; Wednesday;
L; room 14
Longmont; 1880 Sept 8; Wednesday; S
Longmont; 1880 Nov 24; Wednesday;
S; room 13

Crane, Seth M
Star Alliance Opera Co; 1880 June 11;
Friday; D; room 11

Cranston, M P
NY; 1880 Aug 25; Wednesday; S
N Y; 1880 June 7; Monday; D; rm 10

Crary, B F
Golden; 1880 Mar 18; Thursday; L;
room 17

Crawford, J W
Capt Jack; 1880 Apr 22; Thursday; D;
room 17

Crawford, N
Chicago; 1880 July 21; Wednesday; S;
room 1

Crew, Richard
Nederland; 1880 Apr 4; Sunday; S

Crofutt, Geo A
Colo; 1880 Aug 17; Tuesday; S; rm 14

Croler, Hullon
Denver; 1880 Apr 5; Monday; S; rm 3

Cromton, M P
New York; 1880 Oct 27; Wednesday;
L; room 2

Crooks, John L
Massachusetts; 1880 Nov 8; Monday;
S; room 10

Crooks, John S
Massachusetts; 1880 Nov 10; Wednesday; S

Cross, G J
Butler, Pa; 1880 June 1; Tuesday; D;
room 19
Marshall; 1880 June 3; Thursday; L;
room 14
Ouray; 1880 July 3; Saturday; S; rm 14

Crow, Fick
1880 Aug 8; Sunday; D; room 14

Crow, R
Nederland; 1880 June 2; Wednesday;
L; room 10

Crow, Richard
1880 Sept 4; Saturday; D; room 12
1880 Sept 9; Thursday; D; room 32

Crowe, Torn S
Saginaw, Mich; 1880 Aug 13; Friday;
S; room 21

Crudir, A J
NY; 1880 June 7; Monday; S; room 12

Cruise, C T
St Joe; 1880 Aug 16; Monday; D

Crumb, W A
Jackson Coal Co; 1880 Apr 22; Thursday; S; room 12
Jackson Coal Co Erie; 1880 Aug 3;
Tuesday; D

Cue, T M
1880 Mar 22; Monday; L; room 20

Cullacott, J J
Salina; 1880 Mar 15; Sunday; D

Culver, Bessie (Miss)
With Neita Harker; 1880 Mar 10;
Wednesday; S

Culver, Nathan S
Denver; 1880 Aug 21; Saturday; D

Cummings, P L
Denver; 1880 Mar 26; Friday; S; rm 33

Cummings, Pre
1880 Mar 27; Saturday; S; room 33

Curran, J E
New York; 1880 Apr 30; Friday; S;
room 6
NY; 1880 May 1; Saturday; S

Currant, R
Denver; 1880 May 7; Friday; S; rm 8

Curry, E S
Denver; 1880 June 13; Sunday; D

Curry, G W (Mrs)
Denver; 1880 Aug 17; Tuesday; D

Curtice, W J
& Wife; Denver; 1880 Aug 5; Thursday; D; room 8
Denver; 1880 Mar 19; Friday; D
Denver; 1880 Mar 25; Thursday; S

Curtis, H O
Georgetown, Col; 1880 Aug 7; Saturday; S; room 35

Cushman, A
Longmont; 1880 Aug 7; Saturday; S

D

Dailey, D H
Lower Boulder; 1880 Nov 12; Fri; D

Dale, Charles
& Wife; Longmont; 1880 Aug 3;
Tuesday; D

Dalley, Elizabeth
& Child; Caribou; 1880 Dec 14; Tuesday; S; room 5

Daly, C T
& Wife; New York City; 1880 May 17;
Monday; S; room 6

Daniels, A C
Chicago; 1880 Apr 14; Wednesday; S;
room 1
Chicago; 1880 Aug 1; Sunday; D;
room 2
Chicago; 1880 Oct 14; Thursday; S;
room 1

Daniels, George
Youngstown O; 1880 May 13; Thursday; D

Daniels, H T
Chicago; 1880 Oct 30; Saturday; D; room 1

Danon, T H
& Lady; Louisville; 1880 Apr 2; Friday; D

Darrow, H
Louisville; 1880 Dec 7; Tuesday; D

Dartman, M
Cheyenne, WY; 1880 Mar 31; Wednesday; S; room 3

Darwin, Charles
& Wife; Washington, DC; 1880 Dec 15; Wednesday; S; room 12

Daugherty, John M
Delaware; 1880 Sept 10; Friday; S; room 13

Davey, Wm S
Caribou; 1880 June 4; Friday; S; rm 34

Davidson, C W
Nederland; 1880 May 26; Wednesday; S; room 6

Davidson, Mrs
Denver; 1880 Sept 19; Sunday; D; room 10

Davidson, W
Ward; 1880 June 18; Friday; D
Ward; 1880 June 21; Monday; D

Davidson, W A
Ward; 1880 June 25; Friday; D
Ward; 1880 July 10; Saturday; D
Ward; 1880 July 8; Thursday; L; rm 21

Davidson, W S Jr
New York City; 1880 May 13; Thursday; S; room 44

Davidson, Wm A
Ward; 1880 June 24; Thursday; S

Davies, E E
Cleveland, OH; 1880 Mar 27; Saturday; S; room 12
Cleveland, OH; 1880 Mar 28; Sunday; S; room 12

Davis, A
New Haven; 1880 June 21; Monday; S; room 6
Denver; 1880 Dec 7; Tuesday; S

Davis, Ben
Marshall; 1880 Apr 22; Thursday; D

Davis, C
Crisman; 1880 Oct 23; Saturday; D

Davis, Evan R
In jail; Marshall; 1880 Apr 21; Wednesday; B

Davis, G D W
Barnums Show; 1880 Aug 1; Sunday; L; room 14

Davis, H C
Denver; 1880 Aug 21; Saturday; D

Davis, S (Miss)
New Jersey; 1880 Aug 24; Tuesday; D; room 2

Davis, W H
Denver; 1880 Oct 2; Saturday; L; room 6

Davis, Wm
Agent; 1880 May 11; Tues; S; rm 27

Dawley, D L
Saints Rest, Colo; 1880 Apr 29; Thursday; S; room 12

Dawton, John
Marshall; 1880 Apr 23; Friday; B

Day, H
City; 1880 July 19; Monday; S
& Himself; City; 1880 June 28; Monday; S

De Puy, W U
New York; 1880 Oct 3; Sunday; S;
room 12
New York; 1880 Oct 4; Monday; L;
room 12

Dean, Charles
Fort Collins; 1880 Mar 25; Thursday;
L; room 27

DeBerard, W M
Nederland; 1880 Mar 6; Saturday; L;
room 27
Nederland; 1880 Mar 14; Sunday; S;
room 17
Nederland; 1880 Mar 25; Thursday; S;
room 33
Nederland; 1880 Apr 3; Saturday; S
Nederland, Col; 1880 Apr 27; Tues-
day; D
Nederland; 1880 May 11; Tuesday; L;
room 6
Middle Park; 1880 July 8; Thursday; B
Nederland; 1880 July 4; Sunday; S

Debeve, Wm
Dan Castello & Co Circus; 1880 May
23; Sunday

Decker, W S
Denver; 1880 Nov 11; Thursday; D;
room 1

Degenfritz, C E
Leadville; 1880 Sept 2; Thursday; L;
room 3

Deis, Jacob
Minister Plenipotentiary; Cremona
Park Brass Band, Denver; 1880 Aug
21; Saturday

Deitrick, H
UPRR; 1880 June 29; Tuesday; S;
room 3

Deland[e], Emory
Nederland; 1880 May 24; Monday; S;
room 13
Nederland; 1880 Sept 1; Wed; D

DeLand, Frank
North Boulder; 1880 Mar 16; Tues-
day; L; room 28
Smith Batesville; 1880 May 3; Mon-
day; D; room 28
North Boulder; 1880 July 12; Monday;
S; room 13

DeLantry, J M
Central City; 1880 Apr 18; Sunday; D;
room 6

Delen, Geo
Carrabou; 1880 Mar 16; Tuesday; D

Dell, G T
Longmont; 1880 May 22; Saturday; D

Dell, W A
Fla; 1880 Aug 24; Tuesday; S; room 6

Delleket, A (Mrs)
Denver; 1880 Sept 20; Monday; S

DeLong, T
Nederland; 1880 Mar 15; Sunday;
room 27

Denchfield, J W
Greeley, Col; 1880 May 14; Friday; L;
room 18

Denio, J W
Longmont; 1880 Dec 9; Thursday; D;
room 12
Longmont; 1880 June 26; Saturday; D
Longmont; 1880 May 22; Saturday; D

Denison, C W
Nederland; 1880 Apr 28; Wed; B
Nederland; 1880 Apr 28; Wednesday;
S; room 21
Nederland; 1880 May 4; Tuesday; S;
room 11

Denison, C W (cont.)
Nederland; 1880 May 10; Monday; D
Nederland; 1880 May 22; Saturday; D;
room 17
Nederland; 1880 July 18; Sunday; B;
room 10

Denison, Geo
Nederland; 1880 May 24; Monday; S

Dennison, H G
Denver; 1880 July 5; Monday; S
Chihuahua; 1880 Nov 13; Saturday; L;
room 12
Denver; 1880 Nov 25; Thursday,
Thanksgiving; B
Denver; 1880 Dec 15; Wednesday; D

Denny, J P
New York; 1880 July 23; Friday; D

Dentinan, M
Cheyenne; 1880 July 28; Wednesday;
D; room 1

Derbec, E
Paris; 1880 Nov 27; Saturday; S; rm 8

Deverterten, E
New York; 1880 Aug 18; Wednesday;
S; room 12

Devlin, Sam'l S (Hon)
NY City; 1880 Oct 13; Wednesday; D;
room 12
New York; 1880 Oct 18; Monday; D;
room 14

Dewey, S C
Cincinatti, O; 1880 Mar 24; Wednesday; S; room 2

DeWolf, T A
Leavenworth; 1880 June 4; Friday; S;
room 1

Dexter, W H
Omaha; 1880 Aug 30; Monday; L;
room 1

Diamond, John
Philadelphia; 1880 May 27; Thursday;
S; room 19

Dickhart, H E
Caribou; 1880 May 28; Friday; D
Caribou; 1880 Nov 1; Monday; D;
room 34

Dickinson, D C
Longmont; 1880 May 21; Friday; S;
room 18

Dickson, John T
Malta, Col; 1880 May 17; Monday; D

Dickson, L H
Longmont; 1880 Aug 14; Saturday; D
Longmont; 1880 Sept 4; Saturday; D

Dickson, Will E
Malta, Col; 1880 May 17; Monday; D

Dilley, C
Iowa; 1880 Apr 23; Friday; S; room 20

Dillon, R
Leadville; 1880 Mar 10; Wed; D

Dinsmore, H G
St Louis, MO; 1880 Mar 10; Wednesday; D ; 6

Do, J J
Chicago; 1880 June 8; Tuesday; S;
room 1

Dockett, R H
NY; 1880 Mar 24; Wednesday; D

Dockrill, R H
& Wife; Breakfast 6:30; 1880 Aug 3;
Tuesday; B; room 21

Dodge, Dr
Guest of Owen; 1880 June 20; Sun; D

Dodge, F B
Denver; 1880 Apr 26; Monday; L;
room 5

Dodge, Frank
Guest with Kirk; 1880 May 9; Sunday

Dodge, G F
Ft Collins; 1880 Aug 28; Saturday; S;
room 28
Denver; 1880 Aug 30; Monday; S;
room 20

Dodge, H
Denver; 1880 Apr 4; Sunday; D

Dodge, T B
Denver; 1880 Apr 26; Monday; D

Dodson, B W
Chicago; 1880 June 13; Sunday; D

Dolloff, L W
& Wife; 1880 Aug 21; Saturday; D

Donald, Wm
Caribou; 1880 May 1; Saturday; S;
room 5
Caribou; 1880 May 25; Tuesday; S;
room 17
Caribou; 1880 Sept 1; Wednesday; S;
room 25
Caribou; 1880 Oct 21; Thursday; S
& Wife; Caribou; 1880 Oct 25; Monday; D

Donaldson, A M
Beaver City, Neb; 1880 June 28; Monday; L; room 29

Donaldson, W A
& Wife; 1880 May 24; Monday; D

Donnelly, Leo
Caribou; 1880 Mar 7; Sunday; L;
room 28
Caribou; 1880 Mar 8; Monday; S;
room 27
Caribou; 1880 May 18; Tuesday; S;
room 12
Caribou; 1880 Aug 9; Monday; D;
room 13

Donnelly, Leo (cont.)
Caribou; 1880 Aug 10; Tuesday; S;
room 14
New York; 1880 Aug 11; Wednesday;
D; room 14

Donnelly, T L
Ward; 1880 Apr 13; Tuesday; D

Doreald, Jno
Caribou; 1880 Aug 24; Tuesday; S;
room 12

Dormer, Thos L
Central; 1880 July 24; Saturday; D

Dougan, Jas A
Chicago; 1880 Oct 1; Friday; L; rm 3

Dougherty, Jno M
Delaware; 1880 Sept 13; Monday; L;
room 14

Doughty, Miss
North; 1880 June 18; Friday; S; rm 4

Douglass, A J
Gold Hill; 1880 Apr 17; Saturday; L;
room 34

Doune, Miss
Longmont; 1880 Aug 3; Tuesday; D

Dovrot, E
Denver; 1880 Apr 24; Saturday; L;
room 12

Dowell, J M
Kansas City; 1880 Sept 14; Tuesday;
D; room 2

Downer, F M
Longmont, with SD; 1880 Nov 14;
Sunday; B

Downer, John S
Cardinal; 1880 May 27; Thursday; D

Downer, P H
Longmont with DS; 1880 Oct 28;
Thursday; B

Downer, S J
Left after B; 1880 Apr 6; Tuesday; B
Kirm bak [?]; 1880 Apr 7; Wednesday;
D; room 45
Boulder; 1880 Mar 6; Sat
Left after B; 1880 May 18; Tuesday
Boulder; 1880 May 21; Friday; D
City; 1880 Oct 10; Sunday

Downer, S S
With Miss Fulton; 1880 Aug 21;
Saturday; D
& Wife; Boulder; 1880 Dec 16; Thursday; S; room 16
Longmont; 1880 Dec 18; Saturday
Boulder; 1880 Oct 30; Saturday; S

Doyle, P C
1880 Sept 25; Saturday; D; room 27

Doyle, Peter C
Ouray Co, Col; 1880 Sept 21; Tuesday;
S; room 14

Drake, F G
New York; 1880 Aug 23; Monday; D;
room 12

Draper, J S
Chicago; 1880 May 20; Thursday; S

Drenson, C W
Wife & 2 children; N York; 1880 July
6; Tuesday; D; room 10

Drew, E H
Denver; 1880 May 21; Friday; S; rm 2

Droesher, A R
Memphis, Tenn; 1880 July 9; Friday;
S; room 12

Drumm, E R
Hartford, Conn; 1880 Oct 16; Sat; D

Drumm, Henry
City; 1880 Oct 13; Wednesday; L;
room 27
Boulder; 1880 Nov 1; Monday; L;
room 27

Drummond, Daniel
Gold Hill; 1880 Nov 30; Tuesday; L;
room 33
Gold Hill; 1880 Dec 1; Wednesday; D;
room 33

Drury, C J
Atchison; 1880 Oct 12; Tuesday; S;
room 15

Ducas, S
Denver, Col; 1880 Sept 25; Saturday;
L; room 2

Duff, E T
Golden; 1880 May 1; Saturday; S;
room 6

Duffy, Ed
Star Alliance Opera Co; 1880 June 11;
Friday; D; room 29

Duffy, James
Dry Creek; 1880 Apr 1; Thursday; L;
room 27
Dry Creek; 1880 Apr 2; Friday; L;
room 27

Duffy, Jimmie
Dry Creek; 1880 Apr 3; Saturday; L;
room 27

Duffy, Will J
Star Alliance Opera Co; 1880 June 11;
Friday; D; room 33

Dummit, John M
Spanish Bar; 1880 June 8; Tuesday; S;
room 3
Spanish Bar; 1880 June 9; Wednesday;
S; room 6

Dun, J A (see Dunn, J A)
Absent after B; 1880 Mar 8; Mon
Denver; 1880 Apr 20; Tuesday; D;
room 10, 11
Denver; 1880 Apr 22; Thursday; S;
room 10

Dun, J A (see Dunn, J A) (cont.)
& Wife; City; 1880 June 28; Mon; S
City; 1880 Aug 12; Thursday; D
City; 1880 Sept 3; Friday; D
City; 1880 Sept 3; Friday; S
& Wife; City; 1880 Nov 12; Friday; S;
room 16
& Wife; Boulder; 1880 Nov 18; Thursday; S; room 16

Dunagan, C
Nederland; 1880 June 21; Monday; D

Dunagan, E
Nederland; 1880 June 23; Wed; D

Duncan, E
Longmont; 1880 Oct 15; Friday; L;
room 27

Duncan, Elisha
St Vrain; 1880 Aug 9; Monday; S;
room 29

Duncan, G A
Georgetown; 1880 Nov 29; Monday;
L; room 12

Duncan, J B
Breckenridge; 1880 May 5; Wednesday; S; room 27

Duncan, R A
Leadville; 1880 May 4; Tuesday; S

Dunfield, William II
Red Cliff; 1880 Nov 21; Sunday; D;
room 13

Dunfield, Wm H
Red Cliff; 1880 Nov 20; Saturday

Dunlap, F Jeru
Denver; 1880 Nov 11; Thursday; D;
room 17

Dunlap, H N
St Louis; 1880 Sept 14; Tuesday; D;
room 8

Dunlop, Minn (Miss)
1880 Aug 11; Wednesday; L; room 18

Dunn, Geo R
Jamestown; 1880 June 6; Sunday; D
Jamestown, Col; 1880 June 9;
Wednesday; D

Dunn, George R
Philadelphia; 1880 June 4; Friday; S;
room 11

Dunn, J A (see Dun, J A)
& Wife; Boulder; 1880 Aug 10; Tuesday; S
& Wife; 1880 Aug 21; Saturday; D

Dunn, J F
& Wife; New York; 1880 Aug 17;
Tuesday; L; room 8

Dunn, Jno F
& Wife; NY City; 1880 Aug 17; Tuesday; D; room 8

Dunne, Jno W
1880 Apr 22; Thursday; D; room 25

Duons, S
Denver, Col; 1880 Sept 24; Friday; D;
room 2

Durand & Watrigan
Dan Castello & Co Circus; 1880 May
23; Sunday; L; room 26

Durell, E P
Denver, Col; 1880 June 11; Friday; S;
room 6

Durfee, J A
Chicago; 1880 Mar 9; Tuesday; S;
room 1

Durfor, J A
Chicago; 1880 Aug 24; Tuesday; L;
room 2

Dursley, F
Denver; 1880 Aug 28; Saturday; S

Duston, Mrs
1880 Aug 21; Saturday; D

Dwyer, H
Salina; 1880 Apr 26; Monday; D

E

Earan, D A
Greeley; 1880 May 16; Sunday; S

Earhart, Minnie (Miss)
Dinner with E M Styles; 1880 Nov 28; Sunday; D

Earhart, W R (Dr)
Dinner with Cosgrove; 1880 Mar 8; Monday; D

East, James
Cheyenne; 1880 Oct 20; Wednesday; S; room 10

Eaton, B H
Greeley; 1880 Oct 15; Fri; D; rm 17
Greeley; 1880 Oct 16; Saturday; S
Greeley; 1880 Oct 27; Wednesday; D
Greeley, Colo; 1880 Sept 1; Wednesday; D; room 20

Eaton, B W
Greeley; 1880 July 15; Thursday; D

Eaton, C H
Cheyenne, Wyo; 1880 Aug 23; Monday; S; room 2

Eaton, C U
Cheyenne; 1880 Oct 10; Sunday; L; room 33

Eaton, C W
Cheyenne; 1880 Oct 19; Tuesday; S; room 34

Eaton, Geo C
Chicago; 1880 May 12; Wednesday; D; room 2

Eavegens, A
With Egbert; 1880 Dec 8; Wed; S

Eavins, D
Summerville; 1880 May 15; Sat; D

Eckstein, Chas
Chicago; 1880 June 16; Wednesday; L; room 1
Chicago; 1880 July 22; Thursday; D; room 6

Eddours, Ralph Jr
Greeley; 1880 July 5; Monday; D

Eddy, H H
Chihuahua, Col; 1880 May 11; Tuesday; D

Eddy, Miss
Greeley; 1880 Nov 2; Tuesday; S; room 8

Eddy, S E (Miss)
Greeley; 1880 Sept 25; Saturday; S

Edmundson, D W
Denver; 1880 Nov 9; Tuesday; D

Egbert, A A
Denver; 1880 Apr 20; Tuesday; D
Denver; 1880 Aug 17; Tuesday; S; room 6
Denver; 1880 Aug 21; Saturday; D
Denver; 1880 Sept 22; Wednesday; D
Denver; 1880 Oct 15; Friday; S; rm 16
Denver; 1880 Nov 3; Wednesday; S; room 8
Denver; 1880 Dec 6; Monday; S; rm 6

Eggleston, S F
Denver; 1880 Apr 4; Sunday; D

Elan, John
Erie; 1880 July 5; Monday; D

Elbert, S H
Denver; 1880 Mar 25; Thursday; S

Elbring, L A
St Louis, Mo; 1880 Aug 11; Wednesday; L; room 28

Eldridge, S
Dan Castello & Co Circus; 1880 May 23; Sunday; D
1880 May 24; Monday; L; room 17

Eldridge, W W
With RPC; 1880 July 4; Sunday; S

Ellet, Annie (Miss)
1880 Aug 21; Saturday; D

Ellet, Jno A (Col)
& Mrs; guests of JB; 1880 June 29; Tuesday; S

Ellet, Mayor
& Wife; 1880 Aug 21; Saturday; D

Ellingham, Georgia (Miss)
1880 Mar 28; Sunday; D

Ellingham, J J
With Downen; Boulder; 1880 Mar 9; Tuesday; D
1880 Mar 28; Sunday; D
City; 1880 Mar 29; Monday; L; rm 12
City; 1880 May 12; Wednesday; D
Boulder; 1880 Oct 30; Saturday; S

Ellingham, John J
Cheyenne, W T; 1880 June 19; Sat; S

Ellingham, Miss
1880 Sept 19; Sunday; S

Ellingham, Robert
Caribou; 1880 Nov 15; Monday; D

Ellingham, Robt
Caribou; 1880 June 6; Sunday; L; room 27
Caribou; 1880 Aug 16; Monday; D
Guest of JJE; Caribou; 1880 Dec 14; Tuesday; S

Ellingham, Robt (Mrs)
1880 Mar 28; Sunday; D

Ellingham, S
Caribou; 1880 Sept 1; Wednesday; S

Ellingham, Sadie (Miss)
1880 Mar 28; Sunday; D
Albany, Ills; 1880 Aug 23; Monday; D
City; 1880 Sept 4; Saturday; D
JJE; 1880 Sept 5; Sunday; D
JJE; 1880 Nov 15; Monday; D
JJE; 1880 Nov 17; Wednesday; D

Ellingham, Sam E
guest of JJE; Caribou; 1880 Dec 14; Tuesday

Ellingham, Samuel
Caribou; 1880 Aug 23; Monday; D

Ellingham, W A
Caribou; 1880 Apr 16; Friday; D
Kokomo; 1880 Nov 17; Wednesday; D

Ellingham, Wm A
Kokomo; 1880 Nov 16; Tuesday; S
Kokomo; 1880 Nov 18; Thursday; B
Kokomo; 1880 Nov 19; Friday; B
Kokomo; 1880 Nov 20; Saturday; B

Elliot, V A
1880 Aug 21; Saturday; D

Ellsworth, F O
Wakeeney, Kans; 1880 Dec 4; Saturday; S; room 6
Wakeeney, Kans; 1880 Dec 5; Sunday; S; room 6
Wakeeney, Kans; 1880 Dec 6; Monday; D; room 11
Wakeeney; 1880 Dec 8; Wednesday; S; room 3

Ellsworth, F O (Mrs)
Wakeeney, Kans; 1880 Dec 7; Tuesday; S; room 3

Ellsworth, L C
& Wife; Denver; 1880 Apr 24; Saturday; S; room 4

Ellsworth, L C (cont.)
& Wife; Denver; 1880 July 10; Saturday; D; room 4

Elvirnace, C
Absent after B; 1880 Mar 7; Sun

Emans, E
City; 1880 Oct 21; Thursday; S

Emanuel, M, Jr
NZ; 1880 Dec 6; Monday; S; room 2

Emanuel, W H
Nederland; 1880 June 3; Thursday; S; room 25

Emerson, C
Greeley; 1880 Dec 13; Monday; D

Emery, C F
Kas City; 1880 July 17; Saturday; D; room 2

Empfield, G
1880 Mar 16; Tuesday; S; room 27

Engle, E M R
Fla; 1880 Aug 24; Tuesday; S; room 6

Engle, Henry A L
Fla; 1880 Aug 24; Tuesday; S; room 6

Enid, G W
Ward; 1880 Aug 3; Tuesday; L

Ennis, Mrs C C
Rochester, NY; 1880 Apr 19; Monday; S; room 5

Epter, C W
Denver; 1880 Sept 15; Wednesday; D

Erfurt, H
Davenport, Ia; 1880 Sept 21; Tues; S

Erhardt, Dr
& Wife; 1880 Aug 21; Saturday; D

Erhardt, F (Miss)
1880 Aug 21; Saturday; D

Ersinger, Hy
Denver; 1880 Sept 9; Thursday; D
Denver; 1880 Sept 11; Saturday; L; room 3
Denver; 1880 Sept 12; Sunday; L; room 1
Denver; 1880 Oct 18; Monday; D
Denver; 1880 Nov 30; Tuesday; D

Estabrook, Geo H
Denver; 1880 Sept 23; Thursday; D; room 6

Eurgens, A
Wife & Child; Louisville; 1880 Apr 7; Wednesday; S; room 8

Evans, D
Sommerville; 1880 Mar 15; Sunday; S; room 33
Sommerville; 1880 Mar 25; Thurs
Sommerville; 1880 Apr 1; Thurs; D
Sommerville; 1880 Apr 9; Friday; L; room 35
Gold Hill; 1880 Apr 14; Wednesday; L; room 33
Sommerville; 1880 May 3; Monday; D
Summerville; 1880 May 5; Wednesday; D
Sommerville; 1880 July 19; Mon; D
Sommerville; 1880 Aug 17; Tuesday; S; room 13

Evans, Dave
Summerville; 1880 Aug 3; Tuesday; D

Evans, G (Mrs)
Marshall; 1880 June 2; Wednesday; D

Evans, Geo W
Chicago; 1880 June 23; Wednesday; S; room 44
Chicago; 1880 July 28; Wednesday; S; room 2
Chicago; 1880 Sept 10; Friday; D; room 1

Ewart, N D
Estes Park, Col; 1880 July 25; Sunday;
L; room 6
Estes Park, Col; 1880 Aug 8; Sunday;
D; room 6

Ewart, W W
Estes Park; 1880 Aug 13; Friday; S;
room 6

F

Fagan, J M
St Louis; 1880 May 22; Saturday; D;
room 2

Fallons, Bishop
Chicago; 1880 Oct 31; Sunday; S

Farewell, C D
Gold Hill; 1880 Mar 16; Tuesday; D

Farewell, Cy
Gold Hill; 1880 Mar 11; Thursday; D;
room 25

Farnsworth, A C
Chicago; 1880 Mar 12; Friday; S;
room 8

Farrar, B F
St Louis; 1880 Dec 18; Saturday; L;
room 1

Farrar, Fiske
Denver, Col; 1880 Apr 5; Monday; S;
room 17
Marked out; 1880 Apr 6; Tues
Denver, Col; 1880 Apr 20; Tuesday; S;
room 8

Farrington, Ben
Denver; 1880 Aug 4; Wednesday; D;
room 26

Farwell, Ararhu
Gold Hill; 1880 Mar 25; Thursday; S;
room 35

Farwell, C B
Deadwood; 1880 Mar 25; Thursday; S;
room 35

Farwell, C D
Gold Hill; 1880 Apr 28; Wednesday;
D; room 25
Gold Hill; 1880 Apr 6; Tuesday; S;
room 28
Gold Hill; 1880 Apr 8; Thursday; S;
room 25
Gold Hill; 1880 Mar 10; Wed; D
Gold Hill; 1880 Mar 17; Wed; D
Gold Hill; 1880 Mar 23; Tuesday; D
Gold Hill; 1880 Mar 9; Tuesday; L

Farwell, G M
Gold Hill; 1880 Apr 21; Wednesday;
S; room 25

Farwell, J H
Gold Hill; 1880 Apr 23; Friday; S;
room 25
Gold Hill; 1880 Apr 24; Saturday; S;
room 25
Gold Hill; 1880 Apr 26; Monday; D;
room 25
Gold Hill; 1880 Apr 28; Wednesday;
S; room 25
Gold Hill; 1880 Apr 29; Thursday; S;
room 25
Gold Hill; 1880 Apr 30; Friday; S;
room 25
Gold Hill; 1880 May 5; Wednesday;
D; room 25
Gold Hill; 1880 May 8; Saturday; D;
room 25
Gold Hill; 1880 May 11; Tuesday; D;
room 27
Gold Hill; 1880 May 14; Friday; S;
room 27
Gold Hill; 1880 May 15; Saturday; S
Gold Hill; 1880 May 17; Monday; D;
room 25

Farwell, J H (cont.)

Gold Hill; 1880 May 19; Wednesday; D; room 27

Gold Hill; 1880 May 20; Thursday; S; room 27

Gold Hill; 1880 May 21; Friday; S; room 25

Gold Hill; 1880 May 22; Saturday; S; room 27

Gold Hill; 1880 May 24; Monday; D; room 27

Gold Hill; 1880 May 26; Wednesday; D; room 27

Gold Hill; 1880 May 27; Thursday; S; room 26

Gold Hill; 1880 May 28; Friday; S; room 27

Gold Hill; 1880 May 29; Saturday; S; room 27

Gold Hill; 1880 June 1; Tuesday; S; room 27

Gold Hill; 1880 June 2; Wednesday; S; room 27

Gold Hill; 1880 June 4; Friday; D; room 27

Gold Hill; 1880 June 5; Saturday; S; room 27.

Gold Hill; 1880 June 13; Sunday; S; room 27

Gold Hill; 1880 June 14; Monday; S; room 27

Gold Hill; 1880 June 17; Thursday; S; room 27

Gold Hill; 1880 June 19; Saturday; S; room 27

Gold Hill; 1880 June 23; Wednesday; D; room 27

Gold Hill; 1880 June 26; Saturday; D

Gold Hill; 1880 June 29; Tuesday; D; room 27

Gold Hill; 1880 June 30; Wednesday; S; room 27

Gold Hill; 1880 July 1; Thursday; S; room 27

Farwell, J H (cont.)

Gold Hill; 1880 July 3; Saturday; S; room 27

Gold Hill; 1880 July 4; Sunday; S; room 27

Gold Hill; 1880 July 13; Tuesday; S; room 27

Gold Hill; 1880 July 14; Wednesday; S; room 28

Gold Hill; 1880 July 17; Saturday; S; room 27

Gold Hill; 1880 July 19; Monday; S; room 27

Gold Hill; 1880 July 21; Wednesday; S; room 29

Gold Hill; 1880 July 22; Thursday; S; room 27

Gold Hill; 1880 July 24; Saturday; D

Gold Hill; 1880 July 24; Saturday; S; room 27

Gold Hill; 1880 July 26; Monday; S; room 27

Gold Hill; 1880 July 29; Thursday; S; room 27

Gold Hill; 1880 July 31; Saturday; S; room 27

Gold Hill; 1880 Aug 2; Monday; D; room 27

Gold Hill; 1880 Aug 4; Wednesday; D

Gold Hill; 1880 Aug 9; Monday; S; room 27

Gold Hill; 1880 Aug 10; Tuesday; S; room 27

Gold Hill; 1880 Aug 12; Thursday; D

Gold Hill; 1880 Aug 13; Friday; S; room 27

Gold Hill; 1880 Aug 14; Saturday; S; room 27

Gold Hill; 1880 Aug 16; Monday; D; room 27

Gold Hill; 1880 Aug 17; Tuesday; S; room 27

Gold Hill; 1880 Aug 18; Wednesday; S; room 27

Farwell, J H (cont.)

Gold Hill; 1880 Aug 21; Saturday; D; room 24

Gold Hill; 1880 Aug 22; Sunday; L; room 29

Gold Hill; 1880 Aug 23; Monday; S; room 37

Gold Hill; 1880 Aug 27; Friday; S; room 27

Gold Hill; 1880 Aug 28; Saturday; S; room 27

Gold Hill; 1880 Aug 30; Monday; S; room 27

Gold Hill; 1880 Aug 31; Tuesday; S; room 27

Gold Hill; 1880 Sept 1; Wednesday; S; room 27

Gold Hill; 1880 Sept 2; Thursday; S; room 24

Gold Hill; 1880 Sept 3; Friday; S; room 27

Gold Hill; 1880 Sept 4; Saturday; S; room 27

Gold Hill; 1880 Sept 6; Monday; S; room 27

Gold Hill; 1880 Sept 8; Wednesday; D

Gold Hill; 1880 Sept 10; Friday; S; room 27

Gold Hill; 1880 Sept 13; Monday; S; room 24

Gold Hill; 1880 Sept 15; Wednesday; S; room 27

Gold Hill; 1880 Sept 16; Thursday; L; room 27

Gold Hill; 1880 Sept 17; Friday; S; room 27

Gold Hill; 1880 Sept 18; Saturday; S; room 29

Gold Hill; 1880 Sept 19; Sunday; S; room 29

Gold Hill; 1880 Sept 22; Wed; D

Gold Hill; 1880 Sept 23; Thursday; D

Gold Hill; 1880 Sept 23; Thursday; S

Farwell, J H (cont.)

Gold Hill; 1880 Sept 27; Monday; S; room 27

Gold Hill; 1880 Sept 29; Wednesday; S; room 28

Gold Hill; 1880 Sept 30; Thursday; S; room 28

Gold Hill; 1880 Oct 1; Fri; S; rm 28

Gold Hill; 1880 Oct 4; Monday; D

Gold Hill; 1880 Oct 7; Thursday; S; room 28

Gold Hill; 1880 Oct 8; Fri; S; rm 28

Gold Hill; 1880 Oct 13; Wednesday; S; room 28

Gold Hill; 1880 Oct 14; Thursday; S; room 28

Gold Hill; 1880 Oct 15; Friday; S; room 28

Gold Hill; 1880 Oct 23; Saturday; S; room 27

Gold Hill; 1880 Oct 25; Monday; S; room 27

Gold Hill; 1880 Oct 29; Friday; S; room 28

Gold Hill; 1880 Nov 30; Tuesday; S; room 27

Farwell, Jas

Gold Hill; 1880 Sept 26; Sunday; S; room 28

Farwell, Jas H

Gold Hill; 1880 Sept 21; Tuesday; D

Gold Hill; 1880 Sept 28; Tuesday; S; room 28

Gold Hill; 1880 Oct 16; Saturday; S; room 28

Gold Hill; 1880 Oct 19; Tuesday; D; room 28

Gold Hill; 1880 Oct 22; Friday; lD; 27

Gold Hill; 1880 Oct 27; Wednesday; S; room 28

Gold Hill; 1880 Nov 6; Saturday; D; room 28

Gold Hill; 1880 Dec 3; Fri; S; rm 27

Farwell, John
1880 Oct 19; Tuesday

Fasham, B A
NY; 1880 Oct 12; Tuesday; D; rm 12

Fauntleroy, P W
Denver; 1880 Sept 17; Friday; D;
room 10

Faux, William
Denver; 1880 Oct 28; Thursday; S;
room 7

Faux, Wm
Denver; 1880 Mar 26; Friday; S; rm 44
Denver; 1880 Oct 27; Wednesday; D

Faux, Wm J
Denver; 1880 Apr 13; Tuesday; S;
room 21
Denver; 1880 Apr 14; Wednesday; S

Fay, Wm J
Denver; 1880 Aug 22; Sunday; S
Denver; 1880 Aug 2; Monday; S

Fearshein, M
St Joe; 1880 May 7; Friday; S; room 11

Fee, Miss
1880 Aug 21; Saturday; D

Fee, Mr
With Miss Fee & Mrs Duston; 1880
Aug 21; Saturday; D

Fehrmann, Max
Berlin, Germany; 1880 Oct 23; Saturday; D; room 5

Feinple, E J
New Mexico; 1880 Apr 15; Thur; S

Felt, Jas
Omaha; 1880 Mar 24; Wednesday; S;
room 6

Fennis, W H
Milwaukee, Wis; 1880 June 10; Thursday; D

Ferguson, C E
Chicago; 1880 Apr 23; Friday; S; rm 2

Ferguson, N G
Denver; 1880 Dec 15; Wednesday; S

Fest, James Benjamin
Near Louisville, Colo; 1880 Oct 5;
Tuesday; D

Field, I N
1880 Oct 22; Friday; D

Field, Thomas
& Wife; Denver; 1880 Oct 22; Friday;
D; room 16

Field, W M
Denver; 1880 Dec 11; Saturday; D;
room 11

Fillins, Jacob
Georgetown; 1880 Nov 20; Sat; D

Filmore, R H
& Wife; Cedar Rapids, Ia; 1880 July
16; Friday; S; room 3

Fink, El
Leadville; 1880 Mar 10; Wed; D

Firchbach Brothers
Dan Castello & Co Circus; 1880 May
23; Sunday; L; room 32

Firter, A M
Cinti O; 1880 Apr 8; Thursday; S;
room 6

Fischer, F C
Cheyenne; 1880 July 21; Wednesday;
S; room 29
Absent after D; 1880 July 25; Sunday

Fischer, Fred C
Cheyenne; 1880 July 16; Friday; S;
room 35
1880 July 28; Wednesday; S; room 29

Fisher, A W
Caribou; 1880 Apr 21; Wednesday; S;
room 33

Fisher, H C
St Joseph MO; 1880 May 19; Wednesday; S; room 1
St Joseph, Mo; 1880 Sept 2; Thursday; D; room 21
Kansas City; 1880 Nov 8; Monday; L; room 2

Fisher, L (Miss)
Denver; 1880 Aug 29; Sunday; L; room 2

Fisher, L H
& Wife; Denver; 1880 Apr 24; Saturday; S; room 16

Fisher, S M
Chicago; 1880 Apr 3; Saturday; D; room 3

Fisk, A C
Denver; 1880 Aug 21; Saturday; D

Fitch, Geo A
Bellevue, Idaho; 1880 Nov 22; Monday; S; room 6

Fitzgerald, J K
Nederland, Colo; 1880 Aug 3; Tuesday; S; room 29

Flagg, Chas B
Chicago; 1880 July 16; Friday; D; room 3

Flagg, Chas F
Chicago; 1880 Nov 9; Tuesday; D; room 6

Flansbury. Isaac
Longmont; 1880 July 5; Monday; D

Fleck, Mollie (Miss)
Denver; 1880 Apr 13; Tuesday; D; room 17

Fleck, S D
Loveland, Colo; 1880 July 28; Wednesday; L; room 28

Fleischer, T
Denver; 1880 June 17; Thursday; S; room 2

Fleisher, H A
Phila; 1880 Oct 2; Saturday; L; room 8

Fleming, E W
Denver; 1880 May 15; Saturday; S; room 44

Fleming, W E
& Wife; San Francisco; 1880 May 15; Saturday; S; room 4

Flemming, Mrs
Chicago; 1880 Nov 5; Friday; L; rm 12

Flersheim, P S
Kansas City; 1880 Sept 29; Wednesday; D

Flersheins, A S
Kans City; 1880 Apr 30; Friday; D

Fogel, R
Cincy O; 1880 May 13; Thursday; D; room 1
Central City; 1880 Nov 11; Thurs; D

Fogg, J C
Phila, Pa; 1880 July 1; Thursday; S; room 20
Phila; 1880 July 5; Monday; S; room 6
Denver, Co; 1880 Dec 9; Thursday; D

Fogg, John C
Denver; 1880 Sept 9; Thursday; D
New York; 1880 Sept 21; Tuesday; D
New York; 1880 Sept 24; Friday; D
New York; 1880 Sept 28; Tuesday; D
New York; 1880 Oct 16; Saturday; D
New York; 1880 Oct 22; Friday; D
Denver; 1880 Nov 10; Wednesday; S
Denver; 1880 Nov 22; Monday; S
Denver; 1880 Dec 3; Friday; S
NY; 1880 Dec 11; Saturday; S
Denver; 1880 Dec 16; Thursday; D
Denver; 1880 Dec 18; Saturday; S

Foggate, James
Ward; 1880 Oct 23; Saturday; L

Foote, George
Cremona Park Brass Band, Denver;
1880 Aug 21; Saturday

Foote, J B
M C C City; 1880 June 28; Monday; D
Guest of B F Pine Jr; 1880 July 3;
Saturday; D
City; 1880 Aug 23; Monday; D
Boulder; 1880 Aug 24; Tuesday; L;
room 29
City; 1880 Sept 7; Tuesday; S
City; 1880 Sept 25; Saturday; D
Boulder; 1880 Oct 15; Friday; B
City; 1880 Nov 9; Tuesday; D
City; 1880 Nov 24; Wednesday; D

Foote, Jas B
City; 1880 May 12; Wednesday; D

Foote, J Y
City; 1880 Sept 24; Friday; S

Foote, James
& Wife; 1880 Aug 21; Saturday; D

Foote, James B
Boulder; 1880 Oct 17; Sunday; B

Foote, Jas B
City; 1880 Mar 24; Wednesday; D
City; 1880 Apr 21; Wednesday; D
City; 1880 Apr 28; Wednesday; D
City; 1880 May 6; Thursday; D
City; 1880 May 13; Thursday; D
City; 1880 May 24; Monday; D
City; 1880 June 8; Tuesday; B
City; 1880 June 26; Saturday; D
City; 1880 July 12; Monday; D
City; 1880 July 29; Thursday; S
City; 1880 Oct 7; Thursday; D

Foote, S G
1880 Apr 21; Wednesday; L; room 25
Boulder; 1880 Aug 25; Wednesday; L;
room 29

Foote, S G (cont.)
Boulder; 1880 Aug 27; Friday; L;
room 29
Boulder; 1880 Aug 30; Monday; L;
room 29
1880 Sept 2; Thursday; L; room 28
1880 Sept 3; Friday; L; room 29

Forcht, John P
E B Pa; 1880 Aug 5; Thursday; S;
room 3

Ford, H H
Atchison, Ks; 1880 Oct 21; Thursday;
L; room 6

Ford, Jennie F (Miss)
Denver; 1880 July 3; Saturday; L;
room 17

Forgner, Geo
Nederland; 1880 Sept 23; Thursday; D

Fork, Jas H
Breckenridge; 1880 Nov 11; Thursday;
D; room 10

Forman, John W
Ft Smith, Tex; 1880 Aug 20; Friday; S

Fosburgh, I A
Chicago; 1880 Aug 26; Thursday; L;
room 3

Fosburgh, Ira A
Chicago; 1880 Nov 16; Tuesday

Foss, M M
New York; 1880 Aug 25; Wednesday;
L; room 1

Fossett, Frank
Denver; 1880 July 13; Tuesday; D;
room 14

Foster, Ed
Dan Castello & Co Circus; 1880 May
23; Sunday; L; room 27

Foster, H A
Chicago ; 1880 Nov 1; Monday; S;
room 12

Fowler, B E
Hartford, Conn; 1880 Dec 4; Satur-
day; S; room 6
Hartford, Conn; 1880 Dec 5; Sunday;
S; room 6

Fowler, William S
Denver, Colo; 1880 June 17; Thursday;
S; room 13

Fox, A S
Boston, Mass; 1880 Apr 12; Monday;
S; room 2

Fox, J M
Longmont; 1880 Aug 23; Monday; D
Longmont; 1880 Dec 9; Thursday; D;
room 38

Fox, M P
Marshall; 1880 Mar 15; Sunday; D
Marshall; 1880 Aug 14; Saturday; D
Marshall; 1880 Aug 3; Tuesday; D
Marshall; 1880 Nov 9; Tuesday; D

Fox, Mable (Miss)
Longmont; 1880 Aug 3; Tuesday; D

Foycy, John C
New York; 1880 Sept 11; Saturday; S

Francis, Joseph B
Saint Joseph; 1880 Nov 21; Sunday; S

Francisco, C M
Greeley; 1880 July 5; Monday; D

Francisco, J H
Greeley; 1880 July 5; Monday; D

Franger, A P
Denver; 1880 July 13; Tuesday; D;
room 14

Frank, H
San Francisco; 1880 Oct 7; Thursday;
D; room 2

Franklin, P
Denver; 1880 Oct 7; Thursday; D;
room 12
Denver; 1880 Oct 8; Friday; O,
Denver; 1880 Sept 23; Thursday; S;
room 2

Frary, Wm J
Denver; 1880 Aug 21; Saturday; S

Freeman, J M
Greeley; 1880 Nov 23; Tuesday; L;
room 10
Greeley; 1880 Nov 24; Wednesday; S

French, Geo
Denver; 1880 Apr 30; Friday; D

Frendenthal, Max
Left after S; 1880 Apr 5; Monday; S

Friday, W
Denver; 1880 Dec 15; Wednesday; S;
room 25

Friedlander, Max
Nobles Company, New York; 1880
Oct 23; Saturday; D; room 12

Friend, A M
Kansas City; 1880 Sept 3; Friday; D

Frisbee, G
Leadville; 1880 Sept 30; Thursday; S

Frisbie, B H
Gunnison; 1880 Sept 23; Thursday; S;
room 27
Tin Cup; 1880 Sept 27; Monday; S;
room 29

Frost, F P
Greeley; 1880 July 5; Monday; D

Frost, H J
Denver; 1880 June 15; Tuesday; L;
room 27

Fugel, R
Custi, O; 1880 Aug 24; Tuesday; S;
room 3

Fuller, D P
Denver; 1880 Nov 30; Tuesday; S; room 3

Fuller, Geo W
Kansas City; 1880 Dec 15; Wednesday; S; room 6
Kans City; 1880 July 28; Wed; D

Fuller, Isabel
Star Alliance Opera Co; 1880 June 11; Friday; D; room 10

Fulton, Chas E
Chicago; 1880 Nov 10; Wednesday; L; room 6

Fulton, Harry
New York; 1880 June 9; Wednesday; D
Ward; 1880 June 11; Friday; S
NY; 1880 June 14; Monday; D
Ward; 1880 June 18; Friday; D
Denver; 1880 June 20; Sunday; D
NY; 1880 June 21; Monday; D
Ward; 1880 June 24; Thursday; S
Ward; 1880 June 25; Friday; D
Ward; 1880 July 8; Thursday; L; rm 19
New York; 1880 July 10; Saturday; D
Ward; 1880 July 19; Monday; S; rm 3
NiWot; 1880 Aug 10; Tuesday; D
NiWot Ward; 1880 Aug 12; Thursday
Ward; 1880 Aug 29; Sunday; S
Ward; 1880 Aug 31; Tuesday; S; rm 2
Ward; 1880 Sept 18; Saturday; D; room 20
Ward; 1880 Sept 29; Wednesday; D
Ward; 1880 Oct 22; Friday; D; room 5
Ward; 1880 Oct 23; Saturday; S; rm 17
Ward; 1880 Oct 28; Thursday; S
Ward; 1880 Oct 31; Sunday; D
Ward; 1880 Dec 16; Thursday; S; room 3

Fulton, Miss
1880 Aug 21; Saturday; D

Fulton, Wm
Neb City; 1880 July 28; Wednesday; S; room 6

Fulwider, H W
New York; 1880 Sept 10; Friday; D

Fus, H G
1880 Dec 15; Wednesday; X,

Fuzzell, A J
1880 May 12; Wednesday; S; room 13

G

Gaines, Thos E
Kansas City; 1880 July 28; Wednesday; D
Kansas City; 1880 July 29; Thursday; S
Kansas City; 1880 Sept 23; Thursday; S; room 10
Kansas City; 1880 Sept 25; Saturday; L; room 3
Estes Park; 1880 Nov 4; Thursday; L; room 6

Gallagher, C N
Delaware; 1880 Sept 10; Friday; S; room 14

Gallagher, Chas N
Delaware; 1880 Sept 13; Monday; S; room 13

Gallagher, M
St Louis; 1880 July 14; Wednesday; D; room 1

Gallaway, W C
Chicago; 1880 June 22; Tuesday; S; room 2

Gallup, J C
Denver; 1880 July 1; Thursday; D

Galt, E L
Sterling, Ill; 1880 Aug 9; Monday; S; room 8

Galusha, S S
Caribou; 1880 Aug 31; Tuesday; L; room 29

Games, Thos E
KCity; 1880 May 15; Saturday; L; room 6

Ganett, J C
St Louis; 1880 July 22; Thursday; D; room 16

Ganett, R C
St Louis; 1880 July 22; Thursday; D; room 16

Ganse, Henry T
Chicago; 1880 Nov 5; Friday; L; rm 22

Garbarino, L J
1880 Oct 22; Friday; D

Garbarino, Louis
City; 1880 Nov 7; Sunday; L; room 14

Gardner, J G
Boston; 1880 June 4; Friday; D; rm 3

Garner, E S
Central City; 1880 Aug 31; Tuesday; S; room 11
Denver; 1880 Sept 14; Tuesday; D
Denver; 1880 Sept 23; Thursday; S

Garrigues, Thos A
Leavenworth; 1880 Apr 21; Wednesday; S; room 8

Garrigues, Thos A
Leavenworth; 1880 Aug 25; Wednesday; S

Garrison, Philip
Denver, Col; 1880 Nov 26; Friday; D; room 12
Denver; 1880 Nov 27; Saturday; L; room 11

Garudin, H D
Black Hawk; 1880 July 31; Saturday; S; room 29

Gates, Charles
Denver; 1880 Sept 20; Monday; S

Gates, E Landes
London England; 1880 June 25; Friday; S; room 14

Gauster, H J
Chicago; 1880 Aug 12; Thursday; L; room 2

Gaven, Waren
City; 1880 Sept 12; Sunday; S

Gay, I S
Maysville; 1880 June 27; Sunday; D

Gay, WM J
Denver; 1880 Mar 30; Tues

Gayln, Thos
New Guh; 1880 July 19; Monday; S; room 12

Gearch, C H
1880 Apr 22; Thursday; D; room 33

Geegle, J M
Golden; 1880 May 15; Saturday; S

Geer, C
& Wife; Ogdinsburg, NY; 1880 June 12; Saturday; S; room 16

Geer, G F
Absent after B; 1880 Mar 22; Mon
Absent after B; 1880 Apr 19; Mon; B

Geer, G F (Mrs)
Absent after B; 1880 Mar 24; Wednesday; B
Returned; 1880 Mar 29; Monday; S; room 7

Geer, Geo F
Concord, Minn; 1880 Apr 20; Tuesday; S; room 7
Absent after L; 1880 Apr 22; Thursday; L
Left after B; 1880 May 17; Monday

Geer, Geo F (cont.)
Rits; 1880 May 18; Tuesday; D
Return; 1880 May 22; Saturday

Geer, Geo F (Mrs)
Returned at ; 1880 Dec 10; Friday; S

Geer, Geo H
Absent after B; 1880 Mar 18; Thurs
Return; 1880 Mar 20; Saturday; S;
room 7

Geer, Geo P
Peterson; 1880 Mar 16; Tuesday; S;
room 7
Erwin Mine; 1880 Mar 27; Saturday;
S; room 7
Pitnis; 1880 May 12; Wednesday; S

Geer, Geo T
Duncan, MN; 1880 Mar 6; Saturday;
S; room 7
Nederland; 1880 Apr 3; Saturday; S;
room 7
Return; 1880 Apr 5; Monday; S; rm 7
Return; 1880 Apr 10; Saturday; L;
room 7
Return; 1880 Apr 24; Saturday; S
Petr; 1880 May 4; Tuesday; S; room 7
Returned; 1880 June 7; Monday; S;
room 7
& Son; absent after B; 1880 Aug 5;
Thursday
1880 Aug 18; Wednesday; S

Geer, Mrs
Absent after B; 1880 Sept 14; Tues; B

Geer, N S
Returned; 1880 Aug 18; Wednesday;
S; room 7

Geer, Norman S
Absent after B; 1880 Aug 23; Monday
Sextons River, Vt; 1880 July 9; Fri; S

Geer, S F
1880 Mar 6; Saturday; P,

Gerner, E S
Central City; 1880 Sept 2; Thursday; S

Gethraple, _ F
Black Hawk; 1880 May 15; Saturday; S

Gettey, W J
Omaha; 1880 Apr 29; Thursday; D;
room 2
& Wife; Omaha; 1880 July 30; Friday;
L; room 1
Omaha; 1880 Oct 29; Friday; L; rm 2

Ghio, A J
St Louis; 1880 June 24; Thursday; D

Gibbon, Harry
Ouray; 1880 Dec 10; Friday; L; rm 34

Gibbon, R R
Mountains; 1880 Oct 24; Sunday; D

Gibson, Geo A
Leadville, Col; 1880 May 11; Tues; D

Gibson, Geo S
Fitchbury, Mass; 1880 Aug 31; Tuesday; B

Giddings, E J
Denver, Colo; 1880 May 16; Sun; D
Denver, Colo; 1880 Oct 15; Friday; L;
room 6

Gifford, S
& Wife; Boulder; 1880 Apr 3; Saturday; S; room 12

Giggey, G W
County Court Jury; 1880 Mar 11;
Thursday; S

Gilbert, C W
Louisville; 1880 July 24; Saturday; L;
room 3

Gilbert, H D
St Louis; 1880 Apr 27; Tuesday; S;
room 15

Gilds, R M
 Agent; 1880 May 11; Tues; S; rm 27

Gilkison, A T
 & Family; Caribou; 1880 Mar 26;
 Friday; S; room 12
 Ft Collins; 1880 Mar 29; Monday; S;
 room 33
 Ft Collins; 1880 May 4; Tuesday; S
 Ft Collins; 1880 Dec 10; Friday; L;
 room 35
 Collins; 1880 Dec 14; Tuesday; S;
 room 33

Gill, M B
 Greeley; 1880 July 5; Monday; D

Gill, Thos H
 Philada; 1880 June 3; Thursday; S;
 room 16

Gillespie, J
 Ward; 1880 Aug 2; Monday; S

Gillespie, J E
 Denver, Col; 1880 Sept 1; Wed; S

Gillespie, John
 Ward; 1880 Mar 22; Monday; S; rm 33
 Nelson Place; 1880 Nov 29; Monday;
 D; room 35

Gillett, C R
 Chicago; 1880 June 24; Thursday; D;
 room 10
 Chicago; 1880 Sept 16; Thursday; D

Gillett, W L
 Magnolia; 1880 Sept 12; Sunday; D;
 room 29
 Magnolia; 1880 Sept 9; Thursday;
 room 28
 Magnolia; 1880 Oct 15; Friday; S;
 room 34
 Magnolia; 1880 Nov 4; Thursday; D
 & Wife; Magnolia; 1880 Nov 26; Fri-
 day; D; room 3
 Magnolia; 1880 Dec 8; Wednesday; D

Gillett, W L (cont.)
 Magnolia; 1880 Dec 14; Tuesday; B
 Magnolia; 1880 Dec 15; Wednesday; S

Gillette, Anna C (Miss)
 1880 Aug 21; Saturday; D

Gillman, Jas
 Leadville; 1880 Aug 18; Wednesday;
 D; room 29

Gillum, Geo
 Middletown, Conn; 1880 Sept 30;
 Thursday; D

Gilman, A B
 Chicago; 1880 Nov 3; Wednesday; S;
 room 11

Ginisht, A J
 Denver; 1880 June 26; Saturday; S

Gladhill, Theodore
 Summerville; 1880 Apr 1; Thurs; D

Glass, Geo C
 Denver; 1880 Oct 1; Friday; D; rm 6

Gleason, M
 B C; 1880 July 3; Saturday; S

Godd, H
 Wife & Family; Caribou; 1880 Aug 3;
 Tuesday; D; room 25

Goddard, L W
 Sunshine; 1880 Apr 8; Thursday; D

Godding, Frank E
 St Louis; 1880 July 13; Tuesday; D;
 room 5

Godfrey, C O
 Hannibal, MO; 1880 Apr 5; Monday;
 D; room 4
 Hannibal, Mo; 1880 July 5; Monday;
 D; room 20
 Missouri; 1880 July 21; Wednesday; D

Goldstein, S
 New York; 1880 Apr 12; Monday; D;
 room 6

Goldstein, S (cont.)
Chicago; 1880 Nov 18; Thursday; S;
room 10

Good, H H
Atchison, Ks; 1880 Dec 7; Tuesday; L;
room 10

Goodale, E _
Barry, IL; 1880 Apr 1; Thursday; S;
room 33

Goodell, A D
City; 1880 Aug 2; Monday; L; room 27

Goodell, A J
Ward; 1880 Sept 18; Saturday; D;
room 2

Goodell, E
Salina; 1880 Aug 31; Tuesday; D

Goodell, E E
City; 1880 Aug 1; Sunday; B
Absent after S; 1880 Oct 2; Saturday; S

Goodell, Ernest
Salina; 1880 Aug 3; Tuesday; D

Goodhue, A C
Back east; 1880 Apr 1; Thursday; S;
room 35
Rock Creek; 1880 Apr 17; Saturday; D
City; 1880 May 6; Thursday; D
Rock Creek; 1880 June 26; Saturday;
S; room 14
Rock Creek; 1880 June 28; Monday; L;
room 10
Rock Creek; 1880 June 28; Monday; D

Gooding, Chas
Boulder; 1880 May 12; Wednesday; D

Gooding, J F
Chicago; 1880 Oct 16; Saturday; S;
room 12

Goodrich, H
Chicago; 1880 July 20; Tuesday; S;
room 2

Goodwin, R R
Kansas City; 1880 Apr 9; Friday; S;
room 2
Kansas City; 1880 May 22; Saturday;
D; room 46

Gorham, James
Denver; 1880 Sept 21; Tuesday; S

Gorton, E F
Chicago; 1880 May 17; Monday; L;
room 12

Gorton, F S
NY; 1880 May 17; Monday; L; rm 12

Goss, A (Mrs)
Guest of Mrs E Smith; Nederland;
1880 May 27; Thursday; D

Goudge, Ed
Caribou; 1880 Dec 16; Thursday; L;
room 29

Gould, J B
Boulder; 1880 Sept 11; Saturday; S

Gove, E D (Mrs)
Galena, Kans; 1880 Sept 21; Tuesday;
S; room 19

Gove, H
Galena, Kansas; 1880 Aug 24; Tues-
day; S; room 12
Galena, Kans; 1880 Aug 28; Sat; D
Galina, Kansas; 1880 Aug 31; Tues-
day; S; room 10
Salina, Kansas; 1880 Sept 4; Saturday;
D; room 3
Galena, Kas; 1880 Sept 14; Tuesday; D
Salina, Kansas; 1880 Sept 16; Thurs-
day; L; room 17
& Wife; Galena, Kans; 1880 Sept 21;
Tuesday; S; room 20
Galena, Kans; 1880 Sept 28; Tues; S
Galena, Kans; 1880 Oct 18; Monday;
D; room 11

Gove, H C
Absent after supper; 1880 Sept 10;
Friday; S

Gove, John Q A
N Y; 1880 July 22; Thursday; D

Grading, J E
Town; 1880 Apr 17; Saturday; D

Graff, John E
Philadelphia; 1880 Oct 22; Friday; S;
room 8
Phila, Pa; 1880 Oct 26; Tuesday; S;
room 16

Graham, D A
Golden, Col; 1880 Apr 22; Thursday;
S; room 12

Graham, I G
Guest McKinley; 1880 July 16; Fri; S

Graham, Jno T
New York; 1880 Oct 20; Wednesday;
S; room 8

Graham, Jos
1880 Oct 9; Saturday; S; room 8

Graham, Mrs
New Orleans, La; 1880 May 8; Saturday; D; room 10

Graham, T J
Real Estate, Mining & Agt; Boulder;
1880 Mar 6; Sat
Guest of Hoskins; City; 1880 Mar 8;
Monday; D
Boulder; 1880 Mar 17; Wednesday; B
Boulder; 1880 May 28; Friday; S
Guest of J H Jones; 1880 June 3;
Thursday; D
City; 1880 July 20; Tuesday; D

Graham, W J
& Wife; Denver; 1880 Aug 31; Tuesday; D; room 15
& Wife; 1880 Sept 1; Wednesday; L;
room 15

Grandelmyer, Jos
Nevada; 1880 July 3; Saturday; D;
room 10
Nevada; 1880 July 4; Sunday; S; rm 10

Grant, D C
Georgetown; 1880 Sept 4; Saturday; S;
room 25

Grant, H
Denver; 1880 June 13; Sunday; S;
room 10

Grant, J Q
& Lady; Longmont; 1880 July 5;
Monday; D

Grant, U S
& Wife; Galena, Ill; 1880 Aug 21;
Saturday

Grant, W W
Denver; 1880 Aug 4; Wednesday; D;
room 26

Gravelle, A L
Salina; 1880 Dec 7; Tuesday; L; rm 35
Shed Town; 1880 Dec 18; Saturday; D

Graves, Frank
Trenton, NJ; 1880 Oct 12; Tuesday; S

Graves, M L
New York; 1880 Mar 19; Friday; D;
room 17

Gray, C
Caribou; 1880 Apr 25; Sunday; S

Gray, H P
Saint Louis; 1880 Apr 16; Friday; D

Gray, J Thomas
KC; 1880 Nov 21; Sunday; D

Gray, R
Caribou; 1880 Apr 29; Thursday; S
Caribou; 1880 Aug 18; Wednesday; L;
room 29
Caribou; 1880 Nov 15; Monday

Gray, R (cont.)
Caribou; 1880 Oct 13; Wednesday; S; room 12

Gray, Rufus
Caribou; 1880 May 1; Saturday; D
Caribou; 1880 Oct 29; Fri; S; rm 29

Green, G
Greeley; 1880 July 5; Monday; D

Green, M W
1880 Apr 22; Thursday; D; room 35

Greenberg, A H
San Francisco; 1880 Sept 10; Friday; L; room 21
San Francisco; 1880 Dec 13; Monday; D; room 1
San Francisco; 1880 Dec 15; Wednesday; L; room 12

Greffelter, W M
New York; 1880 May 29; Saturday; S; room 6

Gregg, George
Lowell, Mass; 1880 Apr 7; Wed; S

Gregg, W H (MD)
Denver; 1880 Aug 25; Wednesday; S

Gresham, H D
Longmont, Colo; 1880 Nov 18; Thursday; L; room 26

Greub, F R
NiWot; 1880 July 5; Monday; S

Griffin, Chas L
Boston, Mass; 1880 June 5; Saturday; S; room 4

Griffin, Mrs
Boston, Mass; 1880 June 5; Saturday; S; room 44

Griffin, S G
Boston, Mass; 1880 June 5; Saturday; S; room 4

Griffin, William L
Boston, Mass; 1880 June 5; Saturday; S; room 44

Griffith, Mrs
Denver; 1880 June 25; Fri; S; rm 21

Grigsby, A B
Denver; 1880 Nov 13; Saturday; D

Grigsby, L B
Chg H E Washburn - Dun '4 Cover; 1880 Oct 2; Saturday; D; room 12

Grimm, John
Cremona Park Brass Band, Denver; 1880 Aug 21; Saturday

Griswold, A
Gold Hill; 1880 Dec 18; Saturday; D

Griswold, W W
Denver; 1880 Mar 6; Saturday; D
Denver; 1880 Nov 8; Monday; S; room 17
Denver; 1880 Nov 20; Saturday; L; room 5
Denver; 1880 Nov 23; Tuesday; L; room 6
Denver; 1880 Nov 23; Tuesday; L; room 25
Denver; 1880 Nov 24; Wednesday; S

Groesbeck, J D
Leadville; 1880 Oct 28; Thursday; S; room 19
Leadville; 1880 Oct 29; Friday; S; room 19

Gross, W B
Denver; 1880 Sept 8; Wednesday; S; room 1

Grove, H
Nederland; 1880 Aug 16; Monday; D

Grove, J H
Nederland; 1880 Mar 23; Tuesday; D
Cardinal; 1880 Apr 25; Sunday; S; room 5

Grove, J H (cont.)
  Nederland; 1880 May 9; Sunday; S; room 6
  Nederland; 1880 May 11; Tuesday; S; room 6
  Nederland; 1880 May 14; Friday; S; room 4
  Nederland; 1880 May 16; Sunday; D
  Cardinal; 1880 May 17; Monday; D
  Nederland; 1880 June 13; Sunday; S; room 5
  Nederland; 1880 June 22; Tuesday; S; room 11
  Nederland; 1880 June 27; Sunday; S; room 14
  Nederland; 1880 July 24; Saturday; D; room 14
  Nederland; 1880 Aug 3; Tuesday; D
  Nederland; 1880 Aug 7; Saturday; D; room 18
  Nederland; 1880 Aug 13; Friday; D
  Nederland; 1880 Aug 21; Saturday; L; room 15
  Nederland; 1880 Sept 2; Thursday; S; room 11
  Nederland; 1880 Sept 4; Saturday; D; room 11
  Nederland; 1880 Sept 7; Tuesday; S
  Nederland; 1880 Sept 9; Thursday; D
  Nederland; 1880 Sept 22; Wednesday; D; room 33
  Nederland; 1880 Sept 24; Friday; D; room 33
  Nederland; 1880 Oct 18; Monday; L; room 25
  Nederland; 1880 Oct 20; Wednesday; S; room 14
  Nederland; 1880 Nov 16; Tuesday; S; room 26
  Nederland; 1880 Dec 10; Friday; D; room 13

Grove, J O V
  Nederland; 1880 Apr 13; Tuesday; D; room 33

Gruber, Mrs
  Golden; 1880 Aug 31; Tuesday; D; room 10

Gruber, R W
  Cincinnati, Oh; 1880 Oct 16; Saturday; D

Gruber, Wm (Mrs)
  Golden; 1880 July 30; Fri; D; rm 16

Grund, Jun W
  Denver; 1880 Mar 8; Monday; D

Gugsby, Col
  Denver; 1880 Sept 30; Thursday; D

Guild, Jno
  Omaha, Neb; 1880 May 3; Monday; D

Gunster, H J
  Denver; 1880 Oct 5; Tuesday; L; rm 1

Gurley, C L
  Denver; 1880 Nov 9; Tuesday; D

Gurlus, John N
  St Louis; 1880 Apr 17; Saturday; D

Guswold, W R (MD)
  Chicago; 1880 June 1; Tuesday; D; room 11

Gutmann, Emil
  New York; 1880 Mar 21; Sunday; S; room 12

Guy, J H
  Denver; 1880 Sept 14; Tuesday; S; room 20

H

Hageiner, B A
Cheyenne; 1880 June 5; Saturday; S; room 3

Hagen, T W
Chicago; 1880 May 7; Friday; D; rm 6

Hall, A G
KY; 1880 Apr 19; Monday; S; room 3

Hall, G C
Denver; 1880 May 14; Fri; S; rm 29

Hall, Geo
Denver; 1880 Mar 20; Saturday; S; room 6

Hall, Geo W
Chicago; 1880 Sept 16; Thursday; D
Chicago; 1880 Oct 15; Fri; L; rm 11
Chicago; 1880 Dec 15; Wednesday; S; room 2

Hall, John
Erie; 1880 July 5; Monday; D
1880 Aug 3; Tuesday; D

Hall, R D
Golden; 1880 May 12; Wednesday; D; room 6
Golden; 1880 May 15; Saturday; S

Halsted, S D
& Wife; Cold Water, Mich; 1880 July 21; Wednesday; S

Halvorson [Halverson], C
Ward; 1880 Mar 6; Saturday; S; rm 25
Ward; 1880 Mar 7; Sunday; S; rm 28
Ward; 1880 Mar 19; Friday; S; rm 28

Hambin, J
Denver; 1880 June 17; Thursday

Hamill, C M
Hortense, Col; 1880 Dec 2; Thursday; S; room 27
Hortense, Col; 1880 Dec 7; Tues; D

Hammerstine, led W
Buford, Wyo; 1880 Sept 4; Saturday; D

Hammond, C K
Golden; 1880 May 11; Tuesday; S
Crisman; 1880 May 8; Saturday; L; room 33
Crisman; 1880 May 9; Sunday; S; room 33

Hammond, L P
City; 1880 Apr 1; Thursday; L; room 1

Hammond, W A
Chicago; 1880 Aug 29; Sunday; S; room 6
Chicago; 1880 Aug 31; Tuesday; D; room 6

Hanchett, L J
Denver; 1880 May 21; Friday; S; rm 6

Hancock, Winfield S
Salt River; 1880 Nov 16; Tuesday; D

Hanker, I
Denver; 1880 June 2; Wednesday; S

Hannah, Wm
Central City; 1880 June 2; Wednesday; S; room 25

Hannan, E P
Denver; 1880 May 4; Tuesday; D

Hanner, R W
Topeka, Kas; 1880 May 27; Thur; S

Hannount, J W
Chicago; 1880 June 10; Thursday; S; room 3

Hansbaugh, J
Summerville; 1880 June 24; Thur; S

Hansbrough, Geo
Victoria Mine; 1880 Mar 15; Sunday; D; room 33
Victoria Mine; 1880 Mar 23; Tues; D
Victoria Mine, Summerville; 1880 Apr 3; Saturday; D

Hansbrough, Geo (cont.)
Summerville; 1880 Apr 23; Friday; L; room 28
Summerville; 1880 May 15; Saturday; D; room 25
Summerville; 1880 May 17; Monday; D; room 27
Summerville; 1880 May 19; Wednesday; D; room 27
Victoria Mine; 1880 Sept 10; Fri; D
Victoria Mine; 1880 Sept 14; Tues; D
With E G, Summerville; 1880 Sept 23; Thursday; L
1880 Oct 14; Thursday; D
Summerville; 1880 Nov 1; Monday; D

Hansbrough, J J
Sommerville, Colo; 1880 Apr 10; Saturday; D

Hansbrough, J W
Victoria Mine; 1880 Mar 11; Thursday; D; room 17
Victoria Mine; 1880 Mar 27; Sat; D
Salina; 1880 June 8; Tuesday; S
Salina; 1880 July 30; Friday; S
Salina; 1880 July 24; Sat; S; rm 29
With H Gove; 1880 Aug 28; Sat; D
Victoria Mine; 1880 Sept 6; Mon; D
Victoria Mine; 1880 Sept 10; Fri; D
Victoria Mine; 1880 Sept 14; Tues; D
Victoria Mine; 1880 Oct 7; Thurs; S
Wife & Child; Summerville; 1880 Oct 9; Saturday; D
Victoria Mine; 1880 Oct 13; Wednesday; D; room 33
Victoria Mine; 1880 Oct 19; Tues; D
Victoria Mine; 1880 Oct 25; Mon; D
Victoria Mine; 1880 Nov 13; Sat; D
Victoria Mine; 1880 Nov 26; Friday; S
Salina; 1880 Nov 27; Saturday; S; room 17

Hansbrough, O C
County Court Jury; 1880 Mar 11; Thursday; S

Hansbrough, O C (cont.)
Salina; 1880 May 3; Monday; S
Salina; 1880 May 5; Wednesday; S; room 8
Summerville; 1880 May 6; Thursday; S; room 14
Summerville; 1880 Oct 11; Mon; D
Salina; 1880 Oct 12; Tuesday; S; rm 33
Salina; 1880 Oct 23; Saturday; D

Hansbrough, Oliver
Victoria Mine; 1880 Mar 27; Sat; D

Hansbrough, S L
Salina; 1880 Mar 10; Wednesday; D
Victoria Mine; 1880 Mar 11; Thursday; D; room 17
Victoria Mine; 1880 May 12; Wednesday; S; room 32
Salina; 1880 July 31; Sat; S; rm 29
Salina; 1880 Aug 3; Tuesday; D
Summerville; 1880 Aug 4; Wednesday; D
Victoria Mine; 1880 Sept 10; Fri; D
Victoria Mine; 1880 Sept 14; Tues; D
Salina; 1880 Oct 23; Saturday; D

Hansbury, Isaac
Longmont; 1880 June 1; Tuesday; D; room 6

Hanscow, F B
Denver; 1880 Mar 26; Friday; D; room 2

Hansen, O A
Chicago; 1880 Apr 15; Thursday; S; room 6

Hanson, Martin
1880 July 28; Wednesday; Br,

Hanson, Wm
Longmont; 1880 May 8; Saturday; S; room 12

Hantz, D K
Phila, Pa; 1880 July 1; Thursday; S; room 19

Hantz, D K (cont.)
Gold Hill; 1880 July 2; Friday; S
Phila; 1880 July 5; Monday; S; room 6

Hanus, Johanna B
Denver; 1880 Apr 30; Friday; S; rm 16

Hanus, Paul H
City; 1880 May 1; Saturday; D

Hardenbrook, W A
Denver; 1880 May 3; Monday; D;
room 21
Denver; 1880 June 1; Tuesday; D
Denver; 1880 June 4; Friday; D
Denver; 1880 June 18; Friday; D
Denver; 1880 Aug 17; Tuesday; S;
room 10

Hardenbrook, William A
Denver; 1880 July 14; Wednesday; D
Denver; 1880 July 20; Tuesday; D;
room 18
Denver; 1880 July 26; Monday; D
Denver; 1880 Nov 8; Monday; D;
room 11
Denver; 1880 Nov 15; Monday; D;
room 6
Denver; 1880 Dec 6; Monday; S; rm 5

Hare, A W
Orodelfan; 1880 May 2; Sunday; D
Orodelfan; 1880 May 19; Wednesday;
L; room 13
Orodelfan; 1880 July 4; Sunday; L;
room 6
& Wife; Orodelfan; 1880 Sept 8;
Wednesday; D

Harens, G L
& Wife; Denver; 1880 Mar 31;
Wednesday; D

Haris, J M
& Wife; Iowa; 1880 Apr 23; Friday; S;
room 13

Harker, A H
With 3 children; Leadville; 1880 Mar
9; Tuesday; S; room 44

Harker, O H
Leadville; 1880 Dec 3; Friday; S; rm 8

Harland, G R
Cheyenne; 1880 Sept 23; Thursday; S

Harlow, Thos D
Boston; 1880 Nov 29; Monday; D;
room 2

Harmon, I K
Chicago; 1880 June 15; Tuesday; S

Harrington, W C
County Court Jury; 1880 Mar 11;
Thursday; S
Guest Paddock; 1880 July 18; Sun; D
City; 1880 Sept 12; Sunday; B

Harris, A (Miss)
Denver; 1880 Oct 21; Thursday; S;
room 5

Harris, B
1880 Apr 27; Tuesday, Room 6

Harris, Frederick
Clinton, Wis; 1880 Nov 18; Thursday;
L; room 28

Harris, Hattie (Mrs)
Caribou; 1880 July 21; Wednesday; D;
room 17

Harris, J
Longmont, Colo; 1880 Dec 2; Thursday; S; room 33
Longmont, Colo; 1880 Dec 7; Tuesday; L; room 33

Harris, M (Mrs)
Nederland; 1880 July 14; Wednesday;
D; room 17

Harris, Wally
Granite; 1880 Mar 11; Thursday; S

Harris, Walter
Granite, Chaffee County; 1880 Mar 8; Monday; S; room 15

Harris, Wm
Waiter; Chicago; 1880 May 18; Tuesday; S

Harrison, Geo B
Chicago ; 1880 May 8; Saturday; D; room 15
Chicago; 1880 Oct 26; Tuesday; D; room 1

Harrison, James E
Memphis, Ten; 1880 Nov 5; Friday; L; room 14

Harrison, Wm H
Scranton, Pa; 1880 Nov 2; Tuesday; D

Harseet, V H
Leadville; 1880 Oct 16; Saturday; S; room 19

Hart, A
With Pine, Magnolia; 1880 Oct 14; Thursday; D

Hart, Geo V
Denver; 1880 June 6; Sunday; D; room 2

Hart, H J
St Louis; 1880 Apr 11; Sunday; S; room 2

Hart, Mrs
Returned; 1880 Sept 4; Saturday; S

Hart, Ross
Denver; 1880 June 2; Wednesday; S; room 15

Hart, T T
Greeley; 1880 July 5; Monday; D

Hart, W
Denver, Colo; 1880 Mar 24; Wednesday; S; room 6

Hart, W (cont.)
Denver; 1880 Apr 13; Tuesday; S; room 8

Harter, Chas L
Russell Gulch; 1880 Sept 1; Wednesday; S; room 29

Harter, J F
Helena; 1880 Apr 5; Monday; S; rm 27

Harter, John
Grand; 1880 Aug 3; Tuesday; D; rm 28

Harter, W G
Ward, Col; 1880 Oct 3; Sunday; L; room 27
Ward; 1880 Oct 7; Thursday; S; rm 29

Harville, Chas M
Hortense, Col; 1880 Oct 15; Friday; D

Harwell, John
San Francisco, Cal; 1880 June 6; Sunday; S; room 6

Haskell, T N
Denver; 1880 Aug 21; Saturday; D

Haskin, J
Breckenridge; 1880 July 20; Tuesday; D; room 35

Haskins, J
Returned; 1880 May 11; Tuesday; S
& Wife; Denver; 1880 May 8; Saturday; S; room 28

Haskins, J P
Denver; 1880 Nov 3; Wednesday; S; room 11

Hassin, John
Ward; 1880 Apr 17; Saturday; S; rm 25

Hastings, C C
Poland, Ohio; 1880 Oct 19; Tuesday

Hatch, E F
Grouse, Ill; 1880 Oct 16; Saturday; D

Hatch, H S
Michigan; 1880 Mar 27; Saturday; S;
room 12
Michigan; 1880 Mar 28; Sunday; S;
room 12

Hatch, J S
Michigan; 1880 Aug 21; Saturday; D
Michigan; 1880 Aug 31; Tuesday; D;
room 14

Hatch, Miss
1880 Sept 21; Tuesday; D; room 8

Haues, J M
Bananza City; 1880 Aug 23; Monday;
D; room 5

Haveland, G H
Breakfast only; 1880 Aug 3; Tues; B

Havens, H E
Springfield, Mo; 1880 Nov 3; Wednesday; D

Haviland, Chas
Caribou; 1880 Aug 4; Wednesday; B

Haviland, G R
Ogallala; 1880 July 13; Tuesday; S;
room 1

Hawley, C A
Guest M L S; Denver; 1880 July 19;
Monday; S; room 33

Haws, N D
Leominster, Mass; 1880 Dec 9; Thursday; L; room 1

Haxton, S
Denver; 1880 Apr 20; Tuesday; S

Hays, Wm H
Cleveland, O; 1880 Aug 9; Monday; S;
room 35
Cleveland, O; 1880 Aug 12; Thursday;
D; room 3

Hayward, William
Longmont; 1880 Sept 6; Monday; S

Hazen, T W
Chicago; 1880 May 5; Wednesday; S;
room 2

Heaff, J S
Ballerat; 1880 Apr 16; Fri; D; rm 33

Heard, Jesse
Mich; 1880 Oct 6; Wednesday; D

Heber, G W
Nederland; 1880 Aug 21; Saturday; S;
room 5

Hecht, S
New York; 1880 Nov 28; Sunday; S;
room 3

Hectler, E
Denver; 1880 May 15; Saturday; S

Heilner, Samuel
Philada; 1880 July 28; Wednesday; D;
room 6

Heley, Ch
Denver; 1880 June 5; Saturday; S;
room 1

Helfer, J
NY; 1880 May 3; Monday; S; room 2

Helwy, C D
Viltsbery, Wa; 1880 June 30; Wednesday; S; room 6

Henderickson, W M
Dayton, O; 1880 Oct 1; Friday; B

Henderson, A H
& Friend; Denver; 1880 May 27;
Thursday; D

Henderson, D H
Denver, Col; 1880 May 24; Monday; D

Henderson, G E
Crisman, guest of T C Kelsey; 1880
Oct 23; Saturday

Henderson, W L
Greeley, Colo; 1880 Aug 26; Thursday; S; room 10

Henderson, W M (Mrs)
Titusville, Penn; 1880 Aug 26; Thursday; S; room 11

Hendrickson, George G
St Louis; 1880 May 23; Sunday; S; room 12

Hendrickson, W M
Dayton, O; 1880 Aug 9; Monday; S left after breakfast; 1880 Aug 25; Wednesday
Dayton, O; 1880 Sept 18; Saturday; S left after; 1880 Sept 27; Monday; B
Denver; 1880 Sept 30; Thursday; L
Left after ; 1880 Oct 10; Sunday; S
Dayton, O; 1880 Oct 14; Thursday; B
Dayton, O, left after; 1880 Oct 14; Thursday; S
Dayton, O; 1880 Oct 16; Saturday; B

Hendrickson, Wm
Denver; 1880 Aug 2; Monday; L; room 35

Hengette, J
Loveland; 1880 Apr 2; Fri; S; rm 26

Hengstler, J
Loveland; 1880 Sept 22; Wednesday; L; room 30

Henly, Sol
Chicago; 1880 Apr 14; Wednesday; D
Chicago; 1880 July 13; Tuesday; D; room 2
Chicago; 1880 Oct 14; Thursday; S; room 2

Hennish, A
Chicago; 1880 Sept 16; Thursday; D

Henry, O E
Golden; 1880 Aug 25; Wednesday; D
Boulder; 1880 Sept 1; Wednesday; D

Henry, O E (cont.)
Golden; 1880 Sept 18; Saturday; D
Silver Cliff; 1880 Sept 20; Monday; S; room 12
& Son; Golden; 1880 Sept 24; Fri; D
Golden; 1880 Nov 16; Tuesday; S

Henter, L
Denver; 1880 Dec 7; Tuesday; S

Herbach, G H O
Cheyenne; 1880 Nov 19; Friday; L; room 5

Herlity, Charles
De; 1880 July 14; Wednesday; S

Herman, Max
D with No. 3; 1880 July 15; Thur; D

Hermann, James R
Chicago; 1880 Nov 28; Sunday; D; room 37

Herrmann, Max
Guest of 2; 1880 July 13; Tuesday; D
Dinner with No. 3; 1880 July 14; Wednesday; D

Hersey, J C
& Lady; Leadville; 1880 Apr 16; Friday; D

Hersey, W A
Sacorra, NM; 1880 Oct 7; Thursday; S; room 5
Secorra, NM; 1880 Oct 8; Friday; S; room 5

Hershey, B F
& Mrs; Boulder Creek; 1880 July 3; Saturday; S; room 19-20

Hersinger, J F
Loveland; 1880 Mar 18; Thursday; S; room 25

Hertneary, A
Black Hawk; 1880 Oct 22; Friday; D

Hertzel, Mrs
Longmont; 1880 Sept 24; Friday; D

Herzinger, J L
Loveland, Colo; 1880 Apr 16; Friday;
S; room 25
Loveland, Col; 1880 May 18; Tuesday;
S; room 12
Caribou; 1880 May 22; Saturday; D;
room 12

Herzinger, Jno F
Caribou; 1880 July 3; Saturday; D

Herzinger, Jno S
Caribou; 1880 May 22; Saturday; D;
room 26

Hester, W G
Ward, Col; 1880 Aug 3; Tuesday; D;
room 28

Hetrick
Longmont; 1880 Dec 9; Thursday; L;
room 28

Hetser [Hetzer], J W
Ned, Co; 1880 Aug 16; Monday; D

Hetzer, Lois (Miss)
Nederland; 1880 Aug 3; Tuesday; L;
room 14

Hetzinger, M R
Nederland; 1880 May 23; Sunday; S;
room 34

Heue, Chas
Guest of Wm, Todd; 1880 May 27;
Thursday; D

Heusten, E J
Special Agt Colorado Telephone Co,
Denver; 1880 June 11; Friday; D;
room 15

Heuston, J H
Pern India; 1880 Apr 16; Friday; L

Hevells, John
Longmont; 1880 Dec 9; Thursday; L;
room 5

Hewes, J M
& Wife & Daughter; Silver Cliff; 1880
May 27; Thursday; D
Colorado; 1880 Nov 22; Monday; S;
room 19
Bonanza; 1880 Dec 15; Wednesday; S;
room 20

Hewes, Jno M
Absent after dinner; 1880 Sept 13;
Monday; D
Returned; 1880 Sept 15; Wednesday;
D; room 5
Absent after S; 1880 Sept 18; Saturday
City; 1880 Sept 20; Monday; S; room 5

Hewes, Jno M (Mrs)
& Child; Chicago; 1880 Nov 5; Friday;
D; room 19&20

Heyman, Abe
San Francisco; 1880 Apr 27; Tuesday;
L; room 1

Heyn, E
Left after S; 1880 Mar 18; Thursday; S

Heyne, All
Left after B; 1880 Sept 27; Monday

Hickenberger (see Hockinberger)
BVRR; 1880 Mar 14; Sunday; L; rm 26

Hickisch, Joe
Cremona Park Brass Band, Denver;
1880 Aug 21; Saturday

Hickman, C B
Lake City, Colo; 1880 Dec 6; Monday;
S; room 6
& 2 guests; Lake City, Colo; 1880 Dec
7; Tuesday; D

Hickman, N C
Leadville; 1880 May 14; Friday; S;
room 34

Hickman, N C (cont.)
Leadville; 1880 Aug 12; Thursday; D; room 6

Hickman, W C
Leadville; 1880 Dec 13; Monday; S; room 6

Hicks, S R
Black Hawk; 1880 May 15; Saturday; S; room 17

Hilduth, Edward
Chicago; 1880 June 1; Tuesday; D; room 10

Hill, Geo W
Detroit; 1880 Aug 12; Thursday; S; room 21

Hill, H
Chicago; 1880 Nov 14; Sunday; S; room 1

Hill, H H
Chicago; 1880 June 23; Wednesday; S; room 11

Hill, J W
Denver; 1880 Nov 8; Monday; D; room 6

Hilmer, Frank A
Chicago; 1880 Aug 3; Tuesday; D; room 21

Hiltibiddle, C
Platteville, Colo; 1880 Sept 13; Monday; L; room 27

Hines, J
& Wife; Clear Creek; 1880 May 11; Tuesday; S; room 17

Hingstler, J
Greeley; 1880 July 31; Saturday; D

Hingston, S J
N City; 1880 July 25; Sun; D; rm 3

Hinman, M L
NiWot; 1880 July 10; Saturday; D
Lefthand; 1880 Oct 6; Wednesday; D
Lefthand; 1880 Oct 21; Thursday; D
Lefthand; 1880 Nov 10; Wednesday; L; room 27

Hinman, P M
Ni Wot; 1880 Apr 12; Monday; D
NiWot; 1880 May 22; Saturday; D
& Wife; NiWot; 1880 Sept 24; Fri; D

Hinnard, J C
Golden; 1880 May 10; Monday; B

Hoag, T L
Denver; 1880 Aug 28; Saturday; L; room 3
Denver, Col; 1880 Sept 3; Friday; D
Denver, Col; 1880 Sept 3; Friday; L; room 10
Denver, Col; 1880 Sept 5; Sunday; L; room 28

Hobson, W B
Boulder; 1880 Aug 9; Monday; B

Hobson, Wm B
Golden; 1880 Nov 11; Thursday; D; room 25

Hockenberger, Wm (see Hickenberger)
B V Ry; 1880 June 5; Saturday; S
BV Ry; 1880 July 6; Tuesday; D

Hodson, Wm
Ft Collins; 1880 Oct 17; Sunday; L

Hoel, Joseph
Denver; 1880 Sept 20; Monday; S

Hoffman, Chas A
Chicago; 1880 Oct 22; Friday; D

Hoffman, Prof
1880 June 12; Saturday; D; room 25

Hoffords, Wm
Caribou; 1880 Apr 24; Saturday; S; room 15

Hofner, Oscar
Denver; 1880 June 4; Friday; D; rm 35

Hohnan, J W
Central City; 1880 July 19; Monday; D; room 16

Holland, Chas
Longmont Cornet Band; 1880 Sept 23; Thursday; S; room 27

Holland, W
Longmont; 1880 Aug 3; Tuesday; S

Holland, W T
St Louis; 1880 Mar 22; Monday; D; room 6
St Louis; 1880 Apr 19; Monday; D
St Louis; 1880 Apr 26; Monday; D
St Louis; 1880 Aug 7; Saturday; D; room 11
St Louis; 1880 Dec 2; Thursday; S; room 11
St Louis; 1880 Dec 4; Saturday; D; room 11

Holinghead, O
Boulder City; 1880 Mar 10; Wednesday; D

Hollingshead, Oscar
Salina; 1880 May 12; Wednesday; S; room 32
Salina; 1880 Aug 3; Tuesday; D
Summerville; 1880 Sept 24; Friday; S
Salina; 1880 Oct 23; Saturday; L; room 28

Holloway, J M
Kansas City; 1880 Mar 26; Friday; L; room 1
KCity; 1880 May 15; Saturday; L; room 6

Holman, J W (Mrs)
Central; 1880 July 15; Thursday; S; room 16

Holstein, M
1880 June 25; Friday; S; room 17
1880 Nov 12; Friday; S; room 10

Holt, Irw F
& Wife; Detroit, Mich; 1880 Sept 29; Wednesday; S; room 16

Holton, W L
Frankfort, Ky; 1880 Sept 25; Saturday; S; room 6

Homan, B E W
Denver; 1880 Aug 8; Sunday; L
Denver, Col; 1880 Aug 8; Sunday; S; room 3

Homan, B M
Denver; 1880 Dec 11; Saturday; L; room 1

Homan, Ben
Denver; 1880 June 4; Friday; L; rm 12
Denver; 1880 July 9; Friday; D; rm 20
Denver, Colo; 1880 Sept 9; Thur; D

Homs, A F
Collins; 1880 Apr 22; Thursday; S; room 6

Hood, Mrs
& Child; 1880 Sept 9; Thursday; S; room 35

Hood, Thos L
Tinshome; 1880 June 12; Saturday

Hook, Geo F
Leadville; 1880 Mar 10; Wed; D

Horn, H G
Lone Pine, Pa; 1880 Oct 31; Sun; D

Horn, J B
Boulder; 1880 Aug 3; Tuesday; D

Horn, P B
Lone Pine, Pa; 1880 Oct 31; Sun; D

Hornan, J En
Denver, Col; 1880 Oct 11; Monday; B

Horne, Joseph Jr
Greeley; 1880 July 5; Monday; D

Hort, Dean (Rev)
Denver; 1880 June 25; Fri; S; rm 15

Horton, L W
Red Cliff; 1880 Mar 27; Saturday; D

Horton, N W
New York; 1880 June 14; Monday; D
New York; 1880 June 15; Tuesday; D

Hoskin
Summerville; 1880 Mar 11; Thursday;
S; room 5

Hoskin, J
Summerville; 1880 Mar 16; Tuesday;
D; room 35
1880 Mar 25; Thursday
Summerville; 1880 Apr 1; Thur; D
Summerville; 1880 Apr 3; Saturday; D
Summerville; 1880 Apr 8; Thur; D
Summerville; 1880 Apr 12; Mon; D
Summerville; 1880 Apr 23; Friday; L;
room 28
Summerville; 1880 Apr 26; Mon; D
& Wife; Chicago; 1880 Aug 8; Sunday;
S; room 21
& Wife; Chicago; 1880 Aug 15; Sun-
day; B; room 21

Hoskin, John
Summerville; 1880 Mar 29; Mon; D

Hoskins, D T
St Louis; 1880 Apr 5; Monday; D;
room 2

Hoskins, J
& Wife; Salina; 1880 Mar 25; Thurs-
day; S; room 3
& Wife; Salina; 1880 Apr 15; Thurs-
day; D; room 21
& Wife; Summerville; 1880 May 5;
Wednesday; S

Hoskins, J Jr
Summerville; 1880 May 5; Wednesday; S

Hoskins, John
Carbonate Camp Wg; 1880 June 11;
Friday; S; room 28
Summerville; 1880 Mar 8; Monday; D
Summerville; 1880 Oct 11; Monday;
S; room 14

Hoskins, Lottie
Denver; 1880 Apr 30; Friday; S; rm 16

Hoskinser, John
England; 1880 Dec 3; Friday; B

Hoskinson, G
County Court Jury; 1880 Mar 11;
Thursday; S

Hotchiss, E
1880 July 5; Monday; D

Hotchkiss, G S
& Wife; New York; 1880 July 15;
Thursday; S; room 16

Hough, T B
Washington, DC; 1880 Dec 9; Thursday; D

Houseman, E P
Longmont Cornet Band; 1880 Sept
23; Thursday; S

Howan, E A
Kansas; 1880 July 14; Wednesday; D;
room 12

Howard, A T
Denver; 1880 Aug 30; Monday; D

Howard, E A
Fairfield, Ia; 1880 Aug 23; Monday; L;
room 33

Howard, H G
St Louis; 1880 Sept 7; Tuesday; S;
room 11

Howard, J R
Richmond, Ind; 1880 June 10; Thursday; D

Howard, O O
Greeley, guest of A L Welch; 1880 Nov 17; Wednesday; D

Howard, R A
Denver; 1880 June 27; Sunday; S

Howard, W E
Chicago; 1880 Sept 15; Wednesday; L; room 15

Howard, W Eugene
St Joseph, MO; 1880 Apr 21; Wednesday; L; room 6

Howard, W Y
Longmont; 1880 June 4; Friday; L; room 25

Howe, W E
4 mile; 1880 July 23; Friday; S; rm 15

Howe, Walter
Chicago; 1880 Sept 17; Friday; L; room 2

Howell, C C
Leadville; 1880 May 11; Tuesday; L; room 4

Howell, C O
Leadville, Colo; 1880 Oct 22; Friday; S; room 11

Howell, H L
City; 1880 Aug 31; Tuesday; D

Howell, J P
Leadville; 1880 Nov 6; Saturday; L; room 16

Howell, John
San Francisco, Cal; 1880 July 25; Sunday; S; room 15
San Francisco, Cal; 1880 June 3; Thursday; S; room 44

Howell, M L
Erie; 1880 May 16; Sunday; B
City; 1880 July 30; Friday; D; room 14

Howell, O C
Leadville, Colo; 1880 Sept 4; Saturday; L; room 1

Howell, P O
Leadville; 1880 Aug 20; Friday; L; room 3

Howell, S S
Chicago; 1880 Sept 8; Wednesday; D

Howell, W R
& Wife; 1880 Aug 3; Tuesday; S

Howes, J W
County Court Jury; 1880 Mar 11; Thursday; S

Howlin, Miss
& Vale; P T Barnums Great Show Comp; 1880 Aug 3; Tuesday; B; room 16

Hoye, G T
Jamestown; 1880 Mar 27; Saturday; L; room 27

Hoyle, J
Leadville; 1880 July 17; Saturday; S
City; 1880 July 26; Monday; B

Hoyle, James
Boulder; 1880 July 18; Sunday; L; room 35
News & Courier; 1880 Sept 1; Wednesday; L; room 24
City; 1880 Sept 2; Thursday; L; rm 32
City; 1880 Sept 3; Friday; L; room 32
News & Courier; 1880 Sept 6; Monday; L; room 32
News & Courier; 1880 Sept 8; Wednesday; L; room 32
N & C; 1880 Sept 9; Thursday; L; room 32

Hoyle, James (cont.)
No C; 1880 Sept 10; Friday; L; rm 33
News & Courier; 1880 Sept 11; Saturday; L; room 32
News & Courier; 1880 Sept 12; Sunday; L; room 32
News & Courier; 1880 Sept 14; Tuesday; L; room 32
N & C; 1880 Sept 15; Wednesday; L; room 2
N & C; 1880 Sept 16; Thursday; L; room 32
News & Courier; 1880 Sept 17; Friday; L; room 32
N & C; 1880 Sept 18; Saturday; L; room 25
N & Courier; 1880 Sept 26; Sunday; L; room 14
N & C; 1880 Sept 27; Monday; L; room 3
1880 Sept 28; Tuesday; L; room 32
1880 Sept 29; Wednesday; L; room 32
1880 Oct 1; Friday; B

Hoyle, Jas
News & Courier; 1880 Sept 7; Tuesday; L; room 33

Hoyle, Thomas
City; 1880 Sept 5; Sunday; L; room 32

Hoyle, Thos
News & Courier; 1880 Sept 4; Saturday; S; room 32

Hoyt, Harry
Philadelphia, Pa; 1880 Sept 12; Sunday; D; room 20

Hoyt, S J
& Wife; Golden; 1880 June 14; Monday; D
& Wife; Golden; 1880 June 24; Thursday; D; room 1

Hoyt, S Z
Golden; 1880 May 22; Saturday; D

Hoyte, S Z
Golden; 1880 Aug 9; Monday; S; room 3

Hoyte, Sy
& Wife; Golden; 1880 Aug 24; Tuesday; D; room 2

Hubbard, Jno
1880 Aug 24; Tuesday; S

Hubbard, Jno M
Denver; 1880 Sept 23; Thursday; S; room 6

Hubbard, R M
Longmont; 1880 Aug 19; Thursday; S

Hubbell, F B
Chicago; 1880 Sept 15; Wednesday; L; room 12

Hubbell, Kate (Miss)
Longmont; 1880 Sept 23; Thursday; B

Hubbitts, W A
City; 1880 Aug 8; Sunday; L; room 17

Hudson, J A
N York; 1880 May 14; Fri; D; rm 15

Huffman, Dan'l
New York; 1880 June 15; Tuesday; S

Huffman, W S
Colorado Springs; 1880 Aug 25; Wednesday; S; room 19

Huggins, Allen P
Denver; 1880 Oct 12; Tuesday; D; room 33

Hugh, James
N & C; 1880 Sept 13; Monday; L; room 32

Hughes, F C
Kansas City; 1880 May 14; Friday; S; room 6

Hughes, H D
Philada; 1880 Apr 15; Thursday; S; room 2
Philada; 1880 Apr 18; Sunday; S; room 8
Denver; 1880 Apr 19; Monday; S; room 16
Denver; 1880 Apr 22; Thursday; D; room 15

Hughs, A
& Lady; Cheyenne; 1880 Mar 26; Friday; S; room 15

Hugler, Stan
Chicago; 1880 Sept 20; Monday; L; room 8

Hummel, J C
Golden; 1880 May 20; Thursday; D
Golden; 1880 June 2; Wednesday; D
Golden; 1880 July 29; Thursday; D
Golden; 1880 Aug 30; Monday; D
Golden; 1880 Oct 14; Thursday; D
Golden; 1880 Nov 16; Tuesday; S

Humphrey, B P
Kansas City; 1880 Sept 12; Sunday; L; room 3

Hunt, L S
Ft Worth; 1880 Aug 1; Sunday; D; room 16

Hunt, T D
Leavenworth; 1880 Apr 2; Friday; D

Hunter, D M
Longmont; 1880 Aug 3; Tuesday; D

Hunter, J L
Longmont; 1880 May 24; Monday; D

Hunter, J P
New York; 1880 June 9; Wednesday; S; room 10

Hupper, E A
& Wife; Caribou; 1880 June 29; Tuesday; D; room 17

Hupper, W C
Belleville; 1880 July 22; Thursday; D; room 3

Hurd, Jesse
Mich; 1880 Oct 21; Thursday; S; rm 8

Hurd, Pete
Mich; 1880 Oct 20; Wednesday; S; room 3

Hurd, W S
Denver; 1880 Aug 17; Tuesday; S; room 11

Hurlburt, G H
Chicago; 1880 Nov 3; Wednesday; S; room 10

Hurlbut, M P
Chicago; 1880 July 26; Monday; L; room 2

Hurt, A
With Prin Jr City; 1880 Sept 27; Monday; D

Hurthal, J A
Texas; 1880 July 26; Monday; S; rm 17

Huster, Isaac
Reading, Penn; 1880 July 22; Thursday; S; room 4

Hutchinson, D J
Jamestown; 1880 Apr 8; Thursday; S; room 3
Jamestown; 1880 Apr 10; Saturday; L; room 3
Jamestown; 1880 Apr 13; Tuesday; D; room 8

Hutchinson, D J (Mrs)
Denver; 1880 Apr 6; Tuesday; S; rm 3
Denver; 1880 Apr 17; Saturday; S; room 3

Hutchinson, E M
Guest of Owen; 1880 July 5; Mon; D
Liverpool, England; 1880 June 29; Tuesday; S

Hutchinson, J A
& Wife; 1880 Oct 1; Friday; S; room 8

Hutchinson, May P J
Jamestown; 1880 Apr 18; Sunday; S; room 3

Huyck, Martin E
Denver; 1880 Aug 4; Wednesday; S; room 3

Hyde, N C
Vermont; 1880 Apr 26; Monday; S; room 6

I

I M
With G Bev; Denver; 1880 Sept 22; Wednesday; D

Ingeman, J J
Atcheson URS; 1880 Oct 10; Sun; D

Ingols, A B
Denver; 1880 Mar 26; Friday; S; rm 4
Denver; 1880 June 28; Monday; S; room 6
Denver; 1880 Nov 10; Wednesday; S; room 6

Ingraham, Russ
1880 Apr 22; Thursday; D; room 35

Ingram, Mrs
1880 Sept 5; Sunday; S; room 14

Iredale, W J
City; 1880 Oct 10; Sunday; L; room 29

Irlemmir, James A
Denver; 1880 Aug 5; Thursday; S

Irvin, Jas
Louisville, Ky; 1880 Aug 20; Friday; D; room 16

Irwin, J
& Wife; Caribou; 1880 May 14; Friday; S; room 14

Irwin, J (cont.)
New York; 1880 July 20; Tuesday; S; room 26

Irwin, J W
& Wife; Shuger Lofe; 1880 Apr 5; Monday; D

Irwin, Joe
Caribou; 1880 May 5; Wednesday; D; room 27

Irwin, Jos
Caribou; 1880 Dec 9; Thursday; L; room 34
Caribou; 1880 Dec 10; Friday; L; room 28

Irwin, Joseph
Caribou; 1880 Mar 13; Saturday; D; room 33
Caribou; 1880 Mar 15; Sunday; S; room 25
Caribou; 1880 Mar 26; Friday; L; room 28
Caribou; 1880 May 10; Monday; D
Caribou; 1880 July 12; Monday; D; room 35
Caribou; 1880 July 15; Thursday; D
Caribou; 1880 July 19; Monday; S; room 26
Caribou; 1880 June 30; Wednesday; D; room 25
Caribou; 1880 Oct 9; Saturday; S; room 13

J

Jackson, Alfred
1880 Nov 20; Saturday; D

Jackson, D C
Denver; 1880 Aug 17; Tuesday; S

Jackson, Wm
Philada; 1880 Mar 26; Friday; S; rm 6

Jacobi, L
Denver; 1880 July 13; Tuesday; D; room 12
Denver; 1880 July 16; Friday; S; rm 20
1880 Sept 14; Tuesday; L; room 17
1880 Sept 16; Thursday; D
Absent after B; 1880 Sept 21; Tuesday
1880 Sept 23; Thursday
Absent after B; 1880 Sept 30; Thur
Neb; 1880 Oct 1; Friday; S
Absent after B; 1880 Oct 2; Saturday
Returned; 1880 Oct 4; Monday; S
Absent after B; 1880 Oct 15; Friday
Returned; 1880 Oct 16; Saturday; S
Crossed out; absent after ; 1880 Oct 19; Tuesday; D
Absent after B; 1880 Oct 20; Wed
Ret; 1880 Oct 23; Saturday; S
Absent after D; 1880 Oct 27; Wed
1880 Oct 29; Friday; B
Returned; 1880 Oct 30; Saturday; S
Absent after B; 1880 Nov 1; Monday
Returned; 1880 Nov 3; Wednesday; S
Absent after B; 1880 Nov 8; Monday
Returned; 1880 Nov 9; Tuesday; S
Absent after B; 1880 Nov 22; Monday
Returned; 1880 Nov 25; Thursday, Thanksgiving; S
Absent after S; 1880 Nov 26; Friday
Returned at S; 1880 Nov 29; Mon; S
Absent after B; 1880 Dec 7; Tuesday

James, J H
& Wife; Sunshine; 1880 Aug 3; Tuesday; D; room 34

James, Thomas N
Black Hills; 1880 Nov 5; Friday; L; room 4

James, W W
Loveland; 1880 Sept 23; Thursday; S; room 30

James, Will
Star Alliance Opera Co; 1880 June 11; Friday; D; room 12

Jameson, H D
Golden; 1880 May 15; Saturday; S

Janse, John G
Salina; 1880 Oct 25; Monday; D

Janus, Harry
Chicago; 1880 Nov 28; Sunday; D; room 91

Jarner, Allen
BC; 1880 Sept 5; Sunday; B

Jarris, Allen
1880 Oct 11; Monday; L; room 32

Jay, P A
Denver; 1880 July 15; Thursday; D

Jelbert, Martin
& Wife; 1880 Sept 21; Tuesday; S; room 33

Jenkins, Evan
Denver; 1880 Apr 9; Friday; S; room 5

Jenkins, Jno W
Breckinridge; 1880 Sept 20; Monday; S; room 11
Breckinridge; 1880 Sept 21; Tuesday; L; room 4

Jennings, C S
Chicago; 1880 June 3; Thursday; D; room 15

Jennings, D A
& Lady; Castle Rock; 1880 Mar 9; Tuesday; S; room 8

Jennings, M C (Mrs)
Denver; 1880 July 31; Saturday; S; room 17

Jennings, Thomas D
Chicago, Ills; 1880 Nov 2; Tuesday; D

Jenter, J C
Chicago; 1880 July 10; Saturday; S; room 3
Chicago; 1880 July 9; Friday; D; rm 3

Jepson, Joe
Chicago; 1880 Oct 15; Fri; L; rm 10

Jeremy, G W
New York; 1880 June 14; Monday; S; room 12

Jerome, Tour L
Saginaw, Mich; 1880 Aug 9; Mon; S

Jester, John A
& Lady; Gold Hill; 1880 Aug 3; Tuesday; S; room 13

Jewell, D A
Wife & Daughter; 1880 Aug 21; Saturday; D

Joab, A E
Longmont; 1880 Apr 1; Thursday; D; room 12
Longmont; 1880 Apr 3; Saturday; D
Longmont; 1880 July 5; Monday; D
Longmont; 1880 July 26; Monday; L; room 5
Longmont; 1880 July 27; Tuesday; L; room 8
Longmont; 1880 Aug 26; Thursday; L; room 35

Joe Quigly (Prof, Director)
Cremona Park Brass Band, Denver; 1880 Aug 21; Saturday

Johneide, Sam
Kansas City; 1880 Oct 10; Sunday; L; room 15

Johner, J H
Albany, NY; 1880 Oct 4; Monday; S; room 1

Johns, John (Mrs)
Caribou; 1880 Nov 3; Wednesday; L; room 17

Johnson, A B
Agent, Denver Iron Fence Co; 1880 June 15; Tuesday; D; room 12

Johnson, A R
Omaha; 1880 Aug 18; Wednesday; L; room 2

Johnson, D H
Denver; 1880 Oct 14; Thursday; S; room 3

Johnson, D M
Denver; 1880 Apr 23; Friday; S; rm 2
Denver; 1880 June 4; Friday; D
Denver; 1880 July 7; Wednesday; S; room 2
Denver, Colo; 1880 Sept 13; Monday; S; room 1
Denver; 1880 Dec 6; Monday; S; rm 3

Johnson, D S C, Jr
Memphis, Mo; 1880 Dec 5; Sunday; S

Johnson, E
Ward; 1880 Nov 7; Sunday; D; rm 26
Ward; 1880 Nov 8; Monday; S; rm 28

Johnson, Eddie
1880 Aug 22; Sunday; B
Ward; 1880 Nov 30; Tuesday; L; rm 27

Johnson, Edward L
Denver; 1880 Mar 11; Thursday; D
Denver; 1880 June 23; Wednesday; S; room 6
Denver; 1880 Dec 11; Saturday; D

Johnson, Geo
Ward; 1880 Nov 8; Monday; S; rm 28

Johnson, H R
Leadville, Colo; 1880 Mar 7; Sunday; L; room 27
Leadville; 1880 Sept 22; Wednesday; D

Johnson, Jas
Louisville, Colo; 1880 July 26; Monday, room 28

Johnson, Joseph
Caribou; 1880 Dec 8; Wednesday; L; room 29

Johnson, W R
Omaha, NE; 1880 Apr 2; Friday; D; room 15

Johnston, Mamie
Star Alliance Opera Co; 1880 June 11; Friday; D; room 15

Johnston, Sadie
Star Alliance Opera Co; 1880 June 11; Friday; D; room 15

Johnston, U J
City; 1880 Aug 8; Sunday; D

Johnston, W J
City; 1880 Nov 7; Sunday; S

Jones, A H (Capt)
Denver, Col; 1880 Aug 21; Sat; D

Jones, A M
Nevada; 1880 Apr 3; Saturday; S

Jones, C N
Chicago; 1880 June 3; Thursday; D; room 6

Jones, F C
City, AFC Miller & Co; 1880 Apr 19; Monday; D

Jones, Frank
Chicago; 1880 Aug 20; Friday; D; room 32

Jones, G T (Mrs)
Pueblo; 1880 May 3; Monday; D; room 10

Jones, Geo T
Pueblo; 1880 Apr 27; Tuesday; D; room 26

Jones, J G
Salina; 1880 Aug 3; Tuesday; D
Salina; 1880 July 31; Saturday; L; room 29

Jones, J H
Denver; 1880 Mar 20; Saturday; D
Denver; 1880 June 3; Thursday; D
& Wife; Sunshine; 1880 Aug 3; Tuesday

Jones, J J Jr
Janesville; 1880 Aug 20; Friday; S

Jones, J P
Franklin Mine, Sugarloaf; 1880 Mar 16; Tuesday; S; room 17
Franklin Mine, Sugarloaf; 1880 Mar 17; Wednesday; S; room 33
Franklin Mine, Sugarloaf; 1880 Apr 9; Friday; S; room 33
South Sugarloaf; 1880 Apr 17; Saturday; D
Sou Sugarloaf; 1880 Apr 24; Saturday; L; room 35
South Sugarloaf; 1880 May 4; Tuesday; L; room 35
South Sugarloaf; 1880 May 6; Thursday; D
South Sugarloaf; 1880 July 26; Monday; S
Wife & Child; Osborn, Col; 1880 Aug 17; Tuesday; D
Osborn, Col; 1880 Aug 30; Mon; D
Osborn, Colo; 1880 Sept 27; Monday; S; room 33
Osborn, Col; 1880 Sept 4; Saturday; S; room 29
Osborn, Colo; 1880 Oct 2; Satur; D
Osborn, Colo; 1880 Oct 4; Monday; D

Jones, John J Jr
Jonesville, Ky; 1880 July 2; Friday; D; room 12
Jensmith, KY?; 1880 Mar 7; Sun

Jones, M F
Ft Collins; 1880 June 13; Sunday; S; room 14

Jones, M M Jr
Denver; 1880 May 10; Monday; S; room 1

Jones, Mr
& Mrs; Louisville, Colo; 1880 May 7; Friday; D; room BC

Jones, Phineas
New York; 1880 June 20; Sunday; S

Jones, Q P
South Sugarloaf; 1880 July 26; Monday; S

Jones, R__ B
Boulder; 1880 Dec 2; Thursday; S; room 5

Jones, S D
City; 1880 Oct 4; Monday; S

Jones, Thomas
Avon Mine; 1880 Oct 21; Thursday; S; room 28

Jones, W
Perma; 1880 Mar 9; Tuesday; L; rm 17

Jones, W D
City; 1880 Sept 16; Thursday; S
City; 1880 Nov 8; Monday; S
City; 1880 Nov 26; Friday; D

Jones, W F
Kansas City; 1880 May 6; Thursday; D; room 16

Jordan, A J
St Louis; 1880 May 12; Wednesday; D; room 3

Jordan, C W
St Joseph, Mo; 1880 June 4; Friday; L; room 12

Jorlen, J Jug
Denver; 1880 Apr 26; Monday; S; room 6

Jortin, J Jug
Denver; 1880 June 28; Monday; S; room 6

Joseph, M
Boston; 1880 June 29; Tuesday; S; room 6

Joslin, Frank
Denver; 1880 Nov 23; Tuesday; S; room 12
Denver; 1880 Nov 30; Tuesday; D; room 12

Joslin, J Jay
Denver; 1880 June 9; Wednesday; S; room 11
Denver; 1880 July 14; Wednesday; S; room 6

Jotsenburg, M B
& Wife; 1880 Aug 21; Saturday; D

Joyle, James
City; 1880 Sept 16; Thursday; L; rm 32
1880 Sept 30; Thursday; L; room 32

Joyle, Jas
1880 Sept 24; Friday; S

Judd, H P
Golden; 1880 Sept 13; Monday; S; room 35

Judd, I L
St Louis; 1880 July 25; Sunday; D; room 1

Juneman, F W
UP Ry; 1880 Dec 11; Saturday; S; room 10

K

Kach, D C
Greeley; 1880 July 5; Monday; D

Kallemeier, L H
St Louis; 1880 Nov 10; Wednesday; L; room 14

Kambrough, Geo
1880 Mar 20; Saturday; D

Kasson, Wm M
& Wife; Denver; 1880 May 16; Sunday; S; room 12

Kauffman, Luther S
Denver, Col; 1880 Sept 19; Sunday; D

Kavanaugh, R F
Denver; 1880 Sept 25; Saturday; D

Kavanugh, R L
Denver; 1880 Apr 25; Sunday; D; room 17

Kaysar, H Jr
St Vrains; 1880 May 19; Wed; D

Kearney, Theo
Chicago; 1880 July 27; Tuesday; D; room 15

Keating, J M
Dan Castello & Co Circus; 1880 May 23; Sunday; L; room 29

Keeler, J B
Chicago; 1880 May 28; Friday; D

Keeler, N A
Rockford, Ill; 1880 Aug 27; Friday; S

Keeley, D J
Chicago; 1880 Sept 29; Wednesday; D; room 3

Keen, Mrs
Guest of Owen; 1880 Apr 1; Thur; D

Keenan, Matthew
Milwaukee, Wis; 1880 Oct 15; Friday; L; room 6

Keene, H M
& Wife; Denver City; 1880 July 28; Wednesday; D; room 16

Keene, N S
Crisman; 1880 Apr 12; Monday; L; room 26

Keickhoefer, E A
Cremona Park Brass Band, Denver; 1880 Aug 21; Saturday

Keirstadt, John L
Cheyenne, WY; 1880 Apr 22; Thursday; S; room 27

Kelley, C D
Denver; 1880 Mar 20; Saturday; D
Denver; 1880 Oct 16; Saturday; L; room 2

Kelley, D J
Chicago; 1880 May 15; Saturday; D; room 1

Kelley, E D
Denver; 1880 May 1; Saturday; S; room 2
Denver; 1880 Sept 17; Friday; S=D
Denver; 1880 Nov 24; Wednesday; L; room 1

Kelley, Ed
Boulder County; 1880 Mar 31; Wednesday; S

Kelley, J S
Abilene, Ks; 1880 Sept 11; Saturday; S; room 12
Kansas City; 1880 Sept 14; Tuesday; S

Kelley, Jay G
Leadville; 1880 Nov 20; Saturday; S; room 12

Kello, J G
Chillicothe, O; 1880 Sept 13; Monday; L; room 19

Kellogg, D S
Denver; 1880 Sept 4; Saturday; D

Kellogg, E L
Denver, Colo; 1880 Aug 27; Friday; S
Denver; 1880 Sept 4; Saturday; D

Kelly, John
& Wife; Denver, Colo; 1880 Sept 1; Wednesday; S; room 8

Kelsay, Frank J
Leadville; 1880 Apr 29; Thursday; S;
room 12
Leadville; 1880 May 2; Sunday; S;
room 9

Kelsey, T C
Denver; 1880 May 23; Sunday; S
Denver; 1880 Oct 23; Saturday; D

Kempton, James
Magnolia; 1880 Mar 13; Saturday; L;
room 26

Kempton, Jas
with J S Reid; 1880 Nov 4; Thur; D

Kennard, M J
Omaha; 1880 Mar 20; Saturday; D;
room 2

Kennedy, H
Byron, Ill; 1880 May 23; Sunday; S;
room 15

Kent, E P
Rico; 1880 Aug 5; Thursday; S

Kent, T B
Guest of E L Johnas; 1880 Dec 11;
Saturday; D

Kercheval, J G
Cincinnati; 1880 Sept 3; Friday; B;
room 16

Kern, B F
Denver; 1880 Nov 29; Monday; D;
room 12

Kern, J L
Denver; 1880 May 4; Tuesday; S;
room 2

Kernoe, L P
& Wife; Fort Collins; 1880 July 1;
Thursday; S; room 15

Kerr, D
Louisville, guest of A E Lea; 1880 Aug
30; Monday; D

Kesler, Chas
Denver; 1880 June 13; Sunday; S;
room 11

Kesterman, H L
Penna; 1880 July 29; Thursday; S

Kette, Henry
Cremona Park Brass Band, Denver;
1880 Aug 21; Saturday

Kidd, The
R A et; 1880 Sept 27; Monday; S

Kiebler, J K
Chicago; 1880 May 3; Monday; S;
room 6

Kierstead, A B
St Joseph; 1880 Dec 14; Tuesday; L;
room 3

Kilbourn, J B
Middletown, Conn; 1880 Aug 23;
Monday; S; room 1
Middletown, Conn; 1880 Oct 11;
Monday; L; room 15
Conn; 1880 Nov 2; Tuesday; D

Kimball, G W
Saint Louis; 1880 Sept 21; Tuesday; S;
room 44
St Louis; 1880 Dec 2; Thursday; S;
room 1
St Louis; 1880 Dec 5; Sunday; S; rm 12

Kimball, Geo W
St Louis; 1880 Aug 2; Monday; D;
room 6
St Louis; 1880 Aug 4; Wednesday; S;
room 16
St Louis; 1880 Aug 27; Friday; D
St Louis; 1880 Oct 29; Friday; S; rm 6

Kimball, L W
& Lady; Greeley; 1880 July 5; Monday; D

Kimball, R R
Omaha; 1880 Apr 20; Tuesday; D

Kimball, Tho L
  & Wife; Omaha; 1880 Apr 20; Tuesday; D

Kimble, S W
  Virginia City, Nev; 1880 Aug 21; Saturday; D
  Denver, Col; 1880 Sept 15; Wednesday; D
  Denver; 1880 Sept 18; Saturday; S; room 19

Kincaid, George
  Terre Haute, Ind; 1880 May 13; Thursday; L; room 24

Kincanon, J F
  Balarat; 1880 Apr 16; Friday; S

Kiner, J
  Atchison; 1880 Oct 4; Monday; S; room 15

Kiney, W P M
  Valmont; 1880 Nov 20; Saturday; D

King, Geo A
  Denver; 1880 July 5; Monday; S

King, R H
  Agt Barnums Show; 1880 Aug 1; Sunday; L; room 14

King, S C
  Louisville, KY; 1880 Nov 9; Tuesday; L; room 33

Kinkaide, K W
  Denver; 1880 Apr 30; Friday; D

Kinman, M L
  Leadville; 1880 Apr 21; Wednesday; B

Kinnars, C B
  Denver; 1880 July 10; Saturday; S; room 6

Kinnars, J S
  Denver; 1880 July 10; Saturday; S; room 6

Kinnear, N B
  Breckenridge; 1880 Nov 11; Thursday; D; room 10

Kinston, Geo H
  Denver; 1880 May 24; Monday; D

Kinyer, C M
  Nederland; 1880 July 2; Friday; D

Kiper, Julius
  Atchison; 1880 Nov 29; Monday; S; room 10
  Atchison; 1880 Nov 30; Tuesday; L; room 10

Kirby, John E (Mrs)
  Erie; 1880 Aug 3; Tuesday; D

Kirk, Fidel
  City; 1880 Mar 14; Sunday; D

Kirk, T D
  Guest of L C Paddock; 1880 Mar 23; Tuesday; B
  Supper and Tel_; City; 1880 Mar 25; Thursday; S
  Guest Paddock; 1880 Mar 28; Sun; S

Kirk, T DeV
  Guest Paddock; 1880 Apr 11; Sun; S
  City; 1880 Apr 18; Sunday; D
  Guest Paddock; 1880 Apr 25; Sun; D
  City; 1880 May 2; Sunday; D
  City; 1880 May 4; Tuesday; B
  City; 1880 May 5; Wednesday; B
  City; 1880 May 9; Sunday; D
  City; 1880 May 16; Sunday; B
  City; 1880 May 20; Thursday; S
  City; 1880 May 23; Sunday; B
  City; 1880 June 20; Sunday; B
  City; 1880 July 5; Monday; S
  Guest Paddock; 1880 July 18; Sun; D

Kirke, Fred H
  1880 July 20; Tuesday; S; room 33

Kirkendall, F P
Omaha; 1880 Oct 12; Tuesday; L; room 2

Kiser, E
Dan Castello & Co Circus; 1880 May 23; Sunday; L; room 6

Kitchell, William
Central; 1880 May 15; Saturday; S; room 27

Klein, Christ
New York; 1880 May 15; Saturday; S; room 27

Kline, D
Denver; 1880 July 13; Tuesday; D

Klynel, H
Denver; 1880 May 27; Thursday; D

Kneeland, A A
Denver; 1880 May 24; Monday; S; room 25

Knifton, G H
Denver; 1880 Nov 10; Wednesday; D

Knifton, Geo R
Denver, Colo; 1880 Sept 2; Thursday; L; room 14

Knight, F M
Chicago; 1880 Mar 23; Tuesday; S; room 15
Chicago; 1880 Mar 29; Monday; D

Knight, H S
Summerville; 1880 Dec 14; Tues; D

Knowland, Thos
4 Mile; 1880 June 16; Wednesday; S; room 28

Knowles, D M
Louisville, KY; 1880 Mar 29; Monday; S; room 1

Knox, Miss
Denver; 1880 Aug 2; Monday; L; room 11

Kock, Prof
Denver; 1880 Apr 20; Tuesday; S

Koenig, John
Golden; 1880 Dec 9; Thursday; D; room 35

Koenig, R
Golden; 1880 Mar 11; Thursday; S; room 26
Golden; 1880 Mar 13; Saturday; D
Golden; 1880 Mar 22; Monday; D
Golden; 1880 Apr 2; Friday; S
Golden; 1880 Apr 10; Saturday; S; room 33
Golden; 1880 May 15; Saturday; S
Golden Smelting Work; 1880 June 21; Monday; D
Golden; 1880 July 1; Thursday; D
Golden; 1880 July 24; Saturday; D
Golden; 1880 Sept 7; Tuesday; D
Golden; 1880 Sept 10; Friday; S
Golden ; 1880 Sept 22; Wednesday
Golden; 1880 Sept 23; Thursday; D
Golden; 1880 Nov 3; Wednesday; D
Golden; 1880 Nov 18; Thursday; D
Golden; 1880 Dec 4; Saturday; S; room 5
Golden; 1880 Dec 5; Sunday; L; rm 5
Golden; 1880 Dec 9; Thursday; D
Golden; 1880 Dec 18; Saturday; D

Kotthoff, Henry
St Louis; 1880 Mar 18; Thursday; S; room 2

Krieg, L
Burlington, Iowa; 1880 Aug 29; Sunday, Room 11
Burlington, Iowa; 1880 July 20; Tuesday; S; room 12

Krieger, L T
Denver; 1880 Mar 26; Friday; S; rm 33
1880 Mar 27; Saturday; S; room 33

Kun, John F
  South Boulder; 1880 Apr 20; Tuesday;
  L; room 27

Kuppe, Miss
  Denver; 1880 Nov 8; Monday; D;
  room 33

L

Lack, O
  Crisman; 1880 Apr 21; Wednesday; L;
  room 26

Lacke, B H
  Central City; 1880 Sept 12; Sunday; S

Ladden, S W
  Denver; 1880 Apr 30; Friday; D

Lafferty, W A
  Jamestown, NY; 1880 Oct 29; Friday;
  L; room 8

Lake, Miss
  & Mother; Dinner 12; 1880 Aug 3;
  Tuesday; B; room 12

Lakin, Chas W
  Milwaukee; 1880 Sept 8; Wednesday;
  L; room 25

Lamb, C R
  Guest of MAS, Denver; 1880 Nov 11;
  Thursday; D

Lamb, E F
  Denver; 1880 July 20; Tuesday; S;
  room 2
  Denver; 1880 Sept 9; Thursday; D;
  room 10&11
  Denver; 1880 Sept 30; Thursday; B
  Denver; 1880 Oct 5; Tuesday; D;
  room 6
  Denver; 1880 Oct 12; Tuesday; D;
  room 12
  Phila; 1880 Nov 17; Wednesday; S;
  room 17

Lamb, E F (cont.)
  Sunshine; 1880 Nov 22; Monday; D;
  room 26
  Denver, Colo; 1880 Nov 25; Thursday,
  Thanksgiving; D
  Denver; 1880 Dec 7; Tuesday; S

Lambert, Jack
  Denver; 1880 June 5; Saturday; D

Lamson, Ward H
  & Wife; Washington; 1880 Aug 9;
  Monday; S; room 4 & 44

Land, T D
  Nederland; 1880 May 11; Tuesday; D

Lande, E D
  Nederland; 1880 Apr 12; Monday; D;
  room 35

Lande, N D
  Nederland; 1880 Apr 12; Monday; D;
  room 35

Landon, J M
  Denver; 1880 Sept 15; Wednesday; L;
  room 19

Lane, Daniel A
  Nederland; 1880 Aug 3; Tuesday; L

Lane, Jno
  Council Bluffs; 1880 Sept 22; Wednesday; D

Langdon, Geo H
  Boston; 1880 May 11; Tuesday; S;
  room 2
  Boston; 1880 Nov 23; Tuesday; D;
  room 1

Lange, C J
  Denver; 1880 May 15; Saturday; S

Langford, A G
  Denver; 1880 May 1; Saturday; S

Langford, A Q
Denver; 1880 Apr 1; Thursday; D
Denver; 1880 Apr 7; Wednesday; S;
  room 16
Denver; 1880 Apr 20; Tuesday; S;
  room 6
Denver; 1880 Apr 24; Saturday; D
Denver; 1880 Apr 26; Monday; S;
  room 15
Denver; 1880 Apr 29; Thursday; S;
  room 15
Denver; 1880 Apr 30; Friday; S; rm 6
Denver; 1880 May 4; Tuesday; D
Denver; 1880 June 4; Friday; D
Denver; 1880 June 15; Tuesday; D
Denver; 1880 June 22; Tuesday; D
Denver; 1880 July 20; Tuesday; D
Denver; 1880 July 27; Tuesday; S;
  room 12
Denver; 1880 July 28; Wednesday; S
Denver; 1880 July 31; Saturday; B
Denver; 1880 Aug 6; Friday; S
Denver; 1880 Aug 11; Wednesday; S
Denver; 1880 Aug 21; Saturday; D
Denver; 1880 Aug 24; Tuesday; D
Denver; 1880 Aug 26; Thursday; S
Denver; 1880 Sept 3; Friday; S
Denver; 1880 Sept 6; Monday; S
Denver; 1880 Sept 6; Monday; D
Denver; 1880 Sept 8; Wednesday; S
Denver; 1880 Sept 11; Saturday; S
Denver; 1880 Sept 14; Tuesday; S
Denver; 1880 Sept 16; Thursday; S;
  room 20
Denver; 1880 Sept 28; Tuesday; S;
  room 16
Denver; 1880 Sept 29; Wednesday; S
Denver; 1880 Oct 5; Tuesday; S
Denver; 1880 Oct 19; Tuesday; S;
  room 16
Denver; 1880 Oct 21; Thursday; S;
  room 16
Denver; 1880 Oct 22; Friday; S

Langford, A Q (cont.)
Denver; 1880 Oct 26; Tuesday; S;
  room 3
Denver; 1880 Oct 29; Friday; S; rm 3
Denver; 1880 Oct 30; Saturday; S
Denver; 1880 Nov 1; Monday; D
Denver; 1880 Nov 8; Monday; D;
  room 6
Denver; 1880 Nov 13; Saturday; S
Denver; 1880 Nov 15; Monday; S;
  room 2
Denver; 1880 Nov 18; Thursday; S
Denver; 1880 Nov 22; Monday; D
Denver; 1880 Nov 24; Wednesday; S
Denver; 1880 Nov 26; Friday; S; rm 6
Denver; 1880 Nov 29; Monday; S
Denver; 1880 Dec 3; Friday; D
Denver; 1880 Dec 7; Tuesday; D
Denver; 1880 Dec 9; Thursday; S;
  room 6

Langford, J M
Carle's Ranch; 1880 May 5; Wednesday; S; room 35

Langford, L S Q
Denver; 1880 May 6; Thursday; S

Langford, N P
St Paul, Minn; 1880 May 3; Monday;
  D; room 3

Langley, Thos
Ward; 1880 Mar 13; Satur; L; rm 28

Langrishe, J S
& Wife; 1880 Aug 10; Tuesday; D;
  room 19

Langton, W E
Denver; 1880 Sept 19; Sunday; D;
  room 12

Lark, George
Phila; 1880 June 11; Friday; D; room 3

Lars, H H M
Denver; 1880 Dec 7; Tuesday; D

Lasner, A
Chicago; 1880 Mar 24; Wednesday; S; room 3
Chicago; 1880 June 18; Friday; S; room 1
Chicago; 1880 Sept 10; Friday; D; room 2
Chicgao; 1880 Dec 14; Tuesday; D; room 1

Lathrop, Fred N
Boston; 1880 May 12; Wednesday; D; room 1
Boston; 1880 Nov 29; Monday; D; room 1

Lathrop, M A
Leadville; 1880 May 11; Tuesday; S
Leadville; 1880 July 14; Wednesday; S
Leadville; 1880 July 21; Wednesday; S
City; 1880 July 23; Friday; L; room 28

Latimer, Vincent B
Denver; 1880 Oct 5; Tuesday; S; rm 17

Launner, Jno W
St Louis, Mo; 1880 Sept 28; Tuesday; S; room 2

Lawrence, A W
City; 1880 Apr 1; Thursday; D
Omaha; 1880 Apr 12; Monday; S
Columbus, Neb; 1880 Mar 27; Saturday; S; room 2
Denver; 1880 Nov 25; Thursday, Thanksgiving; S; room 5

Laws, H M
Caribou; 1880 June 29; Tuesday; D

Laws, H M (Mrs)
& Son; Caribou; 1880 June 29; Tuesday; D; room 20

Laws, S L
& Wife; Missouri; 1880 Aug 10; Tuesday; S; room 1

Laws, W H
& Wife; 1880 Aug 21; Saturday; D

Lawson, D H
Troy, NY; 1880 June 17; Thursday; D

Lawson, J K
Longmont with S L D; 1880 Nov 3; Wednesday; B

Lawson, W H
& Wife; absent after B; 1880 Oct 29; Friday

Lawson, W N (Col)
& Wife; Washington, D C; 1880 Aug 21; Saturday; D

Lawson, Ward H
& Wife; Washington, D C; 1880 Sept 23; Thursday; S; room 4
& Wife; absent after B; 1880 Sept 29; Wednesday
& Wife; returned at S; 1880 Oct 4; Monday; room 4
& Wife; 1880 Nov 1; Monday; S; room 4&44

Lawyer, H F
& Family; Denver; 1880 Apr 29; Thursday; D; room 8,9

Layd, Louis
Crossed out; 1880 Mar 11; Thur; S

Layer, L W
Boulder; 1880 Aug 16; Monday; L; room 29

Layerment, Wm A
Breckenridge; 1880 Nov 11; Thursday; D; room 11

Lead, William
Caribou; 1880 May 24; Monday; D; room 24

Leake, Charles
City; 1880 Dec 1; Wednes; S; rm 29

Learned, Harry
Denver; 1880 June 6; Sunday; S; rm 25

Learned, Wm
Denver; 1880 Apr 27; Tuesday; S; room 10

Leath, H W
Denver; 1880 Mar 9; Tuesday; D

Lebolt, Joey
St Joe, MO; 1880 Apr 1; Thursday; S; room 6

Lebolt, L E
Chicago; 1880 Mar 29; Monday; S; room 6
Chicago; 1880 June 17; Thursday; D; room 3
Chicago; 1880 Oct 7; Thursday; L; room 3

Ledy, Barney
Trinidad, Colo; 1880 May 4; Tues; S

Lee, Amy (Miss)
Nobles Company, New York; 1880 Oct 23; Saturday; D; room 35

Lee, E B
Denver; 1880 June 28; Monday; S; room 3

Lee, G W
Chicago; 1880 Aug 21; Saturday; D; room 2

Lee, Harry A
Wizard Co; 1880 July 25; Sunday; D; room 11

Leech & Lonergan
Boulder; 1880 Mar 27; Saturday; S

Leeke, H B
Denve; 1880 Mar 6; Saturday; S; rm 8
Denver; 1880 Apr 8; Thursday; S; room 2
Denver; 1880 Apr 30; Friday; S; rm 15
Omaha; 1880 May 13; Thursday; S; room 1

Leeke, H B (cont.)
Omaha; 1880 June 23; Wednesday; D; room 1
Omaha; 1880 Aug 16; Monday; D; room 2
Omaha; 1880 Oct 20; Wednesday; S; room 3
Omaha, Neb; 1880 Nov 22; Monday; S; room 31

Leggate, James
Ward; 1880 Apr 16; Friday; D
& Family; Ward; 1880 Apr 17; Saturday; D; room 12
Ward; 1880 Apr 27; Tuesday; S; rm 21
Ward; 1880 May 1; Saturday; D; rm 17
Ward; 1880 May 17; Monday; S; rm 25
Ward; 1880 June 22; Tues; L; rm 29
Ward; 1880 July 21; Wednesday; S; room 29
Ward; 1880 Dec 11; Saturday; S; rm 3
Ward; 1880 Sept 20; Monday; S; rm 14
Ward; 1880 Nov 13; Sat; L; rm 18

Leggate, Sam'l
Ward; 1880 June 10; Thursday; D

Leggett, J
Lower Boulder; 1880 July 21; Wednesday; S; room 33 & 29

Leggett, Jerry
Louis Bar; 1880 Sept 25, Saturday; L; room C

Lehman, J H
Denver; 1880 Sept 19; Sunday; D; room 12

Lehner, Gilbert
[unreadable]; 1880 Mar 6; Saturday; S; room 11
Caribou; 1880 Mar 13; Saturday; D
Caribou; 1880 Mar 16; Tuesday; D
Caribou; 1880 Mar 23; Tuesday; S; room 5
Caribou; 1880 Mar 26; Friday; S; room 5

Lehner, Gilbert (cont.)
Caribou; 1880 Apr 7; Wednesday; S; room 5
Caribou; 1880 Apr 8; Thursday; S; room 6
Caribou; 1880 Apr 10; Saturday; D
Caribou; 1880 Apr 21; Wednesday; S; room 17
Caribou; 1880 Apr 25; Sunday; S
Caribou; 1880 May 3; Monday; D
Caribou; 1880 May 4; Tuesday; S; room 12
Caribou; 1880 May 9; Sunday; D
Caribou; 1880 May 10; Monday; L; room 12
Caribou; 1880 May 17; Monday; D
Caribou; 1880 May 21; Friday; D
Caribou; 1880 June 11; Friday; D
Caribou; 1880 June 23; Wednesday; D
Caribou; 1880 July 15; Thursday; S; room 12
Caribou; 1880 Aug 11; Wednesday; D; room 5
Caribou; 1880 Aug 23; Monday; D; room 11
Caribou; 1880 Aug 5; Thursday; D; room 14
Caribou; 1880 Sept 2; Thursday; S; room 6
Caribou; 1880 Oct 19; Tuesday; D
Caribou; 1880 Oct 21; Thursday; S; room 14
Caribou; 1880 Nov 10; Wednesday; S; room 17
Caribou; 1880 Nov 14; Sunday; S
Caribou; 1880 Nov 16; Tuesday; D; room 35
Caribou; 1880 Nov 25; Thursday, Thanksgiving; D
Caribou; 1880 Nov 8; Monday; D; room 14

Lehner, John A
Caribou; 1880 Sept 29; Wednesday; D; room 12

Lehrman, I
& Wife; Chicago; 1880 June 21; Monday; S; room 1

Lehrukuhl, Wm
Central; 1880 May 15; Saturday; S; room 13

Leigh, J M
Golden; 1880 May 4; Tuesday; D

Leighton, Harry B
Denver, Colo; 1880 Nov 30; Tuesday; L; room 6

Leimer, C F
Denver; 1880 Aug 6; Friday; S; rm 17

Lenzberg, A
Denver; 1880 June 1; Tuesday; L; room 26

Leonard, E B
Joplin, Mo; 1880 Sept 14; Tuesday; D; room 12

Leonard, I J
Kansas City, Mo; 1880 Aug 28; Saturday; L; room 29
Night watch; 1880 Sept 1; Wednesday

Lerning, Hattie
Nederland; 1880 Aug 3; Tuesday; L; room 32

Lerning, Rosa
Nederland; 1880 Aug 3; Tuesday; L; room 32

Lerryn, H
New York; 1880 Apr 5; Monday; S; room 1

Leslie, Elmer E
Loveland House; 1880 Dec 7; Tuesday; L; room 26

Lessig, Jno M
Denver; 1880 Oct 16; Saturday; S

Lessig, M
Denver; 1880 Aug 10; Tuesday; S

Lessig, Mrs
Denver; 1880 Apr 15; Thursday; D
Denver; 1880 Apr 16; Friday; D
Denver; 1880 June 1; Tuesday; D;
room 44
Denver; 1880 July 15; Thursday; D
Denver; 1880 Oct 15; Friday; S; rm 1
Denver; 1880 Dec 2; Thursday; S;
room 1
Denver; 1880 Dec 3; Friday; S

Lessig, W H
Denver; 1880 Apr 30; Friday; S; rm 8

Lessing, M _
Denver; 1880 Apr 2; Friday; D

Levi, A B
St Louis; 1880 Sept 3; Friday; L

Levison, M
NY; 1880 Sept 11; Saturday; S; room 2

Levy, D
NY; 1880 June 13; Sunday; D; room 2

Levy, J E
Chicago; 1880 June 23; Wednesday; S;
room 10

Lewis, Benj
Summerville, Col; 1880 Aug 3; Tuesday; D
Summerville; 1880 Aug 4; Wednesday; D

Lewis, Billy
& 2 children; Longmont; 1880 Aug 3;
Tuesday; D

Lewis, E L
Ottawa, Ill; 1880 Aug 24; Tuesday; D

Lewis, E N
Altura, Illinois; 1880 Sept 13; Monday; S; room 8

Lewis, Hattie (Miss)
Altura, Illinois; 1880 Sept 13; Monday; S; room 12

Lewis, M L
Dan Castello & Co Circus; 1880 May
23; Sunday; L; room 6

Lewis, Ronnie
Salina; 1880 Oct 25; Monday; D

Lewis, T Jay
St Louis; 1880 Sept 17; Friday; L;
room 29

Lewis, Walter F
St Louis; 1880 Apr 19; Monday; L;
room 8
St Louis; 1880 July 7; Wednesday; L;
room 1
St Louis; 1880 Nov 4; Thursday; D;
room 1

Lewry, Paralls
Central City; 1880 June 2; Wednesday; S; room 25

Leybourn, S K
Denver; 1880 Sept 22; Wednesday; S;
room 25

Libby, H C
1880 Aug 25; Wednesday; S; room 32
1880 Sept 1; Wednesday; S; room 32

Lieu, Minnie (Miss)
All over the state; 1880 Aug 23; Monday; S; room 15

Liey, J E
Chicago; 1880 Oct 14; Thursday; S;
room 6

Light, Edw B
Denver; 1880 Apr 1; Thursday; D

Light, Edw S
Denver, Colo; 1880 Aug 27; Friday; S;
room 19

Light, George
Nederland; 1880 Aug 3; Tuesday; L

Light, W Miern [?]
Denver; 1880 Dec 10; Friday; S; rm 17

Light, William
Calumet, Mich; 1880 July 5; Mon; D
Denver; 1880 May 10; Monday; D;
room 17

Likerman, Henry
Chicago; 1880 July 22; Thursday; D;
room 6

Lindsay, S
Sommerville; 1880 Dec 10; Friday; D;
room 28
Summerville; 1880 Dec 17; Friday; D

Lipholt, J H
Caribou, Colo; 1880 June 12; Saturday; D; room 26

Lippoldt, Henry
Nederland; 1880 Dec 4; Saturday; S;
room 26

Lisqueby, H V
Chicetou, Ills; 1880 Sept 10; Friday; S;
room 19&20

Little, A J
Chicago; 1880 Aug 12; Thursday; D

Livesay, J M D
Leadville, Colo; 1880 Nov 8; Monday;
D; room 29

Livingstone, H W
Leadville City; 1880 Dec 1; Wednesday; S

Lobo, J
& Wife; Longmont; 1880 July 5; Monday; D

Locke, B H
Central; 1880 Aug 9; Monday; S;
room 17

Locke, C F
Hornellsville NY; 1880 May 28; Fri; S

Locke, H F
NY; 1880 Aug 26; Thursday; S; rm 19
NY; 1880 Sept 25; Saturday; S

Locke, H T
New York; 1880 Apr 13; Tuesday; S;
room 44
New York; 1880 Apr 21; Wednesday;
S; room 15
NY; 1880 Aug 23; Monday; S; room 19
NY; 1880 May 1; Saturday; S; room 15
Golden; 1880 May 16; Sunday; D
NY; 1880 May 21; Friday; S; room 1

Locke, Worthington
NY; 1880 Aug 23; Monday; S; room 20

Lodges, R W
Boston, Mass; 1880 June 26; Saturday;
D; room 28

Logenger, L
OM; 1880 June 3; Thursday; D; rm 34

Lokis, M D
Afton, Iowa; 1880 June 4; Friday; S;
room 25

Lonergan (Leech & Lonergan)
Boulder; 1880 Mar 27; Saturday; S

Lonergan, Phil
City; 1880 Oct 21; Thursday; S

Long, D
New York; 1880 July 16; Friday; S;
room 1

Long, S A (Hon)
Erie, Colo; 1880 Dec 12; Sunday; D
Erie, Colo; 1880 Dec 13; Monday; S;
room 12

Long, S Allen
Erie, Colo; 1880 Nov 18; Thursday; L;
room 5
Erie, Colo; 1880 Nov 27; Saturday; L;
room 6

Long, S Allen (Hon)
Erie; 1880 Oct 26; Tuesday; S; rm 10

Long, Samuel Allen
Erie; 1880 Sept 29; Wednesday; S;
room 6

Longley, T S
Ward; 1880 Apr 13; Tuesday; L; rm 34

Loranger, L
Mill City; 1880 Oct 25; Monday; S; room 34
Magnolia; 1880 Dec 14; Tuesday; B
Magnolia; 1880 Dec 15; Wednesday; S

Lorangon, L
George Town; 1880 June 16; Wednesday; D; room 34

Louisburg, E H
Sugar Loaf; 1880 July 27; Tuesday; D; room 28

Louisburg, Edw'd
Sugar Loaf; 1880 July 22; Thursday; D

Lounsbury, E H
Sugar Loaf, Colo; 1880 Mar 13; Saturday; D
Sugarloaf; 1880 Mar 30; Tuesday; D
Sugarloaf; 1880 Apr 24; Saturday; D
Sugar Loaf; 1880 Apr 29; Thursday; D
Sugar Loaf; 1880 May 6; Thursday; D
Sugar Loaf; 1880 May 15; Saturday; D
Sugar Loaf; 1880 May 18; Tuesday; D
Sugar Loaf; 1880 May 25; Tuesday; D
Sugar Loaf; 1880 May 29; Saturday; D
Sugar Loaf; 1880 June 8; Tuesday; D
Sugar Loaf; 1880 June 12; Saturday; D
Sugar Loaf; 1880 June 15; Tuesday; D
Sugar Loaf; 1880 June 26; Saturday; D
Sugar Loaf, Colo; 1880 Aug 5; Thursday; D
Sugar Loaf; 1880 Aug 9; Monday; B
Sugar Loaf; 1880 Aug 14; Saturday; D
Sugar Loaf, Col; 1880 Aug 21; Saturday; D
Sugar Loaf; 1880 Aug 31; Tuesday; D
Boston; 1880 Sept 30; Thursday; S; room 5

Lounsbury, E Haskell
Sugar Loaf, Col; 1880 June 22; Tuesday; D
Sugar Loaf, Col; 1880 Sept 4; Saturday; D

Lounsbury, E W H
Sugar Loaf, Colo; 1880 Apr 8; Thursday; D

Lounsbury, Edw H
Sugar Loaf; 1880 Aug 28; Saturday; D

Loveland, W H H
Denver; 1880 May 16; Sunday; D
Denver; 1880 Sept 22; Wednesday; S

Lovetz, H T
Gold Hill; 1880 May 13; Thursday; D

Low, E A
Col Springs; 1880 Sept 23; Thursday; D; room 6

Lowe, David A
Nederland; 1880 July 24; Saturday; L; room 28
Nederland; 1880 July 25; Sunday; D
Nederland; 1880 Aug 17; Tuesday; L; room 28
Nederland; 1880 Nov 26; Friday; S; room 26

Lowe, J H
Kansas City; 1880 May 27; Thursday; D; room 2

Lowe, Thos H
& Wife; Leadville, Col; 1880 May 2; Sunday; D; room 10

Lowell, Fred J
Guests of JB; Rockford, Ill; 1880 June 15; Tuesday; D

Luce, Minna (Miss)
Grand Rapids, MI; 1880 May 14; Friday; D; room 16

Ludlow, Henry (Mrs)
Boulder; 1880 Mar 29; Monday; D

Lunsreull, F E
Golden; 1880 May 15; Saturday; S

Lybrand, J V
Spring dale; 1880 Sept 27; Monday; D

Lybrandt, J V
Springdale; 1880 Apr 21; Wed; D

Lykins, D J
Guest of Owen; 1880 Apr 1; Thur; D

Lyle, Daniel
& Wife; Dowagina, Mich; 1880 May 3; Monday; S; room 4

Lyman, A A
Absent after ; 1880 Sept 16; Thur; D

Lyman, Geo
Longmont; 1880 Dec 14; Tuesday; D

Lyman, George
Longmont; 1880 Dec 8; Wed; D

Lyman, H A
Denver; 1880 July 5; Monday; D
Absent after dinner; 1880 Aug 24; Tuesday

Lyman, Henry A
New York; 1880 Aug 16; Monday; D; room 35
New York; 1880 Aug 29; Sunday; D; room 35
New York; 1880 Sept 13; Monday; D; room 33
New York; 1880 Sept 17; Friday; S; room 33
Denver; 1880 Dec 3; Friday; D; rm 34

Lyman, P F
New York; 1880 Dec 7; Tuesday; S; room 8

Lyon, J L
D C; 1880 Oct 8; Friday; L; room 12

Lyons, Harry
Cremona Park Brass Band, Denver; 1880 Aug 21; Saturday

Lyons, R
Brainard's Camp; 1880 May 2; Sunday; D

Lytle, H J
Chicago, Ills; 1880 Aug 11; Wednesday; L; room 1

M

M'Nauss
St Louis; 1880 Mar 29; Monday; S; room 2

Maas, B
Golden; 1880 May 15; Saturday; S

MacAllister, J W (Prof)
Wizard Co; 1880 July 25; Sunday; D; room 10

Macdonald, J
Kansas City; 1880 May 3; Monday; S; room 1

MacGermer, C W
Denver; 1880 Dec 3; Friday; D

Mack, H
Allen's Park; 1880 Apr 26; Monday; S; room 2

Mack, Henry
Allens Park, Col; 1880 Oct 21; Thursday; S; room 27

Mack, T W
Denver; 1880 Mar 17; Wednesday; L; room 23

Mackay, H D
New York; 1880 Sept 11; Saturday; S; room 16
New York; 1880 Oct 1; Friday; S; room 15

Mackay, P N
Denver; 1880 May 28; Friday; D

Mackenzie, W R
UP Ry Kas Cy; 1880 May 18; Tuesday;
S; room 44
Kas Cy; 1880 May 19; Wednesday; S

Mackey [Macky], A J
& Wife; 1880 Aug 21; Saturday; D

Mackie, Simon F
New York; 1880 June 16; Wednesday;
S; room 6
New York; 1880 July 2; Friday; S;
room 6
New York; 1880 July 19; Monday; D;
room 2

MacNaughton, P J
Caribou; 1880 June 26; Saturday; D

Madison, A D
& Wife; KC, Mo; 1880 Oct 28; Thursday; S

Magee, M J
Rama; 1880 Sept 6; Monday; D

Magruder, J H
NY; 1880 Sept 1; Wednesday; S; rm 1

Magruder, N D
NY; 1880 Sept 5; Sunday; D; room 14

Maguire & Lewanda
Dan Castello & Co Circus; 1880 May
23; Sunday; L; room 27

Mahan, D
Sunshine; 1880 Aug 4; Wednesday; D

Main, J H
Pittsford, Ills; 1880 July 1; Thursday; L
& Wife; Pittsfield, ill; 1880 Aug 20;
Friday; S

Maisel, John M
Denver, Colo; 1880 May 24; Mon; D

Malden, T J
Denver; 1880 Aug 30; Monday; S;
room 19

Maldon, F J
Ft Collins; 1880 Aug 28; Saturday; S;
room 28

Mallon, B
City; 1880 Mar 6; Saturday; S; rm 27
City; 1880 Mar 12; Friday, room 5
City; 1880 Mar 13; Saturday; L; rm 44
City; 1880 Mar 24; Wednesday; L;
room 33
City; 1880 Mar 25; Thursday; L; rm 28
Middle Park; 1880 Sept 6; Monday; L;
room 28

Malter, E H
San Francisco; 1880 Sept 6; Mon; D
San Francisco; 1880 Sept 7; Tuesday;
D; room 10

Manger, B
Saint Jos Mo; 1880 Aug 13; Friday; S;
room 2

Manhart, F P
Kansas City; 1880 Nov 3; Wednesday;
S; room 12

Manheim, H
Denver; 1880 Sept 20; Monday; S;
room 29

Mann, J
Golden; 1880 Sept 22; Wednesday; D

Mansard, N F
Terre Haute, Ind; 1880 Nov 28; Sunday; D; room 43

Mansfield N G (Miss)
Boulder; 1880 May 12; Wednesday; D

Mansfield, C
Colorado Springs; 1880 July 4; Sunday; D
Colorado Springs; 1880 July 5; Monday; D

Mansfield, E D
Minneapolis; 1880 Mar 24; Wednesday; S; room 6

Mansfield, E L
Greeley; 1880 July 5; Monday; D

Mantz, Chas
Chicago; 1880 May 1; Saturday; S; room 1
Chicago; 1880 July 30; Friday; L; room 12
Chicago; 1880 Oct 16; Saturday; L; room 11

Marce, J W W
Cleveland, O; 1880 Sept 9; Thursday; S; room 12

Maretta, Rose
Dan Castello & Co Circus; 1880 May 23; Sunday; L; room 17

Markell, Chas
Boston; 1880 Sept 17; Friday; L; rm 14

Marks, M
New York; 1880 Oct 1; Friday; D; room 1

Marlow, J U
Denver; 1880 Apr 21; Wednesday; S; room 15

Marquis, Alexander
Milwaukee, Wis; 1880 Aug 29; Sunday; L; room 3

Marquis, Robert
Denver; 1880 Aug 29; Sunday; L; room 3

Marquis, Robt (Mrs)
& Daughter; Denver; 1880 Aug 29; Sunday; L; room 2

Marris, Henry (Mrs)
1880 Apr 1; Thursday; D

Marrs, W F
Denver; 1880 May 6; Thursday; D

Martin, A
Caldwell, Ohio; 1880 Mar 24; Wednesday; S; room 5
Caldwell, Ohio; 1880 Apr 6; Tuesday; L; room 28
Caldwell, Ohio; 1880 Apr 6; Tuesday; S; room 26
Caldwell, Ohio; 1880 Apr 7; Wednesday; L; room 26
Boulder; 1880 Oct 22; Fri; L; rm 35

Martin, A D
1880 July 24; Saturday; S; room 15

Martin, E J
Colorado Tely Sun Co Denver; 1880 Dec 16; Thursday; S; room 5

Martin, Nathan
Guest of T M Finch; Colorado; 1880 Dec 12; Sunday; D

Martinus, D
Denver; 1880 Apr 14; Wednesday; S

Marvin, H C
Mich; 1880 May 17; Monday; S; rm 1

Marx, J L
1880 Apr 22; Thursday; D; room 25

Mather, Wm
Boulder; 1880 Nov 2; Tuesday; D

Mathews, K P
Gold Hill, Colo; 1880 Apr 19; Monday; D; room 25

Mathews, T
Caribou; 1880 Dec 16; Thursday; L; room 29

Matthews, J H
Golden; 1880 Oct 5; Tuesday; S

Matthews, R
Gold Hill; 1880 Apr 28; Wednesday; S; room 27

Matthews, R P
  Gold Hill; 1880 May 11; Tuesday; D; room 27
  Gold Hill; 1880 May 14; Friday; S; room 27

Mauritius, J H
  Kansas City; 1880 July 15; Thursday; S; room 44
  Kans City; 1880 July 17; Saturday; S

Mausbach, B
  Trinidad, Col; 1880 July 29; Thur; D

Maxwell (Miss)
  JJE; 1880 Sept 5; Sunday; D

Maxwell, John M
  Leadville; 1880 Apr 30; Friday; S; room 12
  Leadville, guest of Welch; 1880 July 17; Saturday; D
  Leadville, guest of R R Welch; 1880 Aug 26; Thursday
  & Wife; Leadville; 1880 Aug 29; Sunday; S; room 16

Maxwell, M (Miss)
  JJE; 1880 Nov 15; Monday; D
  JJE; 1880 Nov 17; Wednesday; D

Maxwell, Miss
  1880 Sept 19; Sunday; D

May, John
  Denver; 1880 June 12; Saturday; D

Mayer, A
  Ft Worth; 1880 June 21; Monday; D

Mayer, Ch
  Leavenworth; 1880 Apr 5; Monday; D

Mayer, Chas
  Leavenworth, Ks; 1880 Sept 6; Monday; D

Mazarto
  Dan Castello & Co Circus; 1880 May 23; Sunday; L; room 27

McAffee, S J
  1880 July 5; Monday; D

McAlvin, J H
  Omaha; 1880 June 27; Sunday; S; room 20

McAndrew, Patrick
  Boulder Co Jail; 1880 June 27; Sunday; B

McBurney, H B
  New York; 1880 July 7; Wednesday; D

McCarty, Lyman
  Denver; 1880 Sept 23; Thursday

McCauley, Wm
  Denver; 1880 May 22; Saturday; D

McClair, Sam'l
  Denver; 1880 Oct 10; Sunday; L; room 1

McClallan, R S
  Gold Hill; 1880 Dec 18; Saturday; D

McCleery, S S
  Youngstown, Ohio; 1880 Oct 19; Tuesday

McClure, F D
  Denver; 1880 June 11; Friday; D; room 6

McConnaghey, E (Mrs)
  Sunshine; 1880 Sept 24; Friday; S; room 33

McCorckle, A J
  Newcome Mine; 1880 Aug 17; Tuesday; D

McCorkle, R J
  Jamestown, Col; 1880 July 5; Mon; D

McCornick, C (Miss)
  Erie, Col; 1880 Aug 3; Tuesday; D; room 8

McCrary, D A (Mrs)
Longmont; 1880 June 19; Saturday; D; room 21

McCullough, A W
Butler, Pa; 1880 July 9; Friday; S; rm 6

McDonald, J B
Chicago; 1880 May 24; Monday; D; room 1
Chicago; 1880 Aug 4; Wednesday; S; room 1

McDougall, R
UPRW, Denver; 1880 Aug 23; Monday; S; room 3

McDowell, Ju'd Adair
Chicago; 1880 June 25; Friday; S; room 3

McElrath, T S
St Louis; 1880 Nov 18; Thursday; D; room 2

McFadden, Geo B
Longmont; 1880 May 22; Saturday; D
Longmont; 1880 July 5; Monday; D

McFarland, M
Utica, NY; 1880 May 5; Wednesday; S; room 1
Utica, NY; 1880 July 29; Thursday; S; room 1
Utica, NY; 1880 Nov 19; Friday; S; room 1

McFarland, Sue (Miss)
Longmont; 1880 Sept 23; Thursday; B

McFarland, T M (Miss)
Denver, E M Styles; 1880 Dec 5; Sunday; D

McGetrick, John
& Wife; Ward Dist; 1880 Aug 4; Wednesday; L; room 17

McGetrick, M (see McGitrick)
1880 Oct 3; Sunday; L; room 27

McGie, James A
Golden; 1880 May 15; Saturday; S

McGitrick, M (see McGetrick)
Ward; 1880 Oct 7; Thursday; S; rm 29

McGitrick, Michael
NiWot; 1880 Sept 26; Sun; L; rm 29

McGlenden, J H
& Wife; Nederland; 1880 Aug 17; Tuesday; D; room 1

McGlensay, H H
Philadelphia; 1880 May 23; Sunday; S; room 16

McGrath, James
Saint Louis; 1880 July 26; Monday; D

McHemen, L C
Denver; 1880 Oct 27; Wednesday; S; room 12

McIntosh, Jos
Buena Vista; 1880 June 28; Monday; L; room 33

McIntyre, J (Capt)
Chicago; 1880 July 30; Friday; L; room 12

McIntyre, J W
Chicago; 1880 May 15; Saturday; S; room 3
Chicago; 1880 July 7; Wednesday; S

McIntyre, J W (Capt)
Chicago; 1880 Oct 16; Saturday; L; room 10

McKay, J W
Denver; 1880 Dec 17; Friday; S; rm 29

McKay, John
Denver, Colo; 1880 July 5; Monday; D; room 12

McKay, Miss
Guest of Miss Luce; City; 1880 May 29; Saturday; D

McKay, W T
Denver; 1880 Dec 17; Friday; S; rm 29

McKay, Wm T
City; 1880 May 24; Monday; S

McKee, James
& Wife; Denver; 1880 Sept 22;
Wednesday; S; room 16

McKeirnan, J
& Mrs; Longmont; 1880 Dec 9; Thursday; D

McKenney, D C
Denver; 1880 July 20; Tuesday

McKenney, L C
Denver; 1880 Mar 29; Monday; S;
room 4
Denver; 1880 Apr 26; Monday; D
Denver; 1880 May 17; Monday; S;
room 44
Denver; 1880 May 28; Friday; D
Denver; 1880 June 29; Tuesday; S
Denver; 1880 Sept 10; Friday; D;
room 6
Denver; 1880 Sept 30; Thursday; S;
room 19
1880 Oct 2; Saturday; L; room 5
Denver; 1880 Oct 11; Monday; S;
room 11
Pacific City; 1880 Nov 17; Wednesday; S; room 12

McKenzey, C (see McKinzie)
Nederland; 1880 June 22; Tuesday; S;
room 10
& Wife; Nederland; 1880 July 22;
Thursday; D

McKenzie, Hugh
Cincinnati; 1880 June 2; Wednesday;
S; room 3

McKenzie, M
Nederland; 1880 Apr 6; Tuesday; S;
room 35

McKenzie, N D
& Wife; Nederland; 1880 Mar 11;
Thursday; S; room 8
& Wife; Nederland; 1880 Mar 14;
Sunday; S; room 8
Nederland; 1880 Mar 18; Thursday; D
Nederland; 1880 Mar 19; Friday; D
Nederland; 1880 Mar 23; Tuesday; D
& Wife; Nederland; 1880 Apr 13;
Tuesday; D
Nederland; 1880 Apr 19; Monday; D
Nederland; 1880 Apr 23; Friday; D
Nederland; 1880 Apr 29; Thursday; S;
room 44
Nederland; 1880 May 4; Tuesday; D
Nederland; 1880 May 9; Sunday; S;
room 6
& Wife; Nederland; 1880 July 10;
Saturday; S; room 12
Nederland; 1880 July 11; Sunday
Nederland; 1880 July 20; Tuesday; S
Nederland; 1880 July 21; Wednesday;
S; room 28
Nederland; 1880 July 30; Friday; D
Nederland; 1880 Aug 13; Friday; D
Nederland; 1880 Aug 21; Saturday; D
Nederland; 1880 Aug 7; Saturday; D
Nederland; 1880 Sept 4; Saturday; D;
room 12
Nederland; 1880 Sept 7; Tuesday; S
Nederland; 1880 Sept 9; Thursday; D
1880 Sept 25; Saturday; D; room 27
Nederland; 1880 Oct 5; Tuesday; D
Nederland; 1880 Oct 9; Saturday; D
Nederland; 1880 Oct 16; Saturday; D
Nederland; 1880 Oct 22; Friday; S
Nederland; 1880 Nov 1; Monday; D
Nederland; 1880 Nov 9; Tuesday; D
Nederland; 1880 Nov 20; Saturday; D
Nederland; 1880 Dec 16; Thursday; D;
room 34
Nederland; 1880 Dec 6; Monday; S;
room 13

McKenzie, W
& Wife; Nederland; 1880 May 11; Tuesday; D; room 17

McKingus, C
& Wife; Nederland; 1880 Aug 3; Tuesday; D; room 11

McKinler, C G
Denver; 1880 May 15; Saturday; S

McKinley, C A
Denver; 1880 July 16; Fri; D; rm 24

McKinley, G
Denver; 1880 June 27; Sunday; D

McKinney, D L C
Denver; 1880 Apr 20; Tuesday; S

McKinzie, C (see McKenzey)
Cardinal; 1880 May 23; Sunday; S; room 34
Nederland; 1880 July 4; Sunday; S; room 25
Nederland; 1880 July 12; Monday; D

McKnight
County Court Jury; 1880 Mar 11; Thursday; S

McLaughlin, E
Leadville; 1880 Aug 4; Wednesday; S

McLean, W A
Leadville; 1880 Aug 4; Wednesday; S

McLene, J
& Wife; Denver; 1880 Sept 8; Wednesday; L; room 6
Wife & Daughter; Denver; 1880 Sept 29; Wednesday; S; room 10&11

McMahon, J L
Chicago; 1880 Apr 2; Friday; S; rm 44

McManus, F
Reading, Pa; 1880 Oct 31; Sunday; D

McManus, T P
Reading, Pa; 1880 Nov 8; Monday; S

McMurray, T S
Tax Agent UP Ry; 1880 Dec 13; Monday; L; room 3

McNaughton, H V
Golden; 1880 Apr 9; Friday; S; rm 14

McNaughton, J C
Philada; 1880 Sept 15; Wednesday; D

McNaughton, S V
Denver; 1880 Aug 15; Sunday; S

McNaughton, T D
Absent after B; 1880 Oct 4; Monday

McNaughton, T V
Boulder; 1880 Mar 19; Friday; L; room 26

McNeil, I
Denver; 1880 Apr 13; Tuesday; S; room 2

McNitt, A P
Platteville; 1880 June 10; Thursday; L; room 26

McNoman, B E
Denver; 1880 Nov 9; Tuesday; L; room 14

McNorton, Thos
Leavenworth, Ks; 1880 Aug 20; Friday; D

McNorton, Tom
Boulder; 1880 Mar 19; Friday; L

McWilliams, C K
St Louis; 1880 June 16; Wednesday; D; room 12

Mead, M S
City; 1880 Mar 24; Wednesday; L; room 28

Meehan, R B
Beane City; 1880 Nov 2; Tuesday; L; room 12

Meggeman, F B
Denver; 1880 June 21; Monday; D
Denver; 1880 June 22; Tuesday; S;
room 20

Meinhardt, J H
Denver; 1880 Nov 3; Wednesday; D

Melburn, James Jr
St Louis; 1880 Mar 22; Monday; D;
room 6

Meldrum, N H
Denver; 1880 Mar 13; Saturday; D

Mellett, Nelson (see Millett)
Guest of A L Palsenster; 1880 Oct 6;
Wednesday; S

Mellette, John J
City; 1880 June 10; Thursday; D

Mellor, Barney
Boulder; 1880 Mar 11; Thursday; S;
room 44

Meloille, Maurice
Melbourne, Australia; 1880 Aug 20;
Friday; S

Melton, B
City; 1880 Mar 17; Wednesday; S;
room 27

Melton, Barney
Middle Park; 1880 July 8; Thursday; B

Melton, Barry
City; 1880 Mar 9; Tuesday; L; room 28

Melton, James
Middle Park; 1880 July 8; Thursday; B

Menden, W P
Denver; 1880 Mar 28; Sunday; S;
room 5

Mensell, James
With Mr Barney; 1880 Aug 13; Friday; D

Menson, J
Salina; 1880 June 11; Friday; S; rm 28

Mermel, M B
Longmont; 1880 June 19; Saturday; S;
room 5

Merritt, C A E
Denver; 1880 Sept 11; Saturday; D

Merritt, D D
Leadville; 1880 May 16; Sunday; D;
room 17
Leadville; 1880 May 18; Tuesday; D

Merwin, James
New York; 1880 Sept 16; Thursday; D;
room 12

Metcalf, E J
1880 July 5; Monday; L; room 5

Metcalf, E T
Longmont; 1880 Dec 11; Saturday; S
Longmont; 1880 Nov 6; Saturday; L;
room 26

Metcalf, Eli
Longmont; 1880 Sept 22; Wednesday

Metcalf, Thos
Atchison, Ks; 1880 Aug 20; Friday; D

Metz, M
Chicago; 1880 July 13; Tuesday; D;
room 3
Chicago; 1880 July 15; Thursday; S;
room 6

Meyer, Chas M
& Wife; Terre Haute, Ind; 1880 Aug
20; Friday; S
Terre Haute, Ind; 1880 Aug 21; Saturday; D

Meyer, G F
Salina; 1880 June 21; Monday; D

Meyer, M
Omaha, Neb; 1880 Nov 17; Wednesday; L; room 2

Meyer, Moritz
Omaha; 1880 Apr 6; Tuesday; L; rm 2
Omaha; 1880 July 12; Monday; S;
room 1

Meyering, Henry (see Meyring)
Salina; 1880 July 22; Thursday; D
Wife & 3 children; Salina; 1880 Aug
31; Tuesday; D
Salina; 1880 Sept 28; Tuesday; D;
room 5

Meyers, Lewis
St Jos, Mo; 1880 Nov 4; Thursday; D;
room 11

Meyring, Henry (see Meyering)
& Son; Salina; 1880 Aug 3; Tuesday; D
Salina; 1880 Oct 28; Thursday; D
Salina; 1880 Oct 29; Friday; D
Salina; 1880 Nov 15; Monday; D
Salina; 1880 Nov 18; Thursday; D
Salina; 1880 Nov 29; Monday; D
Salina; 1880 Nov 30; Tuesday; S; rm 5

Mickler, L H S
Denver; 1880 Sept 28; Tuesday; S;
room 3

Middleton, A
Magnolia; 1880 Apr 26; Monday; L;
room 35

Milan, Maggie
Ward; 1880 Dec 16; Thursday; S;
room 11
Nelson Place; 1880 Sept 18; Saturday;
D; room 14

Miles, D C
Mass; 1880 Sept 30; Thursday; L;
room 44
Mass; 1880 Oct 3; Sunday; D; room 19

Millburn, Mrs
& Son; Gold Hill; 1880 Aug 3; Tuesday; D

Miller, E A
Evans, Colo; 1880 Oct 8; Friday; D

Miller, Geo
1880 May 9; Sunday; L; room 26

Miller, J T
Longmont; 1880 July 5; Monday; S

Miller, M T
& Wife; Greeley; 1880 July 5; Mon; D

Miller, Otto
& Wife; Chicago; 1880 June 30;
Wednesday; S; room 15
& Wife; Chicago; 1880 July 20; Tues-
day; S; room 44

Miller, Sm'l
Crisman; 1880 Nov 18; Thursday; D

Miller, W H
Chg B C; 1880 Nov 18; Thursday; S

Millett, Nelson (see Mellett)
Denver; 1880 July 14; Wednesday; D
Denver; 1880 Aug 24; Tuesday; D
Denver; 1880 Oct 8; Friday; D
Denver; 1880 Oct 8; Friday; S

Mills, S
Denver; 1880 Aug 29; Sunday; S
Denver; 1880 Sept 3; Friday; D; rm 35
Denver; 1880 Oct 15; Friday; S; rm 17

Mills, S E
Michigan; 1880 Aug 21; Saturday; D

Mills, Wm B
Denver; 1880 June 3; Thursday; D

Milner, B F
Red Stone; 1880 July 25; Sunday; S;
room 13

Milner, Ben
Red Stone; 1880 Aug 29; Sunday; S;
room 13

Milner, J
Denver; 1880 Mar 6; Saturday; D
Denver; 1880 June 10; Thursday; S;
room 15

Milnor, T J
Leadville; 1880 Oct 27; Wednesday; D
Leadville; 1880 Oct 28; Thursday; S

Minckler, H
Caribou; 1880 Mar 9; Tuesday; S;
room 26
Caribou; 1880 Mar 10; Wednesday; S;
room 12
Caribou; 1880 Apr 7; Wednesday; S;
room 17
Caribou; 1880 Apr 8; Thursday; S;
room 17
Caribou; 1880 May 1; Saturday; D
Caribou; 1880 May 3; Monday; D
Caribou; 1880 May 4; Tuesday; S;
room 9
Caribou; 1880 May 7; Friday; S; rm 8
Caribou; 1880 May 10; Monday; L;
room 12
Caribou; 1880 May 14; Friday; S;
room 12
Caribou; 1880 May 16; Sunday; D;
room 13
Caribou; 1880 May 22; Saturday; D
Caribou; 1880 May 26; Wednesday; D
Caribou; 1880 May 29; Saturday; S;
room 12
Caribou; 1880 June 18; Friday; D;
room 11
Caribou; 1880 Aug 10; Tuesday; S;
room 13
Caribou; 1880 Aug 9; Monday; D;
room 14
Caribou; 1880 Sept 29; Wednesday; D;
room 12
Caribou; 1880 Oct 13; Wednesday; D;
room 12
Caribou; 1880 Oct 2; Saturday; L;
room 12

Minell, Ira T
Sugarloaf; 1880 Apr 7; Wednesday; S;
room 27

Miner, E N
Marshall; 1880 Nov 17; Wednesday;
D; room 12
Denver; 1880 Dec 14; Tuesday; D

Miner, E N (Mrs)
Denver; 1880 Nov 6; Saturday; L;
room 12

Mingan, W C
Georgetown; 1880 Mar 19; Friday; D
Georgetown; 1880 Apr 14; Wednes-
day; D

Minks, G W
Louisville; 1880 July 24; Saturday; L;
room 3

Misier, E P (Miss)
Chicago; 1880 Aug 5; Thursday; S;
room 44

Misier, M (Mrs)
Chicago; 1880 Aug 5; Thursday; S;
room 4

Mitchell, Joseph
Erie; 1880 July 5; Monday; D
Erie; 1880 May 13; Thursday; D

Mitchell, Joseph Jr
Erie; 1880 Apr 16; Friday; D
Wife & Family; 1880 Aug 3; Tues; D

Mitchell, Thomas
Georgetown; 1880 May 4; Tuesday; D;
room 16
Georgetown; 1880 May 10; Monday;
D; room 16
Georgetown; 1880 May 19; Wed; D
Georgetown; 1880 Nov 8; Monday; D;
room 16
Georgetown; 1880 Nov 15; Monday;
D; room 8

Mitchell, Thomas (cont.)
Georgetown; 1880 Nov 23; Tuesday;
D; room 8

Mitchell, Wm
UPRy; 1880 Nov 9; Tuesday; S; rm 6

Mitew, F J
Denver; 1880 Nov 27; Saturday; D

Mitts, Syd
Denver; 1880 Aug 28; Saturday; S;
room 33

Moffett, J C
Boulder; 1880 Nov 19; Friday; S
Boulder; 1880 Dec 4; Saturday; D
St Louis; 1880 Dec 5; Sunday; S

Moffett, Lillie M (Miss)
1880 Sept 5; Sunday; S; room 14

Mollone, B
City; 1880 Mar 8; Monday; L; rm 26

Money, C S
Chicago; 1880 Oct 31; Sunday; S;
room 6

Monhurrier, J
Chicago; 1880 May 13; Thursday; D

Montgomery, J C
Ward; 1880 Apr 3; Saturday; D; rm 28
Ward; 1880 Apr 17; Saturday; S; rm 25
Ward, Col; 1880 May 1; Saturday; D;
room 35

Montgomery, R
Valmont; 1880 June 30; Wednesday; S

Montgomery, R C (Mrs)
Ward; 1880 Sept 4; Saturday; D

Montgomery, Robt
Valmont; 1880 June 26; Saturday; B

Montgomery, Robt C
Valmont; 1880 June 16; Wednesday; D

Moon, James
& Wife; Barnums Show; 1880 Aug 1;
Sunday; L; room 11

Moore, A
Williamsburg; 1880 May 10; Monday;
S; room 25

Moore, A C
County Court Jury; 1880 Mar 11;
Thursday; S

Moore, B F
Denver; 1880 Nov 10; Wednesday; S;
room 6
Denver; 1880 Nov 13; Saturday; D

Moore, E F
New York; 1880 Mar 9; Tuesday; S;
room 6
Denver; 1880 Nov 17; Wednesday; D;
room 17

Moore, Ella
Dan Castello & Co Circus; 1880 May
23; Sunday; L; room 12

Moore, Geo
Guest of Pollock; 1880 May 23; Sunday; D

Moore, H
Nederland; 1880 Aug 24; Tuesday; D

Moore, H C
Chicago; 1880 May 5; Wednesday; S;
room 3
Chicago; 1880 May 7; Friday; D; rm 6

Moore, J G
& Wife; Nederland; 1880 Aug 3; Tuesday; D; room 10

Moore, S S
Denver, Col; 1880 Aug 18; Wednesday; S; room 17

Moore, Tobins
1880 Aug 20; Friday; L; room 29

Moorehead, L
Leadville; 1880 July 17; Saturday; S

Moorhead, J L
City; 1880 July 25; Sunday; D
1880 Sept 24; Friday; S

Morath
City; 1880 July 11; Sunday; L; room 17

Morehouse, P E
Denver; 1880 Mar 8; Monday; S; room 33

Moreley, D C
Jameston; 1880 Apr 11; Sunday; S; room 26

Morey, C S
Chicago; 1880 Apr 27; Tuesday; S
Chicago; 1880 Nov 23; Tuesday; L; room 11

Morgan, C C
Leadville; 1880 Apr 12; Monday; D

Morgan, J D
Longmont; 1880 July 5; Monday; D

Morganroth, J H
New York; 1880 Oct 22; Friday; L; room 11

Morgridge, W O
City; 1880 May 6; Thursday; L; rm 33
City; 1880 May 7; Friday; S; room 44
City; 1880 May 8; Saturday; D
City; 1880 May 8; Saturday; L; room 5
City; 1880 May 9; Sunday; L
City; 1880 May 11; Tuesday; L; rm 6
City; 1880 May 12; Wednesday; D; room 14
City; 1880 May 14; Friday; L; room 5
City; 1880 May 20; Thursday; S; rm 1
City; 1880 May 22; Saturday; L; rm 14
City; 1880 May 23; Sunday; L
City; 1880 May 27; Thursday; L; rm 13
City; 1880 May 28; Friday; S; room 13
City; 1880 May 29; Saturday; S; rm 13

Morgridge, Wm O
Leadville; 1880 Mar 15; Sunday; L; room 25
Boulder; 1880 Mar 16; Tuesday; L; room 25
Boulder; 1880 Mar 17; Wednesday; L; room 25
Boulder; 1880 Mar 19; Friday; L; room 25
Boulder; 1880 Mar 19; Friday; L; room 2
Boulder; 1880 Mar 20; Saturday; L; room 25
Boul; 1880 Mar 21; Sunday; L; rm 25
City; 1880 Mar 22; Monday; L; rm 25
City; 1880 Mar 23; Tuesday; L; rm 25
City; 1880 Mar 24; Wednesday; L; room 25
City; 1880 Mar 25; Thursday; L; rm 25
City; 1880 Mar 26; Friday; L; room 25
City; 1880 Mar 27; Saturday; L; rm 25
City; 1880 Mar 28; Sunday; L; rm 20
City; 1880 Mar 29; Monday; L; rm 25
City; 1880 Mar 30; Tuesday; L; rm 25
City; 1880 Mar 31; Wednesday; L; room 25
City; 1880 Apr 1; Thursday; L; rm 25
City; 1880 Apr 2; Friday; L; room 25
City; 1880 Apr 3; Saturday; L; rm 25
City; 1880 Apr 4; Sunday; L; room 25
City; 1880 Apr 5; Monday; L; room 25
City; 1880 Apr 6; Tuesday; L; room 25
City; 1880 Apr 7; Wed; S; rm 25
City; 1880 Apr 9; Friday; L; room 5
1880 Sept 14; Tuesday; B

Morris, J M
Golden; 1880 May 15; Saturday; S

Morris, T C
1880 Apr 22; Thursday; S; room 28

Morrison, John
County Court Jury; 1880 Mar 11; Thursday; S

Morrison, W M
City; 1880 Sept 1; Wednesday; D

Morse, H B
& Wife; Central; 1880 Aug 11;
Wednesday; L; room 6
Central; 1880 Aug 16; Monday; D;
room 8

Morse, J Hudson
Peabody, Kas; 1880 July 5; Monday; S;
room 15

Mortimore, D (Dr)
Denver; 1880 Mar 13; Saturday; S
Denver; 1880 Apr 20; Tuesday; S
Denver; 1880 June 2; Wednesday; L;
room 44

Mortimore, D MD
Denver; 1880 June 11; Fri; S; rm 44

Morton, C C
Saint Louis; 1880 Apr 16; Friday; D

Morton, H C (Mrs)
MN, absent after supper; 1880 Sept 7;
Tuesday

Morton, John
Louisville; 1880 Nov 1; Monday; D

Moseley, D H
Jamestown; 1880 Mar 22; Monday; L;
room 27
Gold Hill; 1880 June 23; Wednesday;
L; room 28
Gold Hill; 1880 June 29; Tuesday; S;
room 26

Moser, Gus
St Louis; 1880 Aug 25; Wednesday; S;
room 3
St Louis; 1880 Nov 12; Friday; S; rm 2

Mowry, J M
Emerson Camp; 1880 June 6; Sunday;
L; room 27
Ericson Camp; 1880 June 19; Satur-
day; L; room 27

Mowry, J M (cont.)
Emerson Camp; 1880 June 23;
Wednesday; L; room 29
1880 July 3; Saturday; L; room 28
Emerson Camp; 1880 July 5; Monday;
S; room 44
Emerson Camp; 1880 July 31; Satur-
day; L; room 14
1880 Aug 8; Sunday; L; room 35
1880 Aug 11; Wednesday; L; room 30
Crossed out; 1880 Aug 14; Saturday
1880 Aug 15; Sunday; S; room 35
Boulder; 1880 Aug 16; Monday; L;
room 13
Emerson; 1880 Aug 28; Saturday; L;
room 35
Emerson; 1880 Sept 4; Saturday; L;
room 13
Emerson; 1880 Sept 12; Sunday; S;
room 35
Emerson; 1880 Sept 26; Sunday; D;
room 33
Emerson; 1880 Oct 2; Saturday; S;
room 33
Emerson; 1880 Oct 24; Sunday; D;
room 34
1880 Nov 6; Saturday; L; room 34
Emerson; 1880 Nov 13; Saturday; L;
room 33
Magnolia; 1880 Nov 27; Saturday; D
Emerson; 1880 Dec 11; Saturday; L;
room 33
Emerson; 1880 Dec 18; Saturday; L;
room 13

Mowry, John M
Emerson; 1880 Nov 20; Saturday; L;
room 33
Emerson; 1880 Dec 4; Saturday; S;
room 13

Moynahan, T J
Leadville; 1880 May 14; Friday; S;
room 26

Muggatt, Wm R
Oxford, NY; 1880 Aug 4; Wednesday; S; room 12

Mullen, E
Denver; 1880 Apr 6; Tuesday; S; rm 5

Mulligan, J C
1880 Apr 22; Thursday; S; room 25

Mulligan, S H
N land; 1880 June 17; Thursday; D; room 20
New York City; 1880 Sept 17; Fri; D

Munson, Minnie (Miss)
1880 July 26; Monday; S; room 15

Munson, N D
Wife & Son; Quincy, Ill; 1880 July 26; Monday; S; room 16

Murat, A
Absent after dinner; 1880 Aug 21; Saturday

Murphey, Jas J (see Murphy)
Caribou; 1880 May 23; Sunday; L; room 25
Caribou; 1880 June 25; Friday; L; room 29
Caribou; 1880 July 11; Sunday; L; room 13
Caribou; 1880 July 28; Wednesday; S; room 14
Caribou; 1880 Aug 3; Tuesday; S
Caribou; 1880 Dec 8; Wednesday; S; room B

Murphey, Jo
Caribou; 1880 Nov 24; Wednesday; D; room 5

Murphey, Joe
Caribou; 1880 May 11; Tuesday; S; room 12
Caribou; 1880 May 27; Thursday; S; room 25

Murphey, Joe (cont.)
Caribou; 1880 June 7; Monday; L; room 28
Caribou; 1880 Sept 24; Friday; D; room 25
Caribou; 1880 Nov 23; Tuesday; S; room 5

Murphy, Bill
Quincy; 1880 Oct 17; Sunday; L

Murphy, C T
& Wife; Salina; 1880 Dec 6; Monday; S; room 8

Murphy, J M
Emerson Camp; 1880 Aug 8; Sunday; L; room 35

Murphy, Jas J (see Murphey)
Caribou; 1880 Mar 11; Thursday; S; room 12
Caribou; 1880 Mar 23; Tuesday; L; room 35

Myers, A W
Denver; 1880 Dec 1; Wednesday; S; room 12

Myers, L
St Joe; 1880 May 7; Friday; S; room 10

Myers, S
Boston; 1880 June 3; Thursday; S; room 1

Myers, Sydney
Breckenridge; 1880 Nov 11; Thursday; D; room 1

N

Nagle, S H
Denver; 1880 July 10; Saturday; D

Nalli, Miss
New Orleans, La; 1880 May 8; Saturday; D; room 11

Nalod, E
1880 Aug 10; Tuesday; D; room 29

Nash, H R
New York; 1880 June 2; Wednesday; S; room 12

Nathan, J G
Manager, Breakfast only; 1880 Aug 3; Tuesday; B

Naughtan, J A M
Caribou; 1880 May 18; Tuesday; S

Naukirk, W B
St Louis; 1880 June 10; Thursday; L; room 6

Neel, G W
& Wife; Sardis, Miss; 1880 June 11; Friday; S; room 1

Neely, S A J
Pottsville, Pa; 1880 Aug 30; Monday; S; room 6

Neff, Clark
Loveland; 1880 Dec 15; Wednesday; L; room 27

Neihorbt, Sandfour
___, Neb; 1880 July 26; Monday; S; room 8

Neikirk, Carey
Wife & 4 children; City; 1880 Sept 24; Friday; D

Neikirk, H
City; 1880 May 22; Saturday; D

Neikirk, Mr
& Wife; 1880 Aug 21; Saturday; D

Neikirk, T__
Sugar Loaf; 1880 Sept 4; Saturday; D

Neikirk, W
& Wife; Boulder; 1880 Aug 21; Saturday; D

Neil, Gus
Boston; 1880 July 19; Monday; S; room 6

Neilson, D P
S Cliff; 1880 July 21; Wednesday; S; room 6

Nelson, E N
Detroit, Mich; 1880 Oct 12; Tuesday; L; room 3

Nelson, J H
Denver; 1880 Sept 25; Saturday; B

Nesbit, D L
& Wife; 1880 Aug 21; Saturday; D
Guest of L C Paddock; 1880 Aug 29; Sunday; S
City; 1880 Sept 18; Saturday; S

Nestermaver, H L
Denver; 1880 Aug 5; Thursday; S

Neusterstock, H
Chicago; 1880 May 22; Saturday; S; room 25

Nevilly, Arthur
Denver; 1880 June 30; Wednesday; D; room 20

Newcomb, J A
Cleveland, O; 1880 Aug 13; Friday; S; room 21

Newcomb, L L
St Louis, Mo; 1880 Sept 28; Tuesday; S; room 1

Newcome, J A
Cleveland, O; 1880 Aug 17; Tues; D

Newell, C C
Leadville; 1880 Aug 23; Monday; L; room 6

Newell, S
Caribou; 1880 Aug 13; Friday; D; room 35

Newland, Jon
New York City; 1880 Sept 25; Saturday; L; room C

Newland, Q W
Boulder; 1880 Aug 3; Tuesday; D

Newman, H
Russell Gulch; 1880 Sept 1; Wednesday; S; room 29
Russell Gulch; 1880 Sept 2; Thur; S

Newnam, E B
Longmont; 1880 May 22; Saturday; D
& Wife; Longmont; 1880 Aug 3; Tuesday; D
Longmont; 1880 Aug 14; Saturday; D

Newnam, E B (Mrs)
& dau; Longmont; 1880 May 24; Monday; D

Newton, A
Leadville; 1880 May 19; Wednesday; S; room 12

Newton, A P
Denver, Col; 1880 May 19; Wednesday; S; room 12

Newton, E J
Denver; 1880 Sept 21; Tuesday; S; room 28

Nichols, C T Jr
Greeley; 1880 July 5; Monday; D

Nichols, V S
Central City; 1880 Nov 9; Tuesday; L; room 10

Nicholson, John W
City; 1880 Aug 19; Thursday; L; rm 27

Nicholson, Thomas
Brainard's Camp; 1880 May 2; Sun; D
Sunshine; 1880 May 17; Monday; D

Nicholson, W C
Crown Point, IN; 1880 Mar 6; Saturday; S ; 17

Nicholson, Wm C
Chicago; 1880 Apr 6; Tuesday; D

Nickel, Geo D
Del Norte; 1880 Mar 6; Saturday; S
Del Norte; 1880 June 7; Monday; L; room 13
Del Norte; 1880 June 28; Monday; S; room 44

Nickesom, Lee
Denver; 1880 June 10; Thursday; S; room 10

Nield, A D
New York; 1880 Apr 12; Monday; S; room 1

Noble, Wm
La Past Insurance Cy; 1880 Mar 8; Monday; S; room 44

Nobles, Milton
Nobles Company, New York; 1880 Oct 23; Saturday; D; room 19

Nofody, W R
Louisville, KY; 1880 Mar 10; Wednesday; S; room 29

Noland, F H
To Denver with Mr Mackie; 1880 July 19; Monday; D

Noll, F
Leavenworth; 1880 Apr 5; Monday; D

Noll, Geo
Denver; 1880 Mar 11; Thursday; S; room 6

Norcross, W R
1880 July 5; Monday; D

Norris, Chas
1880 Aug 10; Tuesday; D; room 29

North, James M (Hon)
& Lady; 1880 Aug 21; Saturday; D

Northiof, L __
M City; 1880 Mar 16; Tuesday; S; room 12

Norton, H C (Mrs)
Pa; 1880 June 8; Tuesday; D; room 2

Norton, Mrs
New York; 1880 Aug 16; Monday; S; room 25

Norton, W H C (MD)
Franklin, PA; 1880 May 24; Monday; D; room 12

Noyes, N D
Boston; 1880 Nov 3; Wednesday; D

Noyes, T W
Washington, D C; 1880 Sept 13; Monday; D; room 16
Washington, D C; 1880 Sept 17; Friday; D; room 16
Washington, D C; 1880 Sept 18; Saturday; L; room 16
Washington, D C; 1880 Sept 22; Wednesday; S; room 14
Washington, D C; 1880 Sept 25; Saturday; S; room 1
Washington, D C; 1880 Sept 27; Monday; S; room 15

Nugent, Miss
New York; 1880 July 22; Thursday; S; room 33

Nugent, Mrs
Caribou; 1880 June 22; Tuesday; D; room 21
& Child; Caribou; 1880 Nov 4; Thursday; S; room 12

Nulty, J G
Pa; 1880 Apr 23; Friday; S; room 17

Nye, L (Mrs)
New York; 1880 July 13; Tuesday; D; room 16

O

Oberkircher, Val
Denver; 1880 July 8; Thursday; S

O'Conner, L P
Leadville; 1880 Oct 15; Friday; D; room 16
Leadville; 1880 Oct 18; Monday; S; room 16

Olds, Mrs
Albany, Ills; 1880 Aug 23; Monday; D; room 17
Albany, Ill; 1880 Aug 6; Friday; S; room 21

O'Leary, J
Denver; 1880 Dec 13; Monday; S; room 10

Olmirth, Chs F C
St Louis; 1880 Aug 21; Saturday; D

Oppenheim, M J
Chicago; 1880 Nov 9; Tuesday; L; room 1

Oppenheimer, D
Omaha, Neb; 1880 Nov 11; Thursday; D; room 35

Orahood, H M
Central; 1880 May 4; Tuesday; D; room 10
Central; 1880 May 10; Monday; D; room 15
Guest Lins; 1880 Nov 10; Wed; S

Orbenning, James A
Penna; 1880 July 29; Thursday; S

Orparchinney, D
Omaha, Neb; 1880 June 16; Wednesday; S; room 21

Osborn, E
Sugar Loaf; 1880 July 1; Thursday; S; room 29

Otis, C A
Jamestown; 1880 Apr 23; Friday; S;
room 14

Otterbach
Cheyenne, Wy; 1880 Dec 8; Wednesday; S; room 33

Otterback, G H
Cheyenne, Wy; 1880 Dec 7; Tuesday;
L; room 13

Over, H C
Pittsburgh, PA; 1880 Mar 6; Saturday;
S; room 36

Owen, J M
St Louis; 1880 Apr 22; Thursday; S;
room 1

Owen, Jesse T
Loveland; 1880 Dec 7; Tuesday; L;
room 26
Loveland; 1880 Dec 15; Wednesday;
L; room 27

Owen, M G
Unreadable; 1880 Mar 24; Wednesday; S; room 3
St Louis; 1880 Apr 24; Sat
St Louis; 1880 May 11; Tuesday; S;
room 15
St Louis; 1880 July 10; Saturday; S;
room 16
St Louis; 1880 Sept 14; Tuesday; D;
room 15
St Louis; 1880 Aug 2; Monday; D;
room 3
St Louis; 1880 Aug 4; Wednesday; S;
room 16

Owen, M G
St Louis; 1880 Oct 18; Monday; D;
room 3
St Louis; 1880 Nov 22; Monday; D;
room 11
St Louis; 1880 Dec 5; Sunday; S; rm 12

Owen, T R
absent ; 1880 May 11; Tuesday; B
absent after D; 1880 Sept 28; Tues; D

Owen, T R Jr
Returned after D; 1880 Apr 17; Saturday; D
Left after [smudge]; 1880 Apr 24; Sat
Returned; 1880 Apr 24; Sat
Left after; 1880 Apr 29; Thursday; B
Returned; 1880 May 10; Monday; D
Returned after; 1880 May 11; Tuesday; D
Left after D; 1880 June 1; Tuesday
Returned to D; 1880 June 3; Thur; D
Absent after ; 1880 June 24; Thur; S
Returned; 1880 June 25; Friday; S
Returned; 1880 Aug 5; Thursday; S
Left after; 1880 Aug 16; Monday; S
Returned; 1880 Aug 23; Monday; S
Left after; 1880 Aug 30; Monday; D

Owen, Thomas R Jr
Returned to S; 1880 Mar 17; Wed; S
Returned; 1880 Oct 1; Friday; D
Absent after B; 1880 Oct 19; Tues; B
Returned to S; 1880 Dec 10; Friday; S

Owen, Thos R, Jr
Returned; 1880 Apr 8; Thursday; B
Returned after B; 1880 Apr 11; Sun; B
Returned; 1880 Aug 13; Friday; D
Returned to D; 1880 Sept 5; Sun; D
Returned; 1880 Oct 20; Wednesday; S
Left after; 1880 Dec 7; Tuesday; B
Left after; 1880 Dec 16; Thursday; D

Owen, Thos Jr
Left after ; 1880 Aug 3; Tuesday; S

Owen, Thos R
Absent after B; 1880 Apr 17; Sat; B
Absent after supper; 1880 Aug 9;
Monday; S

Owen, Tom
Returned to S; 1880 Mar 20; Sat; S
Left after B; 1880 Apr 6; Tuesday; B

Owen, Tom Jr
Left after S; 1880 Mar 16; Tuesday; S

Owen, W H
St Louis; 1880 June 16; Wednesday; D;
room 12

Owens [Owen]
Left after B; 1880 Mar 25; Thursday; B

Owens [Owen], T J Jr
Left after B; 1880 Apr 9; Friday; B

Owens [Owen], Tom
Left after B; 1880 Mar 20; Saturday; B

Own, M M
St Louis; 1880 June 23; Wednesday; S;
room 2

P

Pabearche, W A
St Louis; 1880 Apr 21; Wednesday; S;
room 3

Pack, J H
1880 Aug 7; Saturday; D

Pack, J W
City; 1880 Aug 2; Monday; L; room 17
City; 1880 Sept 13; Monday; D; rm 3

Pack, W F
St Louis, Mo; 1880 Aug 6; Friday; S;
room 17
1880 Aug 7; Saturday; D

Packard, Wm C
Greeley; 1880 July 8; Thursday; L;
room 5

Packe, Angus L
Leadville; 1880 Nov 4; Thursday; L;
room 28

Paddock
Guest of Kirk, T DeV
1880 Apr 18; Sun

Paddock, C E
Gone after; 1880 Oct 13; Wed; S

Paddock, Chas E
Guest of L C P; 1880 Oct 11; Monday;
S; room 34

Paddock, L C
Guest of T DeV Kirk; 1880 May 2;
Sunday; D
One guest; 1880 May 3; Monday; D
Gone; 1880 May 6; Thursday; D
Leadville; 1880 May 7; Friday; B
Leadville; 1880 Apr 22; Thursday; D
Leadville; 1880 Apr 25; Sun
Leadville; 1880 July 17; Saturday; S;
room 34
Gone after D; 1880 July 31; Saturday
Returned after D; 1880 Aug 2; Mon-
day; S; room 34
News & Courier; 1880 Aug 10; Tues-
day; L; room 34
News & Courier; 1880 Aug 18;
Wednesday; S; room 34
News & Courier; 1880 Sept 17; Friday,
room 34
Gone after; 1880 Oct 13; Wed; D

Pagby, Malison
Sunshine, Colo; 1880 Apr 24; Sat; D

Page, D H
Chicago; 1880 May 24; Monday; S;
room 44

Page, Lynx F
Butler, Mo; 1880 Sept 4; Saturday; D;
room 35

Palenertord, A L
Denver; 1880 Aug 2; Monday; L;
room 35

Palevertor, A M
Left after supper; 1880 Sept 3; Fri; S

Palinerton, Thos
Denver; 1880 Sept 20; Monday; D

Palmanton, C W
& Wife; Denver, Col; 1880 June 11;
Friday; D; room 14

Palmer, Frank
1880 Oct 24; Sunday; L; room 28

Palmer, W B
Denver; 1880 July 28; Wednesday; D

Palmer, W W
Chicago; 1880 Mar 31; Wednesday; S;
room 3
Chicago; 1880 Apr 19; Monday; S;
room 12
Chicago; 1880 May 10; Monday; D;
room 2
Chicago; 1880 June 16; Wednesday;
D; room 2
Chicago; 1880 June 30; Wednesday; S;
room 2
& Wife; Chicago; 1880 Aug 7; Satur-
day; S; room 1
Chicago; 1880 Sept 6; Monday; D;
room 1
Chicago; 1880 Oct 6; Wednesday; L;
room 1
Chicago; 1880 Nov 22; Monday; D;
room 10

Palmerten, C W
Denver, Col; 1880 Oct 13; Wednesday; S; room 10

Palmerton, A H
Denver; 1880 Aug 14; Saturday; S

Pappa, L
Loveland, Col; 1880 Aug 29; Sunday;
L; room 28

Paps, A H
Caribou; 1880 Nov 16; Tuesday; B;
room 17

Park, H W
Absent after breakfast; 1880 June 5;
Saturday

Park, J H
City; 1880 Oct 11; Monday; S

Parker, C E
Denver; 1880 July 20; Tuesday; S;
room 6

Parker, C J
Valmont; 1880 Mar 20; Saturday; D
Valmont; 1880 May 19; Wednesday; D
Ward; 1880 Sept 4; Saturday; D

Parker, C W
Chicago; 1880 July 26; Monday; L;
room 3

Parker, E D
Denver; 1880 Aug 24; Tuesday; D

Parker, E J
Valmont; 1880 Mar 6; Saturday; D
Valmont; 1880 Mar 15; Sunday; D
Valmont; 1880 Mar 17; Wednesday; D
Valmont; 1880 June 7; Monday; D
Valmont; 1880 June 16; Wednesday; D
Valmont; 1880 June 26; Saturday; B
Valmont; 1880 June 29; Tuesday; D
Valmont; 1880 June 30; Wednesday; S
Valmont; 1880 July 2; Friday; D
Ward; 1880 July 5; Monday; D; rm 29
Ward; 1880 July 8; Thursday; S; rm 28
Ward; 1880 July 17; Saturday; D;
room 27
Ward; 1880 July 18; Sunday; L; rm 29
Ward; 1880 Aug 3; Tuesday; L
Ward; 1880 Aug 9; Monday; S; rm 28
Ward; 1880 Aug 12; Thursday; S;
room 28
Ward; 1880 Sept 6; Monday; D

Parker, E J (cont.)
Ward; 1880 Sept 8; Wednesday; S; room 28
Ward; 1880 Sept 1; Wednesday; S; room 28
Ward; 1880 Sept 28; Tuesday; S; rm 29
Ward; 1880 Oct 1; Friday; S; room 29
Ward; 1880 Oct 6; Wednesday; S; room 28
Ward; 1880 Oct 13; Wednesday; D; room 28
Ward; 1880 Nov 7; Sunday; D
Ward; 1880 Nov 8; Monday; D; rm 28
Ward; 1880 Nov 16; Tuesday; S; rm 28

Parker, Ed
Ward; 1880 Dec 17; Friday; D; rm 28

Parker, Edward
Longmont; 1880 Nov 18; Thursday; S

Parker, Jim
1880 Sept 21; Tuesday; S; room 28

Parkhill, E W
St Louis; 1880 Dec 2; Thursday; S; room 6

Parkinson, W
Denver; 1880 Apr 5; Monday; S; rm 5
Denver; 1880 Apr 29; Thursday; D

Parkinson, W J
Denver; 1880 July 14; Wednesday; S; room 20
Denver; 1880 July 16; Friday; S; rm 2
Denver; 1880 Sept 23; Thursday; S; room 1

Parks, E F
With Winch, Paw Paw, Mich; 1880 Aug 9; Monday; D

Parlin, David
With Eben Smith; 1880 Sept 3; Fri; S

Parrott, W L
Albany; 1880 Apr 21; Wednesday; S; room 6
Chicago; 1880 July 15; Thursday; S; room 2

Parrotte, W L
Chicago; 1880 Oct 18; Monday; L; room 6

Pasmore, E J
Denver; 1880 Sept 24; Friday; D; room 11

Paterson, A M
Gold Hill; 1880 Apr 10; Saturday; S; room 25
Gold Hill; 1880 Apr 17; Saturday; S; room 34

Paterson, S H
Gold Hill; 1880 Apr 19; Monday; S; room 25

Paterson, S M
Gold Hill; 1880 Mar 30; Tuesday; S; room 28

Pateson, A M
Gold Hill; 1880 Apr 8; Thursday; S; room 25

Paton, Jas S
Cheyenne; 1880 July 16; Friday; S; room 35
Cheyenne; 1880 July 17; Saturday; D; room 29
1880 July 26; Monday; S; room 29

Patriarch, P H
St Louis, MO; 1880 Apr 1; Thursday; S; room 15
St Louis, Mo; 1880 Oct 11; Monday; L; room 3

Patrick, Thos
Washington Ave; 1880 Mar 8; Monday; L; room 25

Patterson, Arthur
1880 Aug 11; Wednesday; L; room 28

Patterson, F
Longmont; 1880 July 5; Monday; D

Patterson, M C
Georgetown; 1880 Nov 9; Tuesday; S

Pattinson, B W
Albany, NY; 1880 July 5; Monday; D

Pattison, H R
Longmont; 1880 Dec 13; Monday; D

Pattison, Harwen
Albany, NY; 1880 Aug 18; Wed; S

Patton, C L
Denver; 1880 July 17; Saturday; S; room 33

Patton, J N
London, England; 1880 Aug 18; Wednesday; S

Paulsoce, James
St Louis; 1880 Mar 10; Wednesday; L; room 2

Paxton, B F
St Joseph; 1880 June 26; Saturday; S

Payne, M
Nobles Company, New York; 1880 Oct 23; Saturday; D; room 6

Payne, Mrs
Chicago; 1880 July 12; Monday; S; room 4

Payntor, E C
Guests of JB; Rockford, Ill; 1880 June 15; Tuesday; D

Peacock, L C
City; 1880 Mar 22; Monday; D; rm 17

Pearce, John
Salina; 1880 Dec 14; Tuesday; D

Pease, L
Montana; 1880 Aug 31; Tuesday; D; room 6

Pease, L Fred
Mouland; 1880 Aug 29; Sunday; S; room 6

Peat, George
Gold Hill; 1880 Sept 22; Wednesday; D; room 25

Peck, Ai
Denver; 1880 Sept 30; Thursday; S

Peck, Delavan
& Wife; Nelson Place; 1880 Apr 11; Sunday; S; room 16
& Wife; Nelson Place; 1880 Apr 15; Thursday; D; room 16
Wife & servant; Nelson Place; 1880 Apr 17; Saturday; D; room 4, 44
Nelson Place - Ward; 1880 Aug 7; Saturday; D; room 16
& Wife; Nelson Place - Ward; 1880 Aug 10; Tuesday; D
& Wife; Nelson Place - Ward; 1880 Aug 12; Thursday; S; room 18
Nelson Place - Ward; 1880 Aug 15; Sunday; L; room 12
Nelson Place - Ward; 1880 Aug 18; Wednesday; S; room 16
& Wife; Nelson Place Ward; 1880 May 12; Wednesday; S; room 4
& Wife; Nelson Place Ward; 1880 June 30; Wednesday; D; room 16
& Wife; Ward; 1880 July 20; Tuesday; S; room 4
& Wife; Nelson Place; 1880 Sept 18; Saturday; D; room 6
& Wife; Nelson Place Ward; 1880 Oct 22; Friday; D; room 8
& Wife; Ward; 1880 Dec 16; Thursday; S; room 10

Peck, Geo A
Denver; 1880 Aug 21; Saturday; D

Peck, Mr
& Wife; Nelson Place Ward; 1880 Oct 23; Saturday; S; room 16

Pell, Chas C
Dan Castello & Co; 1880 May 11; Tuesday; S; room 4

Pell, W G
& Wife; 1880 Aug 21; Saturday; D

Pendit, L
NY; 1880 Mar 26; Friday; D; room 16

Pennock, Carrie
Longmont; 1880 Apr 3; Saturday; D

Peobrige, Mrs
Sunshine; 1880 Aug 3; Tuesday; D

Peppard, C D
Golden; 1880 May 1; Saturday; S; room 6

Peppin, Todd & Co
Baltimore, MD; 1880 May 25; Tuesday; D

Perin, C M
UPRR; 1880 Dec 10; Friday; S

Perkins, Eli
Omaha, Neb; 1880 Oct 10; Sunday; D

Perkins, G M B
Denver; 1880 June 15; Tuesday; S; room 13

Perkins, H C
Denver; 1880 June 25; Fri; S; rm 10

Perrin, C M
UPRy; 1880 Nov 9; Tuesday; S; rm 6

Perrin, H H
Boston; 1880 June 20; Sunday; D; room 1
Boston; 1880 June 4; Friday; D; rm 2

Perry, A
Caribou; 1880 May 22; Saturday; D
Caribou; 1880 May 26; Wednesday; S; room 26
Caribou; 1880 Oct 13; Wednesday; D; room 12
Caribou; 1880 Nov 25; Thursday, Thanksgiving; D; room 33

Perry, L T
New Orleans, La; 1880 Apr 22; Thursday; D; room 25

Person, Chas
Denver; 1880 Sept 23; Thursday; S; room 27

Pesci, H F
& Wife; 1880 Aug 21; Saturday; D

Peter, Samuel
Conger Me; 1880 Apr 1; Thurs

Peterbaugh, Geo
Breckenridge; 1880 Nov 11; Thursday; D; room 11

Peters, E A
Denver; 1880 Mar 19; Friday; D; room 6
Denver; 1880 May 13; Thursday; S; room 2
Denver; 1880 July 21; Wednesday; S; room 2
Denver; 1880 Oct 14; Thursday; D; room 11
Denver; 1880 Nov 29; Monday; L; room 11
Denver; 1880 Nov 30; Tuesday; L; room 11

Peterson, A
Magnolia; 1880 Nov 4; Thursday; D

Peterson, An
Magnolia; 1880 Dec 8; Wednesday; D

Peterson, J M
Magnolia; 1880 Nov 27; Saturday; D

Peterson, M
Magnolia; 1880 Sept 4; Saturday; D
Magnolia; 1880 Sept 12; Sunday; D;
room 29
Magnolia; 1880 Sept 27; Monday; D

Peterson, Martin
Magnolia; 1880 Nov 22; Monday; D
Matnolia; 1880 Oct 28; Thursday; D

Peterson, N
Magnolia; 1880 Nov 13; Saturday; D

Petherbridge, C L
Buena Vista; 1880 Sept 24; Friday; D;
room 1

Pettebone, Payne
Golden; 1880 May 15; Saturday; S;
room 14

Pettibone, P F
Chicago; 1880 Nov 11; Thursday; L;
room 13

Petty, Geo F
St Louis; 1880 May 6; Thursday; S

Pfaiffer, G W
St Louis, Mo; 1880 Oct 6; Wednesday;
L; room 11

Pfeiffer, G W
St Louis; 1880 Dec 2; Thursday; L;
room 35

Phelps, W H
Leavenworth; 1880 Apr 1; Thursday;
S; room 40
Leavenworth, Kas; 1880 Sept 1;
Wednesday; S; room 6

Philip, George G
Salina; 1880 May 4; Tuesday; D
Salina; 1880 July 28; Wednesday; D
Salina; 1880 July 30; Friday; D

Philips, George
Salina; 1880 Nov 6; Saturday; D

Phillbuck, Frank
Doniphan, Ks; 1880 Aug 20; Friday; D

Phillips, C B
New York; 1880 Oct 3; Sunday; S;
room 12
New York; 1880 Oct 4; Monday; L

Phillips, Florence C (Miss)
Longmont; 1880 Sept 6; Monday; S

Phillips, G M
Northfield Mine; 1880 July 27; Tuesday; S; room 6

Phillips, Morris
St Louis; 1880 Nov 10; Wednesday; L;
room 1

Phillips, Wm
& Wife; 1880 June 7; Monday; S;
room 4

Philpot, R S
Denver; 1880 Oct 28; Thursday; D

Phily, George G
Salina; 1880 July 30; Friday; D

Pickel, J Lee
& Lady; Nederland; 1880 Aug 3;
Tuesday; L

Pierce
Denver; 1880 Apr 13; Tuesday; S;
room 35
Denver; 1880 Apr 14; Wednesday; S;
room 5

Pierce, Geo
Denver; 1880 May 17; Monday; D

Pierce, W R
Denver; 1880 Sept 18; Saturday; L;
room 5
Denver; 1880 Nov 4; Thursday; L;
room 17

Pierce, Wm H
Denver; 1880 May 8; Saturday; S;
room 16

Piercely, L D (Mrs)
Denver; 1880 July 29; Thursday; D

Pierson, S F
Denver; 1880 Apr 20; Tuesday; D

Pilmor, Richard
Osborn; 1880 Oct 13; Wednesday; D

Pine, B F
With Craig; 1880 June 21; Monday; D
Boulder; 1880 Aug 11; Wednesday; S

Pine, B F Jr
Boulder; 1880 June 18; Friday; D
Guest of Leeke; 1880 June 23;
Wednesday; D
With R R Craig; 1880 June 28; Monday; D
Boulder; 1880 July 3; Saturday; D
Boulder; 1880 Sept 10; Friday; B
Returned at B; 1880 Oct 4; Monday; B

Pine, Frank
Guest of Tom Owen
1880 Mar 14; Sunday; S
Took dinner with me today, Tom
Owen; 1880 Mar 16; Tuesday; D
Guest of Leeke; 1880 Nov 23; Tuesday; D

Pine, I S
City; 1880 Mar 21; Sunday; S

Pine, Isaac S
City; 1880 Mar 14; Sunday; D

Pine, J H
Greeley; 1880 July 5; Monday; D

Pine, J S
Boulder; 1880 Oct 18; Monday; B
Magnolia; 1880 Oct 23; Saturday; S
Boulder; 1880 Nov 3; Wednesday; D
Boulder, Co; 1880 Nov 18; Thur; B

Pine, W R
Denver; 1880 June 3; Thursday; D;
room 14

Pinger, John E
Leadville; 1880 Apr 26; Monday; S;
room 12

Pingree, Geo H
Prussian Mine; 1880 Mar 14; Sunday;
L; room 27

Pinkney, C C
Chicago; 1880 Apr 23; Friday; S; rm 6
Denver; 1880 May 26; Wednesday; S;
room 3
Denver; 1880 May 27; Thursday; S;
room 4
Chicago; 1880 May 27; Thursday; S;
room 33
Babcock with CCP; 1880 Aug 12;
Thursday; S
Denver; 1880 Aug 12; Thursday; D;
room 1

Pippin, J C
City, guest of J R; 1880 May 24; Monday; D

Pippin, Jim
Guest of Owen; 1880 May 20; Thursday; D

Pitkin, F W
Denver; 1880 Aug 21; Saturday; D

Plattenburg, C J A
Chicago; 1880 Oct 2; Saturday; D

Plattenburg, Chas
Chicago; 1880 Apr 22; Thursday; S;
room 3

Plumb, H T
NY; 1880 Apr 19; Monday; S; room 2
N Y; 1880 June 9; Wednesday; D;
room 2

Plumb, S J
Wife & 2 children; Erie; 1880 Aug 3;
Tuesday; D

Plummer, C H
City; 1880 Apr 1; Thurs; room 28

Plummer, D
Iowa; 1880 May 28; Friday; S; room 15

Plunkett, Blanche (Miss)
Plunket Troup; 1880 July 19; Monday;
D; room 19

Plunkett, Carra (Miss)
Plunket Troup; 1880 July 19; Monday;
D; room 20

Plunkett, Chas
& Wife; Mng Plunket Troup; 1880
July 19; Monday; D; room 8 & 9
Plunkett Troupe; 1880 Sept 19; Sun-
day; S; room 8

Plunkett, Chas (Mrs)
Plunkett Troupe; 1880 Sept 19; Sunday; S; room 8

Plunkett, Sue (Miss)
Plunket Troup; 1880 July 19; Monday;
D; room 20

Podner, G
Blopsburg, PA; 1880 Mar 14; Sunday;
D; room 6

Polanski, S
San Francisco; 1880 May 12; Wednesday; S; room 2

Polaski, Sam
San Francisco; 1880 Nov 9; Tues; D

Polaski, Sam S
San Fred [?]; 1880 Mar 14; Sunday; D;
room 1

Poleck, Jas
Boulder; 1880 Sept 15; Wednesday; D

Pollin, A H
City with R P Craig; 1880 June 27;
Sunday; S; room 12

Pollock, Alex
St Louis; 1880 July 25; Sunday; S;
room 2

Pond, John
Erie; 1880 Sept 29; Wednesday; S;
room 12

Pontices, N
Denver; 1880 Aug 5; Thursday; S

Porstions, N
Penna; 1880 July 29; Thursday; S

Porter, Benj
Jayon, Mich; 1880 Oct 6; Wed; D

Porter, J M
& Wife; Denver; 1880 July 29; Thursday; D

Posthethwaite, A G
Philada; 1880 Sept 15; Wednesday; D

Potlitzer, H
New York; 1880 July 17; Saturday; S;
room 1

Pound, Ch
City; 1880 May 25; Tuesday; L; rm 25

Pound, E
County Court Jury; 1880 Mar 11;
Thursday; S

Pound, F
City; 1880 June 27; Sunday; D

Pound, H
City; 1880 Aug 29; Sunday; D

Pound, T
City; 1880 Apr 25; Sunday; D

Powell, A C
Omaha; 1880 Sept 22; Wednesday; D

Powell, F T
St Louis; 1880 Dec 4; Saturday; D;
room 1

Powell, J E
Kas City; 1880 Sept 17; Friday; D;
room 11

Powell, S F
Denver; 1880 May 4; Tuesday; S;
room 44

Powers, Edw'd
Denver; 1880 Nov 3; Wednesday; S;
room 6

Pratt, Sam
New York; 1880 Sept 18; Saturday; S;
room 5

Price, Chas & Brown
Dan Castello & Co Circus; 1880 May
23; Sunday; B

Price, Hugh P
Denver; 1880 Dec 16; Thursday; S;
room 17

Price, Hugh T
Leadville; 1880 Dec 8; Wednesday; L;
room 17

Price, Jno
Marshall; 1880 Apr 6; Tuesday; S;
room 27

Prichard, C H
Denver; 1880 Aug 7; Saturday; S;
room 12

Pritchard, N N
Greeley; 1880 July 5; Monday; D

Procter, Thomas
Longmont; 1880 May 26; Wed; D

Proncpont, Owen
St Louis; 1880 Sept 17; Friday; L;
room 1

Prostwith, J M & Lady
1880 June 12; Saturday; D

Prunswick, S
St Louis; 1880 Dec 10; Friday; L; rm 1

Pugh, Ulysses
Caribou; 1880 June 24; Thursday; D
1880 Aug 2; Monday; S; room 28
Caribou; 1880 Nov 22; Monday; S;
room 27

Pughe, J
Gold Hill; 1880 Mar 20; Saturday; S;
room 17
Gold Hill; 1880 Mar 21; Sunday; L;
room 5
Sunshine; 1880 Apr 14; Wednesday; L;
room 25
& Wife; Gold Hill; 1880 Sept 17; Friday; S; room 4

Pughe, John
Gold Hill; 1880 Mar 6; Saturday; D;
room 26
Gold Hill; 1880 Mar 13; Saturday; D;
room 17
Gold Hill; 1880 May 29; Saturday; S
Gold Hill; 1880 June 1; Tuesday; D
Gold Hill; 1880 June 2; Wednesday; D
Gold Hill; 1880 June 7; Monday; L;
room 27
Gold Hill; 1880 June 12; Saturday; D
Gold Hill; 1880 June 26; Saturday; D
Gold Hill; 1880 June 27; Sunday; S
Gold Hill; 1880 July 19; Monday; S
Gold Hill; 1880 Dec 1; Wednesday; S;
room 13

Pughy, Nadine
Sunshine; 1880 Apr 13; Tuesday; D

Puiger, John E
Leadville; 1880 May 2; Sunday; S;
room 8

Pumphrey, Lloy W
1880 Mar 11; Thursday; S; room 28

Punsell, A B
St Louis; 1880 Dec 8; Wednesday; S;
room 11

Purce, W R
Denver; 1880 Sept 13; Monday; S; room 5

Purmort, H C
Chicago; 1880 Mar 6; Saturday; S; room 1
Chicago; 1880 May 11; Tuesday; S; room 9
Chicago; 1880 Oct 7; Thursday; L; room 15

Pursel, John
Central City; 1880 Aug 14; Saturday; S; room 28

Purser, W H
Denver; 1880 May 16; Sunday; S; room 17

Putnam, Bayard T
US Geol Survey NY; 1880 Oct 5; Tuesday
New York; 1880 Oct 7; Thursday

Pynchon, J H
Omaha; 1880 July 26; Monday; L; room 1

Q

Quimby, Wells
& 2 Ladies; Greeley; 1880 July 5; Monday; D

R

Rabbitts, W D
City; 1880 Apr 26; Monday; D

Rabbitts, W S
City; 1880 Aug 9; Monday; L; room 11
City; 1880 Aug 10; Tuesday; L; room 3
City; 1880 Aug 11; Wednesday; L; room 5
Gone to Longmont; 1880 Dec 12; Sunday

Ragland, B R
Denver; 1880 Dec 3; Friday; S; room 3

Rainford, Clara (Miss)
1880 Aug 10; Tuesday; D; room 10

Rainkingame, E E
Denver; 1880 Apr 15; Thursday; S; room 12

Rand, Geo
Ralston; 1880 June 28; Monday; D
Louisville; 1880 June 28; Monday; L; room 11
Louisville; 1880 Nov 1; Monday; D

Rand, George
Louisville; 1880 Oct 9; Saturday; D

Randall, Mo F
St Louis; 1880 Aug 17; Tuesday; S

Randell, B F
Denver; 1880 Mar 25; Thursday; D; room 16

Randolph, Peter F
NYC; 1880 Mar 14; Sunday; S; rm 15
NYC; 1880 Aug 12; Thur; L; rm 12

Rangell, B _
Denver; 1880 Mar 29; Monday; S; room 16

Ranken, E H
Denver; 1880 May 11; Tuesday; S; room 14

Rankin, E H
Denver; 1880 June 28; Monday; D

Ransom, D
Magnolia; 1880 Apr 10; Saturday; D
Magnolia; 1880 Aug 16; Monday; S; room 5
Magnolia; 1880 Aug 24; Tuesday; D
Magnolia; 1880 July 12; Monday; S
Magnolia; 1880 June 19; Saturday; D
Magnolia; 1880 June 19; Saturday; S

Ransom, Daniel
St Joseph, MO; 1880 Apr 6; Tuesday;
D; room 33
Magnolia; 1880 Apr 14; Wednesday;
L; room 26
Magnolia; 1880 May 14; Friday; D
Magnolia; 1880 May 21; Friday; S
Magnolia; 1880 May 27; Thursday; D
Magnolia; 1880 June 8; Tuesday; S
Magnolia; 1880 June 12; Saturday; D
Magnolia; 1880 July 7; Wednesday; D
Magnolia; 1880 Aug 19; Thursday; D
Magnolia; 1880 Aug 19; Thursday; S;
room 5
1880 Aug 21; Saturday; D
Magnolia; 1880 Sept 2; Thursday; D

Ransom, H A
Longmont; 1880 Aug 3; Tuesday; S

Ransom, J
Magnolia; 1880 May 17; Monday; D

Raske, Henry
Denver; 1880 Mar 10; Wednesday; S;
room 8

Rawhn, R H
Chicago; 1880 Nov 10; Wednesday; L;
room 13

Ray, John
Denver; 1880 Nov 20; Saturday; S

Raymond, B B
St Louis; 1880 Sept 7; Tuesday; S;
room 19

Raymond, Chas W
Boulder; 1880 May 11; Tuesday; S

Raymond, L W
Guest with Kirk; 1880 May 9; Sun; D

Raynolds, J O
& boy; Denver; 1880 Apr 6; Tuesday;
S; room 16
Denver; 1880 Dec 2; Thursday; S;
room 8

Read, W H
Cheyenne; 1880 Mar 15; Sunday; S;
room 6

Ream, D S
& Lady; 1880 Aug 21; Saturday; D;
room 17

Reech, L H
Lowell, Mass; 1880 Aug 21; Sat; D

Reed, Burt
Longmont; 1880 Sept 17; Friday; S

Reed, Christin
Leadville; 1880 Sept 20; Monday; S;
room 10

Reed, Emma (Miss)
NiWot; 1880 Aug 3; Tuesday; D

Reed, Miss
Longmont; 1880 Aug 3; Tuesday; D

Reed, P J
Golden; 1880 Sept 22; Wednesday; D

Rees, B F
Columbus, O; 1880 Aug 17; Tues; D

Regue, L S
Decorah, IA; 1880 July 13; Tuesday; S;
room 35

Reid, Ben
Longmont; 1880 Nov 8; Monday; L;
room 27

Reid, Jno S
Leadville; 1880 Nov 3; Wednesday; D
1880 Nov 4; Thursday; D; room 17
1880 Nov 5; Friday; L; room 8
1880 Nov 13; Saturday; D
1880 Nov 25; Thursday, Thanksgiving;
D; room 12
1880 Dec 2; Thursday; D; room 13
Leadville; 1880 Dec 6; Monday; S;
room 6
Magnolia; 1880 Dec 18; Saturday; S;
room 14

Reid, Mrs
Longmont; 1880 Aug 4; Wednesday;
L; room 26

Reilley, Henry B
Frankfort; 1880 Nov 21; Sunday; S

Remington, William
DeWitt, Nebr; 1880 June 17; Thursday; S; room 28

Renn, J N
Col Springs; 1880 Apr 17; Saturday; S

Reuter, G A
Denver; 1880 July 19; Monday; D

Revolcott, Edw'd
Georgetown; 1880 Oct 12; Tuesday;
D; room 11

Revolcott, Henry
Black Hawk; 1880 Oct 12; Tuesday; D;
room 10

Reynolds, C H
& Wife; Denver; 1880 July 3; Saturday; S; room 15

Reynolds, J C
Denver; 1880 Apr 27; Tuesday; D

Reynolds, J O
Denver; 1880 July 7; Wednesday; S;
room 6
Denver; 1880 Oct 6; Wednesday; S;
room 1
Denver; 1880 Dec 3; Friday; D; rm 8

Rhoads, A G
Denver; 1880 Sept 7; Tuesday; S;
room 2

Rhodes, C B
Philada; 1880 Aug 4; Wednesday; S;
room 6

Rhodes, D
Sunshine; 1880 June 20; Sunday; D;
room 5

Rhodes, Daniel
Denver; 1880 June 13; Sunday
Denver; 1880 June 4; Friday; S

Rhodes, J B
& Lady; Longmont; 1880 July 5;
Monday; S

Rhodes, N H
Chicago; 1880 Sept 21; Tuesday; S;
room 2

Richards, C D
Denver; 1880 Nov 9; Tuesday; L;
room 17
Denver; 1880 Nov 10; Wednesday; D;
room 11

Richards, H (Mrs)
& 2 children; Caribou; 1880 July 28;
Wednesday; D; room 17
& 2 children; Caribou; 1880 July 30;
Friday; D; room 17

Richards, J H
Golden; 1880 Aug 8; Sunday; D

Richards, S (Mrs)
& Family; Caribou; 1880 July 27;
Tuesday; D

Richardson, A G
St Louis; 1880 Dec 7; Tuesday; S;
room 2

Richardson, R M
Syracuse, NY; 1880 June 30; Wednesday; S; room 44
Denver; 1880 Oct 19; Tuesday; S;
room 19
Denver; 1880 Oct 21; Thursday; S;
room 10

Richardson, R M Jr
Denver; 1880 Oct 19; Tuesday; S;
room 20
Denver; 1880 Oct 21; Thursday; S;
room 11

Richardson, R M Jr (cont.)
Denver; 1880 Oct 28; Thursday; S; room 17
Denver; 1880 Oct 30; Saturday; S; room 17
Denver; 1880 Nov 2; Tues; S; rm 17
Denver; 1880 Nov 22; Monday; S; room 26
Denver; 1880 Nov 30; Tuesday; D; room 26

Richmond, E G
Denver; 1880 Apr 30; Friday; S; rm 9

Richthofen, W Baron
Fort Lupton; 1880 Sept 22; Wednesday; D; room 13

Rico, Sol
New York & Leadville; 1880 Oct 30; Saturday; S; room 8

Rife, Jno N
Middletown, Pa; 1880 Oct 26; Tuesday; S; room 19

Riley, J E
New York; 1880 June 18; Friday; S; room 3

Riley, J G
San Francisco; 1880 May 14; Friday; S; room 4
San Francisco; 1880 May 16; Sun; D
New York; 1880 Sept 4; Saturday; D; room 10
New York; 1880 Sept 7; Tuesday; D; room 14

Riley, Thomas
Denver; 1880 May 21; Friday; S; rm 6
Denver; 1880 July 14; Wednesday; D; room 12
Denver; 1880 July 29; Thursday; S
Denver; 1880 Aug 5; Thursday; S
Omaha, Neb; 1880 Aug 18; Wednesday; S; room 5

Ringon, W Par
Denver; 1880 Dec 8; Wednesday; S; room 10

Rinkenbeck, L
Chicago; 1880 Nov 9; Tuesday; D; room 3

Ripley, C H
New York; 1880 Oct 28; Thursday; S

Ripley, Chas
St Louis; 1880 Mar 27; Saturday; D

Ripley, Chas H
New York; 1880 Nov 8; Monday; S; room 11
New York; 1880 Oct 27; Wed; D

Ripley, Chas P H
New York; 1880 Nov 10; Wed; S

Ripley, Geo
St Louis; 1880 Mar 27; Saturday; D

Rivoleatt, H
Denver; 1880 Oct 9; Saturday; L; room 11

Robbins, E
St Louis; 1880 Mar 31; Wednesday; S; room 1
St Louis; 1880 Sept 14; Tuesday; S; room 12

Robbins, Isaac
City; 1880 Dec 8; Wednesday; S

Roberts, C A
Denver, Col; 1880 Nov 8; Monday; D

Roberts, Caesar
Denver, Col; 1880 Nov 5; Friday; D

Roberts, J F
Rih___; 1880 Mar 11; Thursday; S; room 3
Gold Hill; 1880 Mar 29; Monday; S; room 5
Gold Hill; 1880 Apr 1; Thursday; D; room 3

Roberts, R J
  & Wife; Somerville; 1880 May 15; Saturday; D; room 17
  With J H S; 1880 Oct 21; Thursday; D; room 34
  Crossed out; Somerville, Colo; 1880 Oct 23; Saturday
  Summerville; 1880 Oct 24; Sunday; D
  Summerville; 1880 Nov 16; Tuesday; S; room 33
  Summerville; 1880 Nov 26; Friday; D
  Summerville; 1880 Dec 1; Wednesday; S; room 34
  Sommerville; 1880 Dec 6; Monday; L; room 26
  Summerville; 1880 Dec 10; Friday; S; room 29

Robertson, Jehu
  Denver; 1880 June 7; Monday; S
  Denver; 1880 June 13; Sunday; D

Robertson, John
  St Louis; 1880 Sept 18; Saturday; S

Robertson, Victor
  Denver; 1880 June 24; Thursday; S; room 20
  Denver; 1880 June 26; Saturday; L; room 21
  Denver; 1880 June 27; Sunday; L; room 15
  Denver; 1880 July 5; Mon; S; rm 13
  Denver; 1880 Aug 18; Wednesday; L; room 6
  Denver; 1880 Sept 19; Sunday; S
  Denver; 1880 Sept 20; Monday; S
  Denver; 1880 Sept 24; Friday; S
  Denver; 1880 Sept 26; Sunday; S
  Denver; 1880 Oct 24; Sunday
  Denver; 1880 Oct 25; Monday; B

Robeskey, Jacks
  St Louis; 1880 May 17; Monday; S; room 34

Robinson, A
  Denver, Colo; 1880 Apr 18; Sunday; D

Robinson, H C
  Denver, Colo; 1880 July 11; Sunday; D
  Denver; 1880 July 26; Monday; D

Robinson, J M
  Sunshine; 1880 Apr 13; Tuesday; D

Robinson, V
  Marshall Mine; 1880 Apr 26; Monday; L; room 2

Robinson, Victor
  Denver; 1880 Apr 19; Monday; D
  Denver; 1880 Apr 21; Wednesday; S
  Denver; 1880 Apr 22; Thursday; D
  Denver; 1880 Apr 23; Friday; D
  Denver; 1880 Apr 24; Saturday; D
  Denver; 1880 Apr 28; Wednesday; S; room 8

Robinson, W A
  St Louis; 1880 May 22; Saturday; D; room 15

Robinson, W W
  Denver; 1880 Mar 11; Thursday; S; room 15
  Denver; 1880 June 17; Thursday; S; room 19
  Denver; 1880 Dec 2; Thursday; S; room 10
  Denver; 1880 Dec 4; Saturday; D; room 10

Rockwell, J E
  Central; 1880 May 4; Tuesday; D

Rodgers, Chas
  Claymore; 1880 Mar 6; Saturday; S; room 25

Rodgers, John
  1880 July 19; Monday

Rodgers, R H
  Greeley; 1880 July 5; Monday; D

Roesch, Seward
Denver; 1880 May 15; Saturday; S

Rogers, E L
Denver; 1880 Mar 26; Friday; S; rm 35

Rogers, George
Boulder; 1880 Nov 14; Sunday; D

Rogers, Henry
NY; 1880 Oct 14; Thursday; S; rm 27

Rogers, Jno A
Wilmington, Del; 1880 Aug 10; Tuesday; S

Rogers, John A
Boulder; 1880 Mar 6; Sat

Rogers, M A
& Wife; Denver; 1880 Apr 9; Friday, room 16

Rogers, Platt
Boulder; 1880 Oct 14; Thursday; B

Rogers, S S
Chicago; 1880 May 29; Saturday; S; room 15

Rollins, J Q A
Rollinsville; 1880 Nov 8; Monday; S; room 26

Rollins, John D A
Rollinsville, Col; 1880 Oct 10; Sun; D

Rollins, Y S A
Rollinsville; 1880 Sept 30; Thur; D

Romer, A
Denver; 1880 Oct 30; Saturday; S; room 12
With L J; 1880 Nov 3; Wednesday; S

Ronik, Dave
San Francisco; 1880 May 15; Saturday; S; room 15

Roop, Oscar
& Wife; Denver; 1880 Sept 24; Friday; D; room 1

Roper, E J
Denver; 1880 Aug 23; Monday; S

Roper, J Jr
Absent after breakfast; 1880 June 19; Saturday

Roper, Jas Jr
City; 1880 Sept 3; Friday

Roper, Joe Jr
City; 1880 June 3; Thursday; S
City; 1880 June 9; Wednesday; D
City; 1880 June 10; Thursday; B
City; 1880 June 21; Monday; S
Absent after S; 1880 June 28; Mon; S
Boulder; 1880 July 27; Tuesday; D
Boulder; 1880 Aug 8; Sunday; S

Roper, Jos Jr
1880 Sept 2; Thursday; D

Rosa, Wm L
& Wife; Chicago; 1880 June 13; Sunday; S; room 21

Rose, D M (Mrs)
1880 Aug 21; Saturday; D

Rose, J B
Chicago; 1880 Oct 21; Thursday; S; room 1

Rosenberg, Chas W
Philada; 1880 Apr 8; Thursday; S

Rosengarten, F P
Jamestown; 1880 Nov 15; Monday; D

Rosenthal, E R
Chicago; 1880 Apr 12; Monday; D; room 1

Ross, A D
Denver, Col; 1880 May 8; Saturday; S

Rothschild, Chas (Mrs)
Denver; 1880 Nov 18; Thursday; S; room 11

Rothschild, Chas S
Denver; 1880 Apr 30; Friday; D; rm 2

Rou, J B
Chicago; 1880 June 8; Tuesday; D; room 2

Rouse, Herbert
Denver; 1880 Sept 22; Wednesday; S

Routt, John L
Denver; 1880 Aug 21; Saturday; D

Rowen, A A
& Wife; Canesville, Ia; 1880 Sept 17; Friday; S; room 20

Rowland, E (Capt)
& Wife; 1880 Aug 21; Saturday; D

Rudolph, Peter F
NY City; 1880 Nov 17; Wednesday; L; room 1

Ruey, H Serc
Rockville, O; 1880 Nov 8; Monday; S; room 12

Ruiser, C T
St Joe; 1880 Sept 30; Thursday; L; room 6

Rulings, C X
Chicago; 1880 Mar 22; Monday; D; room 15

Rummig, R
Detroit; 1880 Sept 22; Wednesday; S; room 1

Rumsey, W C
St Louis; 1880 May 4; Tuesday; S; room 15

Ruple, J Good
Denver; 1880 Apr 29; Thursday; D

Rush, Geo O
& Wife; 1880 Aug 21; Saturday; D

Russell, G R
Tampa, FL; 1880 Mar 9; Tues

Russell, H M
& Wife; City; 1880 Nov 25; Thursday, Thanksgiving; D

Russell, J M
San Francisco; 1880 Mar 8; Monday; S; room 1

Ruter, Chas
Denver; 1880 Aug 19; Thursday; S; room 3

Ruth, D (Mrs)
Pistol Shots of the World; 1880 June 12; Saturday; D; room 3

Ruth, J
Champion Rifle; 1880 June 12; Saturday; D; room 3

Ruth, Van B
Chicago; 1880 July 7; Wednesday; D; room 5

Ruttles, Chera (Miss)
[prob Miss Clara Buttles]
Neita Harker; 1880 Mar 10; Wed; S

Ruty, H
Paris; 1880 June 16; Wednesday; S; room 6

Ryan, M A
Denver, Co; 1880 Nov 10; Wed; S

Ryan, Sam E
1880 Oct 23; Saturday; D; room 29

S

Sabin, W H H
1880 July 22; Thursday
New York; 1880 July 23; Friday; D; room 1

Sackett, J E
Agt Hoss Bitters; 1880 June 9; Wednesday; S; room 12

Safely, A F
1880 Aug 21; Saturday; D
& Wife; 1880 Aug 21; Saturday; D
Boulder, Co; 1880 Nov 18; Thur; B

Safely, Frank
& Wife; New York City; 1880 Nov 25;
Thursday, Thanksgiving; D

Safley [Safely], Miss
Denver; 1880 Apr 27; Tuesday; D

Safley [Safely], Wm
Denver; 1880 Apr 27; Tuesday; D

Sales, Geo
Denver; 1880 Sept 22; Wednesday; D

Salisbury, M L (see Salsbury)
& Wife; 1880 Aug 21; Saturday; D

Salsbury, J A Jr
City; 1880 June 27; Sunday; B

Salsbury, M A
& Wife; City; 1880 July 4; Sunday; B

Salsbury, M L (see Salsbury)
City; 1880 May 11; Tuesday; D
City; 1880 June 17; Thursday; D
Deputy Sheriff City; 1880 June 24;
Thursday; D
City; 1880 June 25; Friday; B
Valmont; 1880 June 26; Saturday; D
& Wife; City; 1880 June 27; Sunday; B
Tinmouth, Vt; 1880 June 29; Tues; D
City; 1880 July 20; Tuesday; D
Wife & Child; City; 1880 Sept 6;
Monday; D
& Wife; City; 1880 Sept 9; Thur; D
Boulder; 1880 Sept 10; Friday; D;
room 25
Absent after B; 1880 Oct 12; Tues; B
1880 Oct 18; Monday; D
City; 1880 Oct 29; Friday; B
City; 1880 Nov 3; Wednesday; B
City; 1880 Nov 6; Saturday; B
City; 1880 Nov 8; Monday; B

Salsbury, M L (see Salisbury) (cont.)
City; 1880 Nov 9; Tuesday; B
City; 1880 Nov 10; Wednesday; B

Salsbury, M L (Mrs)
& Son; Denver; 1880 Oct 11; Monday;
S; room 12

Saltenstall, C R
St Louis; 1880 Mar 30; Tuesday; S;
room 6

Sampson, A J
Silver Cliff; 1880 Oct 26; Tuesday; S;
room 12

Sampson, Edwin E
Philadelphia; 1880 June 4; Friday; S;
room 16

Samuals
Dan Castello & Co Circus; 1880 May
23; Sunday; L; room 13

Samuels, Isaac
Hong Kong, Jap; 1880 July 14;
Wednesday; S

Sanborn, Wm
Denver; 1880 Apr 3; Saturday; D

Sanders, S
Caribou; 1880 Mar 16; Tuesday; S;
room 28
Guest of A E Lea; 1880 Oct 21; Thursday; D

Sands, O
Gunnison Cty; 1880 Apr 10; Saturday;
D; room 6
Gunnison; 1880 Apr 26; Monday; S;
room 15
Gunnison; 1880 May 18; Tuesday; S;
room 4

Sanquiette, William
Leadville; 1880 Aug 15; Sunday; D

Sansbury, P Jr
City; 1880 May 20; Thursday; D

Sargent, W O
Boston, Mass; 1880 June 26; Saturday; D; room 28

Sarwask, N
1880 Apr 12; Monday

Sattrithwait, B
& Wife; Chicago; 1880 June 15; Tuesday; D; room 1

Sauley, O
Denver; 1880 July 10; Saturday; S; room 28

Saulsberey, M L Jr (see Salsbury)
City; 1880 Mar 11; Thurs

Saulsbury, M L (see Salsbury)
Q B; 1880 Mar 24; Wednesday; D
Returned; 1880 Aug 11; Wednesday; S
Boulder; 1880 Aug 17; Tuesday; D

Savage, E R
Denver; 1880 May 5; Wednesday; S; room 44
Denver; 1880 May 7; Friday; D
Denver; 1880 May 7; Friday; D; rm 15

Savory, O
& Children; Gold Hill; 1880 May 29; Saturday; D

Sawhill, H F
Chicago; 1880 Apr 2; Friday; S; rm 1
Chicago; 1880 Oct 9; Saturday; D; room 2

Sawyer, B C
Denver; 1880 Dec 12; Sunday; D
Denver; 1880 Dec 13; Monday; S

Sawyer, H F
Denver; 1880 Apr 23; Friday; S; rm 17

Sawyer, N F
St Vrain; 1880 Apr 16; Fri; S; rm 17

Sayler, D H
Salina, Colo; 1880 Mar 22; Monday; D

Scales, Geo
Denver; 1880 Aug 17; Tuesday; S; room 6

Scales, R R
Denver; 1880 Nov 3; Wednesday; S; room 14

Schaefer, Fred
Chicago; 1880 June 1; Tuesday; S; room 3
Chicago; 1880 Nov 19; Friday; D
Chicago; 1880 Sept 10; Friday; S; room 3

Schaeffer, Chas (see Shafer)
Absent after S; 1880 Sept 21; Tues; S

Schaeffer, J H (See Shaeffer)
Left after; 1880 Oct 1; Friday; L

Schaeffer, Jno H
Summerville; 1880 June 3; Thursday; S; room 12
Summerville; 1880 June 7; Monday; S; room 12
Summerville; 1880 June 22; Tuesday; D; room 19
Summerville, Col; 1880 July 6; Tuesday; D; room 17
Summerville, Col; 1880 July 22; Thursday; S; room 17
Summerville, Col; 1880 July 24; Saturday; S; room 17
Summerville, Col; 1880 Aug 3; Tuesday; D; room B
Summerville; 1880 Sept 15; Wednesday; D
Summerville; 1880 Sept 18; Sat; D
Left after; 1880 Oct 15; Friday; B
Summerville, Col; 1880 Oct 19; Tuesday; D; room 17

Schaeffer, John H
Philada; 1880 May 1; Saturday; D; room 12

Schaeffer, John H (cont.)
Boulder; 1880 May 11; Tuesday; D
Summerville, Col; 1880 July 12; Monday; D; room 17
Summerville, Col; 1880 Oct 12; Tuesday; S; room 17

Schaeffer, W E
Philada; 1880 May 5; Wednesday; D

Schaeffer, W W
Summerville; 1880 June 13; Sunday; L; room 28

Schaf, J C
Denver, Colo; 1880 Apr 16; Friday; S; room 27

Schaffer, H
Cheyenne; 1880 Oct 20; Wednesday; S; room 11

Scheaffer, W E
Middletown; 1880 May 1; Saturday; D; room 12

Scheuch, D
Denver; 1880 May 15; Saturday; S

Schiffer, G
St Louis; 1880 July 23; Friday; S; rm 6

Schinck, J M
Denver; 1880 Oct 23; Saturday; S; room 10

Schlurs, L
Chicago; 1880 Apr 22; Thursday; S; room 10

Schmidt, George
B.C; 1880 June 9; Wednesday; S

Schmitt, Geo
Left Hand; 1880 Aug 12; Thursday; S

Schneffey, Geo H
Summerville, Col; 1880 Sept 29; Wednesday; D; room 14

Schneider, Louis
Denver; 1880 Oct 23; Saturday; S; room 23

Schneider, Louis P
Boulder; 1880 Mar 6; Sat
Boulder; 1880 Aug 3; Tuesday

Scholer, Thos
Lawrence, KS; 1880 Mar 27; Saturday; S; room 3

Scholes, Mos
Lawrence, KS; 1880 Mar 16; Tues; D

Schrader, H
St Louis; 1880 Nov 4; Thursday; D; room 10

Schuck, C W
Denver; 1880 Dec 9; Thursday; S; room 10
Denver; 1880 Nov 20; Saturday; S; room 3

Schultz, Otto M (Rev)
Central City; 1880 May 5; Wednesday; S; room 6

Schultz, Wilbur F
Secorro, NM; 1880 Dec 18; Saturday; S; room 33

Schwarts, John
Louisville, Ky; 1880 Aug 20; Friday; D; room 32

Schwartz, Alonzo
1880 Oct 23; Saturday; D; room 13

Schweitzer, C
Chicago; 1880 Oct 5; Tuesday; D; room 2

Schweizer, Chas
New York; 1880 July 8; Thursday; S; room 1

Scott, A R
Phone [?] & C; 1880 May 10; Monday; D; room 33

Scott, A R (cont.)
Trout Dale; 1880 May 3; Monday; S;
room 33

Scott, Charles
Crisman; 1880 Apr 21; Wednesday; L;
room 28

Scott, Charles G
Balarat; 1880 Apr 16; Friday; S
St Louis; 1880 Apr 17; Saturday; D

Scott, Ed H
Central City; 1880 June 18; Friday; L;
room 26

Scott, Geo
Gothic, Col; 1880 Mar 21; Sunday; B
Caribou; 1880 Aug 6; Fri; D; rm 14
Caribou; 1880 Sept 16; Thursday; S
Caribou; 1880 Sept 18; Saturday; D
Caribou; 1880 Oct 19; Tuesday; S
Caribou; 1880 Oct 20; Wednesday; S;
room 5

Scott, Mrs
Marshall; 1880 May 12; Wednesday; D

Scott, W R
Troutdale; 1880 Nov 8; Monday; D;
room 36

Scott, Wm
Marshall; 1880 May 16; Sunday; S

Scribner, W T
1880 Oct 14; Thursday; S; room 34

Scukez, W N
St Louis; 1880 May 12; Wednesday; D

Seabury, R F Jr
Peoria; 1880 Mar 14; Sunday; D; rm 2
St Joseph, Mo; 1880 Sept 14; Tues; D

Seal, Bessie E
New York; 1880 July 21; Wednesday;
S; room 44
NY; 1880 Aug 1; Sunday; L; room 49

Seal, G T
NY; 1880 Mar 11; Thursday; S
NY; 1880 June 2; Wednesday; D
NY; 1880 June 3; Thursday; S; room 3
New York; 1880 July 21; Wednesday;
S; room 4
NY; 1880 Mar 6; Saturday; S; room 2
NY; 1880 Aug 1; Sunday; L; room 4

Seales, George
Denver; 1880 Sept 10; Friday; S; rm 29
Denver; 1880 Sept 16; Thursday; S;
room 13

Searles, C F
Ohio; 1880 Dec 4; Saturday; L; rm 17
Tiffin, Ohio; 1880 Dec 5; Sunday; L;
room 17
Ohio; 1880 Dec 7; Tuesday; L; rm 17
Ohio; 1880 Dec 8; Wednesday; D;
room 17

Searles, C Fran
Tiffin, Ohio; 1880 Nov 27; Saturday;
S; room 17

Sears, H D
Chicago; 1880 Oct 2; Saturday; S;
room 5

Sears, L D
Denver; 1880 July 2; Friday; S; rm 21

Sears, T D
Denver; 1880 May 26; Wednesday; S
Denver; 1880 June 14; Monday; D
Denver; 1880 June 15; Tuesday; D

Seater, G G
Denver; 1880 Sept 23; Thursday; D

Sebastian
& Wife; Supper 5:30; 1880 Aug 3;
Tuesday; B; room 17

Sebillot, A
New York; 1880 May 18; Tuesday; S

Secor, D E
& Wife; Longmont; 1880 Aug 3; Tuesday; S; room 34

Secor, G
Home; 1880 Dec 1; Wednesday; L; room 13
Spring Creek; 1880 Nov 3; Wednesday; L; room 26

Secor, W W
Longmont; 1880 May 10; Monday; S; room 13
Longmont; 1880 May 25; Tuesday; S; room 26
Longmont; 1880 May 29; Saturday; S; room 26
Longmont; 1880 Aug 7; Saturday; S
Longmont; 1880 Oct 26; Tuesday; D; room 5
Longmont; 1880 Nov 6; Saturday; L; room 14
Longmont; 1880 Nov 10; Wednesday; D; room 29
Longmont; 1880 Dec 9; Thursday; D

Seely, Jonas
Denver; 1880 July 5; Monday; S

Seely, W L
Cheyenne; 1880 Oct 20; Wednesday; S; room 12

Seer, Sert
Return; 1880 Mar 26; Friday; S; rm 7

Segnitz, Miss
Chicago; 1880 July 12; Monday; S; room 44

Seller, H M
Central City; 1880 Oct 13; Wednesday; D

Sellers, S D
Philadelphia; 1880 July 1; Thursday; S; room 1

Semmer, Phillip
Chicago; 1880 Nov 3; Wednesday; L; room 2

Setzer, T
Nederland; 1880 Aug 3; Tuesday; S; room 29

Seymour, E N
NY; 1880 May 12; Wednesday; D; room 44

Seymour, J F
New York; 1880 Mar 19; Friday; L; room 16

Seymour, J F (Col)
Denver; 1880 Mar 15; Sunday; S; room 16

Shaeffer, J H (see Schaeffer)
Left after supper; 1880 Aug 7; Saturday; S

Shaeffer, Jno H (see Schaeffer)
Summerville, Col; 1880 Sept 1; Wednesday; S; room 13

Shafer, Charley (see Schaeffer)
Boulder; 1880 June 10; Thursday; L; room 28

Shallenberger, Chas
Loveland, Col; 1880 May 29; Saturday; S; room 34

Shattuck, _____
Denver; 1880 Aug 21; Saturday; D

Shaw, Joe
Caribou; 1880 June 19; Saturday; S

Shaw, Joseph
1880 Mar 22; Monday; S; room 12
Denver; 1880 Mar 27; Saturday; D
Denver; 1880 Mar 29; Monday; S; room 12

Shaw, Oscar
Sugar Loaf; 1880 May 5; Wed; D

Shaw, Wm
Louisville, Colo; 1880 July 26; Monday, room 28

Shea, C E
& Wife; England; 1880 Oct 8; Friday; S; room 15

Sheaffer, W E
Summerville; 1880 May 8; Sat; D

Sheaffer, Wm E
Summerville; 1880 Aug 18; Wed; D

Sheaffer, WM E
Middletown, PA; 1880 May 15; Sat; D

Sheaffer, Wm E
Summerville; 1880 May 20; Thur; D
Summerville; 1880 May 28; Friday; D
Summerville, Col; 1880 Oct 22; Friday; D; room 17

Sheafley, T G
City; 1880 Sept 21; Tuesday; L; rm 15

Shedd, Wm E
Leadville; 1880 June 1; Tuesday; L; room 25

Sheehan, William
Silver Plume; 1880 Apr 12; Mon; D
Ward; 1880 Apr 17; Saturday; S; rm 25
Ward; 1880 May 8; Saturday; D
Ward; 1880 July 1; Thursday; D
Ward; 1880 Sept 1; Wednesday; D
Ward; 1880 Oct 3; Sunday; D; rm 29
Ward; 1880 Oct 12; Tuesday; S

Sheehan, Wm
Ward; 1880 Aug 2; Monday; L; rm 27

Sheets, __ W
Louisville; 1880 Oct 24; Sunday; D

Shepard, J S
Sunshine; 1880 Apr 1; Thursday; D
Sunshine; 1880 May 2; Sunday; D
Fareplay; 1880 Aug 31; Tuesday; S; room 25

Shepard, J S (cont.)
Fairplay, Colo; 1880 Aug 6; Friday; S; room 25
Fareplay; 1880 Sept 1; Wednesday; S; room 25
City; 1880 Sept 4; Saturday; D
Sunshine; 1880 Sept 22; Wed; D
Sunshine; 1880 Sept 29; Wed; D
Sunshine; 1880 Oct 1; Friday; S; rm 27
Sunshine; 1880 Oct 11; Monday; S; room 26
Sunshine; 1880 Oct 2; Saturday; L; room 27
Sunshine; 1880 Oct 30; Saturday; L; room 13
Sunshine; 1880 Nov 1; Monday; S; room 28

Shepherd, Jas S
Sunshine; 1880 Apr 3; Saturday; D; room 27
Sunshine; 1880 Apr 11; Sunday; D
Sunshine; 1880 Apr 16; Friday; D

Sherman, Arthur
Chicago; 1880 May 2; Sunday; D
Ward, Boulder, Co; 1880 May 11; Tuesday; D
Chicago; 1880 May 18; Tuesday; D
Ward; 1880 May 29; Saturday; D
Chicago; 1880 Nov 13; Saturday; S

Sherman, T
New York; 1880 May 24; Monday; D; room 3

Sherman, W Arthur
Pa; 1880 Aug 5; Thursday; S
Kittanning, PA; 1880 July 29; Thur; S

Sherwood, C E
Gold Hill; 1880 June 2; Wednesday; S; room 27
Gold Hill; 1880 June 4; Friday; D

Sherwood, F
Magnolia; 1880 Mar 18; Thursday; D
Magnolia; 1880 Apr 20; Tuesday; D
Magnolia; 1880 Apr 23; Friday; S;
room 35
Magnolia; 1880 Apr 30; Friday; D
Magnolia; 1880 July 15; Thursday; D
Magnolia; 1880 July 21; Wed; D
Magnolia; 1880 July 26; Monday; D

Sherwood, F W
Fort Collins; 1880 Aug 10; Tuesday; S;
room 35

Sherwood, J M
Fort Collins; 1880 Sept 12; Sunday; L;
room 17

Sherwood, J M (Mrs)
Chicago; 1880 Sept 12; Sunday; L;
room 12

Shiek, W J
& Wife; Golden; 1880 Aug 6; Fri; D

Shields, C O
Golden; 1880 Nov 23; Tuesday; D;
room 26

Shigler, W N
C___, Colo; 1880 Mar 15; Sunday; D

Shink, A A
Guest of Coffin, Denver; 1880 July 26;
Monday; D

Shonerman, J M
NY; 1880 Apr 15; Thursday; S; room 8

Shorb, E H
NY; 1880 Aug 10; Tuesday; S; room 6
New York; 1880 Mar 7; Sunday; S;
room 2

Shortridge, W T
Denver; 1880 June 21; Monday; S;
room 10

Shoup, C H
Atchison; 1880 June 9; Wednesday; D

Shpear [?], D G
Longmont; 1880 May 10; Monday; S;
room 27

Shull, M L
Longmont; 1880 July 5; Monday; D

Sieler, Geo W
Denver; 1880 Oct 29; Friday; S; rm 12

Sifer, Geo W
Denver; 1880 Sept 28; Tuesday; D;
room 27

Sigler, Geo W
Denver; 1880 Sept 27; Monday; S;
room 28

Sill, Joseph
Kalamazoo, Mich; 1880 May 27;
Thursday; S; room 44

Silsbee, S
Star Alliance Opera Co; 1880 June 11;
Friday; D; room 35

Silver, Martin
& Wife; 1880 Sept 15; Wednesday; D;
room 3

Silver, P
Chicago; 1880 July 9; Friday; S; rm 2

Simmer, H
Golden; 1880 June 14; Monday; D

Simmons, G E
Philada; 1880 Nov 30; Tuesday; S;
room 2

Simmons, Geo E
Philadelphia; 1880 May 27; Thursday;
D; room 3

Simmons, John
Caribou; 1880 Mar 13; Saturday; S;
room 25
Caribou; 1880 Apr 4; Sun; S; rm 28
Caribou; 1880 May 23; Sunday; D
Caribou; 1880 May 26; Wednesday; D

Simmons, John (cont.)
& Wife; 1880 July 10; Saturday; S; room 21
Caribou; 1880 Aug 3; Tuesday; S
Caribou; 1880 Aug 26; Thursday; S; room 14
Caribou; 1880 Dec 15; Wednesday; S; room 13&14

Simmons, Thomas
Caribou; 1880 Apr 4; Sun; S; rm 28

Simmons, William
Caribou G Crisman Company; 1880 May 13; Thursday; D

Simmons, Wm
Caribou; 1880 May 10; Monday; D
1880 May 14; Friday; S; room 27

Simon, D
Chicago; 1880 May 15; Saturday; S
Chicago; 1880 May 15; Saturday; S

Simons, R M
Chicago; 1880 Mar 11; Thursday; D

Simpson, Frank
City; 1880 Nov 6; Saturday; L; rm 14

Simpson, Henry T
Frankfort; 1880 Nov 2; Tuesday; D

Simpson, J M
Boulder & Caribou S C; 1880 May 6; Thursday; S; room 25
Caribou Ruge [?] Co; 1880 May 8; Saturday; L; room 22
Caribou Rags Co; 1880 May 9; Sunday; L
Caribou Rags Co; 1880 May 15; Saturday; S; room 28
Caribou Rags Co; 1880 May 16; Sunday; S; room 27
Caribou Stage Co; 1880 May 18; Tuesday; L; room 27
Caribou Stage Co; 1880 May 20; Thursday; S; room 27

Simpson, J M (cont.)
Caribou Stage Co; 1880 May 22; Saturday; L; room 27
Caribou Stage Co; 1880 May 25; Tuesday; S; room 27
1880 May 27; Thursday; S; room 27
Caribou Stage Co; 1880 May 29; Saturday; S; room 27
Caribou Stage Line; 1880 June 1; Tuesday; S; room 27
City; 1880 June 4; Friday; S; room 27
Caribou; 1880 July 13; Tuesday; D; room 28
Caribou; 1880 July 14; Wednesday; S; room 34

Simpson, Jas
Caribou; 1880 June 7; Monday; L; room 28

Simpson, R
& Wife; Cincinnati; 1880 Apr 15; Thursday; S; room 4
& Wife; Cincinnati; 1880 Apr 25; Sunday; S; room 12

Simpson, R C (Mrs)
Chicago; 1880 July 10; Saturday; D; room 44

Simpson, Sam'l
Denver; 1880 Nov 28; Sunday; S; room 22

Simpson, Wm
& Wife; Louisville; 1880 July 7; Wednesday; D
& Wife & Sister; Louisville; 1880 July 17; Saturday; D; room 19 & 20
Louisville; 1880 Aug 19; Thursday; D
Louisville; 1880 Nov 1; Monday; D
Louisville; 1880 Dec 7; Tuesday; D

Sinclair, W E
Treasurer, Breakfast only; 1880 Aug 3; Tuesday; B

Sinley, E H
St Louis, Mo; 1880 Sept 13; Monday;
L; room 11

Sirth, John G
Ward; 1880 June 19; Saturday; S;
room 6

Skaggs, W O
St Vrain; 1880 Oct 13; Wednesday
St Vrain; 1880 Oct 14; Thursday; D

Slanton, R B
Denver; 1880 Dec 3; Friday; S

Sleight, W W
Carbonatsville; 1880 May 10; Monday; S; room 25
Carbonatsville; 1880 May 11; Tuesday;
S; room 32

Sliter, E F
Fort Collins; 1880 July 3; Saturday; S;
room 35

Slitt, W S
Chicago; 1880 Nov 23; Tuesday; L;
room 1

Slicum, T J
Denver; 1880 Sept 20; Monday; S;
room 24

Sloan, A C
St Louis, MO; 1880 Apr 15; Thursday;
S; room 15

Sloan, Andrew
Savanah, Ga; 1880 Sept 2; Thur; D

Sloan, R C
St Louis; 1880 June 9; Wednesday; D

Smails, J D
Denver; 1880 Oct 26; Tuesday; D

Small, Wm (Mrs)
North; 1880 June 18; Friday; S; rm 21

Smead, E C
Kansas City; 1880 Nov 3; Wednesday;
S; room 12

Smeaton, W H
New York City; 1880 July 14; Wednesday; S; room 6

Smith, A L (Mr)
Phila; 1880 Aug 14; Saturday; D;
room 3

Smith, A W (Miss)
Phila; 1880 Aug 14; Saturday; D;
room 6

Smith, Abraham
St Louis, MO; 1880 Mar 8; Monday; S;
room 33

Smith, Anne
Chicago; 1880 July 22; Thursday; D

Smith, Ben
Nederland, Colo; 1880 Aug 31; Tuesday; D

Smith, C (Mrs)
Chicago; 1880 June 7; Monday; D

Smith, C B
Denver, Colo; 1880 Apr 18; Sunday; D

Smith, C E
Nederland; 1880 Mar 6; Saturday; S;
room 4

Smith, C Edgar
& Family; New York; 1880 May 22;
Saturday; S; room 10 and 11

Smith, C Edw
& boy; Boulder; 1880 Sept 2; Thursday; D

Smith, D E
Longmont; 1880 June 19; Saturday; S;
room 33
St Louis; 1880 July 14; Wednesday; S;
room 19
St Louis; 1880 Dec 11; Saturday; L;
room 3

Smith, Dudley

St Joseph; 1880 Mar 9; Tuesday; S; room 6

St Joseph; 1880 Apr 20; Tuesday; D

St Joseph MO; 1880 June 2; Wednesday; S; room 3

St Joseph; 1880 Aug 7; Saturday; D; room 10

Estes Park; 1880 Sept 13; Monday; S; room 2

St Joseph; 1880 Nov 4; Thursday; L; room 6

St Joseph; 1880 Dec 9; Thursday; L; room 11

Smith, E

Brhall, NY; 1880 June 17; Thursday; S; room 29

Smith, E B

Marshall; 1880 May 9; Sunday; S; room 12

Marshall; 1880 May 29; Saturday; L; room 14

Boulder; 1880 June 13; Sunday; D

Central City; 1880 June 17; Thursday; S; room 29

Boulder; 1880 Aug 18; Wednesday; L; room 6

Guest of E M Styles; 1880 Sept 5; Sunday

Chg E M Styles; 1880 Oct 4; Mon; S

Smith, Eben

Absent after H; 1880 Mar 7; Sunday; S

Nederland; 1880 Mar 15; Sun; rm 19

Left after breakfast; 1880 Mar 17; Wed

Nederland; 1880 Mar 18; Thursday; S; room 19

New York; 1880 May 17; Monday; D; room 19

Absent after B; 1880 May 19; Wed

Caribou; 1880 May 21; Friday; D; room 19&20

Smith, Eben (cont.)

Boulder; 1880 May 24; Monday; S; room 19

Nederland; 1880 June 3; Thursday; S; room 10

Nederland, Colo; 1880 June 7; Monday; D; room 19

Nederland; 1880 June 15; Tuesday; D

Allarvunel; 1880 June 17; Thursday; D; room 12

& Wife; Nederland; 1880 June 26; Saturday; S; room 19-20

Nederland; 1880 July 19; Monday; D; room 4

& Wife; Nederland; 1880 July 21; Wednesday; D; room 21

& Family; Nederland; 1880 Aug 2; Monday; D; room 19

Nederland; 1880 Aug 10; Tuesday; D

& Wife; 1880 Aug 27; Friday; S; rm 16

Nederland; 1880 Sept 3; Friday; S; room 1

Wife & two children; 1880 Sept 8; Wednesday; D

Wife & 2 children; City; 1880 Nov 25; Thursday, Thanksgiving; D

Smith, Eben (Mrs)

1880 Aug 24; Tuesday; D

Smith, Edward B

Denver; 1880 May 21; Friday; S

Smith, Edward P

Marshall; 1880 May 8; Saturday; L; room 6

Marshall; 1880 May 10; Monday; D

Smith, Elmer B

With D J Cross; Boulder; 1880 July 4; Sunday; D

Smith, Fin

& Wife; Nederland; 1880 June 25; Friday; D; room 20

Smith, Geo A
Leadville, Colo; 1880 June 10; Thursday; S; room 14
Jamestown, Colo; 1880 Oct 26; Tuesday; L; room 13
Gold Hill; 1880 Dec 18; Saturday; D; room 14

Smith, Geo S
Chicago; 1880 June 14; Monday; D; room 2
Chicago; 1880 Oct 16; Saturday; L; room 3

Smith, H H
1880 Sept 22; Wednesday

Smith, H R
Denver; 1880 July 5; Monday; S
New York; 1880 Sept 30; Thursday; S
NY; 1880 Oct 26; Tuesday; L

Smith, Harry R
Canton, Miss; 1880 Nov 11; Thursday; D; room 1

Smith, Herbert R
NY; 1880 Apr 22; Thursday; S; room 3

Smith, I N
Jachn Springs; 1880 Sept 13; Monday; S; room 15

Smith, J R
Atchison, Ks; 1880 Aug 20; Friday; D

Smith, J Washington
All the World; 1880 Dec 11; Saturday; L; room 44

Smith, John
1880 Oct 21; Thursday; L; room 33

Smith, Jos
1880 June 12; Saturday; D; room 14

Smith, L E
Nederland; 1880 Mar 30; Tuesday; S; room 15
Menerwood; 1880 May 19; Wednesday; S; room 14

Smith, L E (cont.)
Nederland; 1880 May 22; Saturday; D
Nederland; 1880 May 26; Wed; D
Denver; 1880 June 4; Friday; S
Nederland; 1880 June 22; Tuesday; S; room 17
Neverwood; 1880 June 26; Sat; D

Smith, L E Jr
Denver; 1880 June 13; Sunday

Smith, Lou
Nederland; 1880 July 5; Monday; D; room 16

Smith, Lowell H
Springdale; 1880 Mar 12; Friday; D

Smith, M A
NY; 1880 May 1; Saturday; D
NY; 1880 May 3; Monday; D
NY; 1880 May 4; Tuesday; S; room 8
NY; 1880 May 7; Friday; S; room 9
NC; 1880 May 11; Tuesday; D; rm 12
NY; 1880 May 17; Monday; S; rm 14
NY; 1880 Aug 13; Friday; S; room 12
NY; 1880 Aug 18; Wednesday; D
NY; 1880 Aug 23; Monday; S; room 6
NY; 1880 Sept 28; Tuesday; D; rm 17
NY; 1880 Oct 2; Saturday; L; room 20
NY; 1880 Oct 13; Wednesday; S
NY; 1880 Oct 14; Thursday; S; rm 10
Nederland; 1880 Oct 8; Friday; D; room 17
NY; 1880 Oct 9; Saturday; room 17
New York; 1880 Oct 21; Thursday; D

Smith, M W (Miss)
Phila; 1880 Aug 14; Saturday; D; room 6

Smith, Martin L S
Phila; 1880 Aug 14; Saturday; D; room 3

Smith, N A
New York; 1880 May 15; Saturday; S; room 12

Smith, O E
St Louis; 1880 May 5; Wednesday; D

Smith, O J
Worcester, Mass; 1880 Nov 8; Monday; S; room 12

Smith, O L
Agt Denver Republican; 1880 Nov 8; Monday; D; room 2

Smith, P Henry (Mrs)
Burlington, Iowa; 1880 July 22; Thursday; S; room 4

Smith, R
Chicago; 1880 May 22; Saturday; D

Smith, R B
News & Courier; 1880 June 8; Tuesday; S; room 33

Smith, R Pearsall
& Wife; Phila; 1880 Aug 14; Saturday; D; room 1

Smith, S C
Columbus, Neb; 1880 Oct 23; Saturday; D

Smith, Samuel
Chicago; 1880 July 22; Thursday; D
1880 Nov 13; Saturday; S; room 14

Smith, W A
NY; 1880 Aug 19; Thursday; S; rm 12
NY; 1880 May 22; Saturday; D

Smith, W H
Denver; 1880 Oct 18; Monday; D; room 17

Smith, W N
Denver; 1880 July 15; Thursday; D

Smith, W W
City; 1880 May 19; Wednesday; L; room 2
City; 1880 May 20; Thursday; L; rm 3
Washington, Pa; 1880 Aug 21; Saturday; D

Smith, Walter H
Mgr Silver Cliff Stage Line; 1880 June 25; Friday; D

Smith, Walter V
Colorado; 1880 Dec 8; Wednesday; S; room 26

Smyth, James D
Burlington, Iowa; 1880 Aug 29; Sunday; S; room 10
Burlington, Iowa; 1880 July 22; Thursday; S; room 44

Smyth, Wm A
Quincy, Ill; 1880 Sept 25; Saturday; D; room 11

Snyder, John H
Chicago; 1880 July 13; Tuesday; D; room 6

Snyder, John J
K C; 1880 Mar 23; Tuesday; D; room 3
Kansas City; 1880 May 15; Sat; D
Kans City; 1880 May 17; Monday; D
K C; 1880 July 29; Thursday; D
Kans City; 1880 Aug 24; Tuesday; D
K C; 1880 Sept 28; Tuesday; D
Kans City; 1880 Sept 28; Tuesday; L; room 6

Snyder, L C
Black Hawk; 1880 Apr 18; Sunday; D; room 6
Black Hawk; 1880 May 15; Saturday; D; room 25
& Wife; Black Hawk; 1880 Nov 8; Monday; S; room 1

Soden, Chas S D
Omaha; 1880 May 18; Tuesday; S; room 3

Soderberg, Pont
Hastings, Neb; 1880 July 15; Thursday; S; room 3

Sollade, Frank
Longmont; 1880 Sept 25; Saturday; S

Soloman, J
San Francisco; 1880 Apr 27; Tuesday; D; room 1

Sopris, P
Denver; 1880 Apr 3; Saturday; S; room 44

Southworth, D P
& Wife; Denver; 1880 July 2; Friday; S; room 16

Southworth, J
Longmont Cornet Band; 1880 Sept 23; Thursday; S; room 3

Soward, C
Guest of H Day; 1880 July 19; Monday; S

Spain, Henry
New York; 1880 Oct 22; Friday; S

Spain, O Henry
New York; 1880 Aug 21; Saturday; D

Speck, S H
Star Alliance Opera Co; 1880 June 11; Friday; D; room 35

Spencer, W T
Nederland; 1880 May 22; Saturday; D

Spencer, Wm
Nederland; 1880 May 26; Wed; D

Spenser, W
Golden; 1880 June 26; Saturday; D

Sperber, Geo
Longmont; 1880 Aug 4; Wednesday; B

Sperry, L L
New York; 1880 Apr 23; Friday; S; room 3
Westfield, Mass; 1880 Oct 9; Saturday; D; room 1

Sperry, W F
Denver; 1880 Sept 23; Thursday; S; room 6

Spirer, R
New York; 1880 Oct 20; Wed; D

Sprangler, E (Mrs)
Erie; 1880 Mar 15; Sunday; S; room 17

Springstein, A B
Castleton, NY; 1880 June 8; Tues; D

Squire, Howell
Waterloo, Wis; 1880 May 18; Tuesday; D; room 15
Waterloo, Wis; 1880 May 19; Wednesday; S; room 12

Stack, A H
Longmont; 1880 Aug 3; Tuesday; D

Stack, Edw'd J
San Francisco; 1880 July 28; Wednesday; D; room 3

Staivitz, C
St Louis; 1880 Oct 25; Monday; L; room 3

Stallcup, Jno C
Denver; 1880 Sept 30; Thursday; D

Stallcup, Jno C (Hon)
Denver; 1880 Oct 2; Saturday; D; room 12

Standish, O T
Coal Creek; 1880 May 25; Tuesday; D

Stansberg, I
& Family; Longmont; 1880 Aug 3; Tuesday; L; room 12

Stansbury, Isaac
Longmont; 1880 June 4; Friday; D
Longmont; 1880 Aug 13; Friday; B

Stanton, C E
& Wife; Louisville; 1880 Apr 29; Thursday; D; room 10,11
1880 June 5; Saturday; L; room 28

Stanton, R B
Denver; 1880 Nov 3; Wednesday; S

Stanton, Robt B
Denver; 1880 Nov 19; Friday; S

Starbird, Geo A
Longmont; 1880 June 30; Wednesday;
S; room 14

Stark, A E
City; 1880 Mar 16; Tuesday; L; rm 26
& Wife; B&MRR; 1880 Mar 31;
Wednesday; L; room 8

Stark, Annie (Miss)
1880 Apr 22; Thursday; D; room 9

Stark, S
Denver; 1880 July 23; Friday; S; rm 2
Denver; 1880 Nov 3; Wednesday; D

Starr, Geo O
P T Barnum's Show; 1880 July 19;
Monday; S; room 12

Starr, Geo P
Philada; 1880 July 21; Wednesday; D;
room 1

Stawetz, C
St Louis; 1880 June 8; Tuesday; S

Stearns, J C (Mrs)
Rocky Butte; 1880 June 4; Friday; L;
room 32

Stearns, Mack
Longmont; 1880 Aug 3; Tuesday; D
1880 Nov 7; Sunday; S; room 28

Stein, E L
San Francisco; 1880 June 26; Saturday; S; room 2

Steinbeck, G
San Antonio, Tx; 1880 Nov 5; Friday;
L; room 29

Stelle, Geo R
Chicago; 1880 Mar 13; Saturday; L;
room 2

Stephen, Elijah
Central; 1880 May 15; Saturday; S;
room 27

Stephens, J A
Omaha; 1880 Mar 20; Saturday; D;
room 2

Steppler, Joseph
Gold Hill; 1880 Nov 25; Thursday,
Thanksgiving; L; room 13

Steppter, Joseph
Denver; 1880 Nov 8; Monday; S;
room 13

Stern, E L
San Francisco; 1880 Apr 1; Thursday;
S; room 2

Stern, Geo T
Sugarloaf; 1880 Mar 8; Monday; S;
room 7

Stern, N
1880 Nov 5; Friday; L; room 28

Stevens, John M
Greensburgh, Ind; 1880 July 21;
Wednesday; S; room 3

Stevens, R H
New York; 1880 Aug 9; Monday; S;
room 1

Stevenson, E J
Denver; 1880 Sept 23; Thursday; L;
room 33

Stewart, Albert P
Evans; 1880 Sept 27; Monday; D

Stewart, W
City; 1880 Aug 2; Monday; L; room 29

Stewart, W F
Boulder; 1880 July 5; Monday; D

Stewart, Wm R
New York City; 1880 July 20; Tuesday;
S; room 12

Stewart, Wm R (cont.)
New York City; 1880 Aug 17; Tuesday; S; room 1

Stickey, Geo
Guest of Blake; 1880 Sept 27; Monday; S

Stickney, Charles H
Pauger, Mo; 1880 Sept 24; Friday; S

Stiles, E G
Chicago; 1880 Apr 15; Thursday; S; room 6

Stilwell, T J
St Louis; 1880 Apr 28; Wednesday; S; room 15
St Louis; 1880 Sept 21; Tuesday; L; room 16

Stimpson, James
Louisville, Colo; 1880 Mar 28; Sunday; D

Stimpson, Wm
& Wife; Louisville, Colo; 1880 Mar 28; Sunday; D

Stine, Geo
1880 July 12; Monday; L; room 29

Stoah, Jno C
Leadville, Colo; 1880 Apr 13; Tuesday; S; room 26

Stoddard, F R
Hartford, Conn; 1880 Sept 18; Saturday; S; room 12

Stokes, G A
Jamestown, Col; 1880 July 5; Mon; D

Stone, W B
Galena, Ks; 1880 July 29; Thursday; S

Stone, W C
Denver; 1880 May 1; Saturday; S; room 27
1880 May 16; Sunday; D; room 25

Stone, W C (cont.)
1880 May 25; Tuesday; D; room 25
Salina; 1880 June 11; Friday; S; rm 28
Leadville; 1880 Aug 11; Wednesday; S; room 26
1880 Aug 31; Tuesday; S; room 27
Absent after breakfast; 1880 Sept 6; Monday
Returned; 1880 Sept 7; Tuesday; S; room 27
Absent after B; 1880 Sept 9; Thursday
1880 Sept 15; Wednesday; D
Absent; 1880 Sept 29; Wednesday; B
Rocky Mountains ; 1880 Oct 23; Saturday; D; room 28
Rocky Mountains ; 1880 Nov 11; Thursday; S; room 24

Stone, W G M (Mrs)
& Daughter; Denver; 1880 Apr 28; Wednesday; S; room 3

Stotembury, W B
& 4 children; Philadelphia, PA; 1880 June 5; Saturday; S; room 10, 11, 12

Stouder, Ira
Cheyenne; 1880 Nov 27; Saturday; L; room 23

Stout, E
& Son; La Grange J; 1880 May 13; Thursday, room 26

Stowe, F E
Denver; 1880 Mar 8; Monday; D; room 12

Stowruhr, John
Louisville; 1880 Apr 7; Wednesday; S; room 33

Strahan, Robt E
& Wife; Union Pacific Ry; 1880 June 14; Monday; S; room 10

Strasberger, S
Absent after S; 1880 July 24; Sat; S

Strasburger, M
City; 1880 Sept 6; Monday; S
Absent after B; 1880 Sept 21; Tuesday
City, returned; 1880 Sept 30; Thur; S

Strauss, M
St Louis; 1880 Nov 20; Saturday; D;
room 3
St Louis; 1880 Sept 1; Wednesday; L;
room 2

Straw, W C
Jamestown; 1880 Apr 12; Monday; S;
room 27

Streamer, F M
Ills; 1880 June 4; Friday; D

Strebig, I V
& Wife; Wizard Co; 1880 July 25;
Sunday; D; room 21

Streeter, R
Longmont; 1880 May 22; Saturday; D
Longmont; 1880 Sept 24; Friday
Longmont; 1880 Oct 14; Thursday; L;
room 32

Strock, B G
Jamestown; 1880 June 6; Sunday; D
Jamestown; 1880 Dec 10; Friday; S;
room 35

Strock, Cyrus G
Jamestown; 1880 Nov 9; Tuesday; S

Strycker, D H
1880 Aug 30; Monday; D

Strycker, Dr
Denver; 1880 Sept 27; Monday; D

Strycker, L A
Denver; 1880 June 29; Tuesday; S;
room 10

Styles, E M
Absent after Bkfst; 1880 Aug 12;
Thursday; D
Absent after breakfast; 1880 Aug 13;
Friday; B
Boulder; 1880 Aug 18; Wednesday; L;
room 6
Returned; 1880 Aug 19; Thursday; R,
St Vrain; 1880 May 10; Monday; D

Styles, Eugene M
Boulder; 1880 June 28; Monday; D

Sueker, W N
St Louis; 1880 July 29; Thursday; D

Sullivan, J W
Denver; 1880 June 23; Wednesday; S;
room 17
Denver; 1880 June 24; Thursday; S;
room 17

Sulwell, T J
St Louis; 1880 Apr 26; Monday; S;
room 8

Sumner, B E (Mrs)
Skyler, Neb; 1880 July 19; Monday; S;
room 21

Sumner, Frank
Denver; 1880 Aug 19; Thursday; D

Sumner, Geo T
Sheboygan, Wis; 1880 July 19; Monday; S; room 14

Sumner, H
Golden ; 1880 Apr 16; Friday; D

Sumner, H (Mrs)
Golden; 1880 June 24; Thursday; D;
room 1

Sun, George
Chicago; 1880 June 15; Tuesday; D;
room 2

Sutphen, R G
Jamestown; 1880 July 6; Tuesday; D

Swazey, M J (Mrs)
Skyler, Neb; 1880 July 19; Monday; S; room 21

Sweet, E T
Silverton; 1880 Apr 6; Tuesday; D; room 14

Sweney, James P
St Louis; 1880 June 24; Thursday; D

Swifts, Frank S
Nederland; 1880 July 7; Wednesday; S; room 16

Swigart, G__m
Chicago; 1880 Mar 8; Monday; S; room 8

Swittle, S Elbridge
Denver; 1880 Oct 1; Friday; D; rm 6

T

Taiselor, Henry
Miller & Co; 1880 Oct 22; Friday; S

Tallans, Hy P
Boston; 1880 Apr 29; Thursday; S; room 10

Talley, J D
& Wife; Lafayette; 1880 June 16; Wednesday; D; room 1

Tankersley, E D
City; 1880 June 28; Monday; S

Tansill, R W
Chicago; 1880 July 16; Friday; S

Tarrey, A J
Jamestown; 1880 Dec 9; Thursday

Taylor, Bush N
Madison, Ind; 1880 July 21; Wednesday; S; room 3

Taylor, J A
Greeley; 1880 July 5; Monday; D

Taylor, W D
Boulder; 1880 Nov 15; Monday; D; room 14

Teal, Geo
1880 Aug 21; Saturday; D

Teal, George
Guest of Campbell; 1880 Apr 11; Sunday; D
& Wife; Gold Hill; 1880 Oct 6; Wednesday; D
Gold Hill; 1880 Oct 11; Monday; S; room 10
Gold Hill; 1880 Oct 13; Wednesday; D
Gold Hill; 1880 Oct 23; Saturday; D
Gold Hill; 1880 Nov 1; Monday; D
Gold Hill; 1880 Nov 12; Friday; D; room 14
Gold Hill; 1880 Nov 15; Monday; S; room 6
Gold Hill; 1880 Nov 18; Thursday; S; room 6
Gold Hill; 1880 Dec 4; Saturday; S; room 12
Gold Hill; 1880 Dec 10; Friday; D; room 5

Teal, J
Portland, O; 1880 Sept 11; Sat; D

Teal, Thomas H
Gold Hill to Jacobi; 1880 Nov 7; Sunday; L; room 13

Teller, W M
Central City; 1880 Oct 23; Saturday; L
Central City; 1880 Nov 26; Friday; D; room 8

Teller, Willard
Denver; 1880 July 6; Tuesday; D

Templeton, Fay
Star Alliance Opera Co; 1880 June 11; Friday; D; room 15

Templeton, John
Star Alliance Opera Co; 1880 June 11; Friday; D; room 21

Templeton, Little Lady Lee
Star Alliance Opera Co; 1880 June 11; Friday; D; room 20

Tenne, D J
Sterling, Ills; 1880 Nov 5; Friday; L; room 6

Terry, A Q
Jamestown; 1880 Dec 10; Friday; S; room 6

Terry, J E
Chicago; 1880 Mar 12; Friday; S

Terry, Milo L
Longmont; 1880 Aug 3; Tuesday; D

Terry, Nora (Miss)
Longmont; 1880 Aug 4; Wednesday; L; room 26

Thacher, W H
Phila; 1880 Nov 23; Tuesday; L; rm 2

Thacker, W A
St Louis; 1880 June 28; Monday; D; room 2

Thacker, W H
St Louis; 1880 Mar 19; Friday; S; rm 2

Theadore, Chas
Plunket Troup; 1880 July 19; Monday; D; room 5
Plunkett Troupe; 1880 Sept 19; Sunday; S; room 32

Thomas, F A
KC; 1880 Oct 16; Saturday; D

Thomas, J E
Phila Pa; 1880 May 10; Monday; S; room 9
Phila; 1880 May 11; Tuesday; S

Thomas, Robt
Denver; 1880 Sept 14; Tuesday; L; room 24
with JJE; 1880 Sept 23; Thursday; S

Thomas, W W
Denver; 1880 May 18; Tuesday; S; room 6
Denver; 1880 May 19; Wednesday; S; room 6

Thomason, J A
& Wife; Sunshine; 1880 Aug 3; Tuesday; D

Thome, Geo W
New York; 1880 July 19; Monday; S; room 6

Thompson, A H
Symens, NY; 1880 July 23; Friday; D

Thompson, B Frank
KC; 1880 Nov 21; Sunday; D

Thompson, C
Chicago; 1880 Oct 19; Tuesday; S; room 11

Thompson, C H
Boston; 1880 May 29; Saturday; S; room 6

Thompson, D F
St Louis, Mo; 1880 Sept 5; Sunday; D; room 21

Thompson, E
Chicago; 1880 Aug 5; Thursday; L; room 10
Chicago; 1880 Apr 14; Wednesday; S; room 15

Thompson, H
City; 1880 Dec 7; Tuesday; D

Thompson, J B
Longmont; 1880 May 22; Saturday; D
Longmont; 1880 June 7; Monday; D; room 20

Thompson, J B (cont.)
Longmont; 1880 June 15; Tuesday; D; room 33
Longmont; 1880 July 5; Monday; D; room 14
Wth a P; 1880 July 5; Monday; D
Longmont; 1880 July 19; Monday; D
Longmont; 1880 Aug 2; Monday; D; room 6
Longmont; 1880 Aug 9; Monday; L; room 5
Longmont; 1880 Sept 13; Monday; D
Longmont; 1880 Oct 8; Friday; D; room 6
Longmont; 1880 Oct 11; Monday; D; room 17
Longmont; 1880 Dec 6; Monday; S; room 12

Thompson, J W
Kansas City; 1880 Sept 28; Tuesday; L; room 12

Thompson, W
& Wife; 1880 Aug 21; Saturday; D

Thompson, William H
Racine, Wis; 1880 Nov 5; Friday; L; room 15

Thomson, A G
Westfield, Mass; 1880 Sept 18; Saturday; S; room 2

Thorrey, E A
Denver; 1880 May 23; Sunday; S

Tibbon, W T
Ft D A Russell, Wyo; 1880 Oct 24; Sunday; S; room 5
Ft D A Russell, Wyo; 1880 Dec 15; Wednesday; S; room 34

Tidball, W H
Chicago; 1880 May 14; Friday; S; room 6

Tillotson, M G
New Bern; 1880 June 28; Monday; S; room 15

Tinker, W N
St Louis; 1880 Oct 28; Thursday; D

Tippett, C K
Caribou, Colo; 1880 June 12; Saturday; D; room 26

Tippett, Charles B
Caribou; 1880 Apr 4; Sun; S; rm 28

Titus, Frank
Cremona Park Brass Band, Denver; 1880 Aug 21; Saturday

Todd (Peppin, Todd & Co)
Baltimore, MD; 1880 May 25; Tuesday; D

Todd, William
Caribou; 1880 Aug 6; Friday; S; rm 29
Caribou; 1880 Aug 11; Wednesday; L; room 25
Caribou; 1880 Aug 12; Thursday; S; room 27

Toll, Chas H
Del Norte; 1880 Oct 9; Saturday; L; room 12

Topping, J
England; 1880 May 28; Friday; S; room 25

Torado, John
Erie, Col; 1880 Aug 3; Tuesday; D; room 30

Totton [Totten], F B
1880 Mar 6; Saturday; L; room 28

Towger, Abram W
& Wife; Denver; 1880 Apr 24; Saturday; D; room 3

Towner, E E
Sugarloaf; 1880 Apr 17; Saturday; D

Traddell, B G
East Branch, New York; 1880 Aug 13;
Friday; S; room 28

Tradell, Wm
1880 Aug 13; Friday; S; room 12

Tranton, Miss
& Friend; 1880 Sept 16; Thursday; D

Trettea, Evan
1880 Oct 6; Wednesday; D

Tritch, Geo
Denver; 1880 Oct 9; Saturday; S

Trounstine, Phil (Col)
Denver, Col; 1880 Aug 21; Sat; D

Trounstine, Wm
Denver, Colo; 1880 Mar 24; Wednesday; S; room 12
Denver; 1880 June 3; Thursday; S; room 2
Denver, Colo; 1880 Aug 26; Thursday; S; room 2

Tuesnel, E A
St Louis; 1880 June 6; Sunday; D; room 3

Turck, John
Georgetown; 1880 Apr 26; Monday; D

Turner, E H
Denver; 1880 Mar 15; Sunday; S; room 28

Turner, Otis A
Quincy, Ills; 1880 Apr 10; Saturday; D; room 6
Jerusalem; 1880 May 18; Tuesday; S; room 4
Quincy, Ills; 1880 Sept 25; Saturday; D; room 10

Turner, Thos J
Schuyler, Neb; 1880 July 19; Monday; S; room 14

Turrell, J W
Gold Hill; 1880 May 6; Thursday; S; room 25
Longmont; 1880 May 6; Thursday; D

Tussey, S Dean
Hastings, Neb; 1880 July 17; Saturday; D; room 12

Tuttle, C R
With George H Estabrook; 1880 Sept 23; Thursday; D

Twety, H F
Gold Hill; 1880 May 11; Tuesday; D; room 27

Two Headed Lady Combination
1880 June 12; Saturday

Tydensdeo, C F
Sunshine; 1880 Aug 11; Wed; D

U

Udy, Isaad
Leadville; 1880 Nov 3; Wednesday; S

Ullman, Cole
St Louis; 1880 June 9; Wednesday; S; room 3

Ulrich, Allen
Longmont; 1880 May 10; Monday; D

Ulrich, Charles
Caribou; 1880 Oct 9; Saturday; S; room 14

Ulrich, E O
Caribou; 1880 May 11; Tuesday; D; room 26
Caribou; 1880 May 28; Friday; D
Caribou; 1880 July 6; Tuesday; S; room 20
Caribou; 1880 Aug 2; Monday; D; room 27
Caribou; 1880 Oct 3; Sunday; D

Ulrich, E O (cont.)
Caribou; 1880 Oct 14; Thursday; D; room 33
Caribou; 1880 Oct 22; Friday; D; room 33
Caribou; 1880 Oct 29; Friday; D; room 33

Ulrich, Ed
Caribou; 1880 Sept 4; Saturday; S
Caribou; 1880 Sept 6; Monday; S; room 35

Ulrictz, E O (see Ulrich)
Caribou; 1880 June 26; Saturday; D; room 27

Underhill, Ellen
New York; 1880 Aug 27; Friday; S; room 20

Underhill, Miss
Denver; 1880 July 28; Wednesday; S; room 44

Underhill, Mr
NY; 1880 Aug 26; Thursday; D

Underwood, Jno H
Denver; 1880 Nov 3; Wednesday; S; room 14

Upinser, T N
Denver; 1880 May 25; Tuesday; D; room 6

Upton, E N
St Louis; 1880 Apr 19; Monday; S; room 1

Ureble, Mrs
Longmont; 1880 July 5; Monday; S

V

Vader, Frank
Longmont; 1880 July 5; Monday; D

Valencia, C
Star Alliance Opera Co; 1880 June 11; Friday; D; room 29

Valiquette, Chas G
Rutland, Utah; 1880 Aug 14; Sat; S

Valle, Nereo
Aspine, Colo; 1880 Aug 11; Wednesday; L; room 6

Van Doren, H _
St Jo, MO; 1880 Mar 9; Tuesday; S; room 17

Van Dorff, H C
Central City; 1880 Dec 1; Wed; D

Van Fleet, Chas G
City; 1880 May 3; Mon
City; 1880 May 4; Tuesday; D

Van Gahren, Ed
Greeley; 1880 July 5; Monday; D

Van Kleeck, H
New York; 1880 June 8; Tuesday; S; room 19

Van Riper, C
& Wife; 1880 Aug 21; Saturday; D

Van Valkenburg, G
& Wife; Longmont; 1880 Sept 24; Friday; S

Van Vert, J H
Denver; 1880 Dec 16; Thursday; D
Denver; 1880 Dec 18; Saturday; S

Van Wagenon, T F
Denver; 1880 Apr 14; Wednesday; S

Vandenburgh, J W
Washington with Larson; 1880 Sept 4; Saturday; S; room 8

Vandercamp, J H
Crisman, Colo; 1880 Oct 16; Saturday; D

Vanderver, John J
Denver; 1880 Nov 9; Tuesday; L; room 13

Vane, Alice
Star Alliance Opera Co; 1880 June 11; Friday; D; room 19

VanKirk, W B
St Louis; 1880 June 11; Friday; L; room 2
St Louis; 1880 July 12; Monday; L; room 6

Veal, J L
Atlantic City, NJ; 1880 Oct 27; Wednesday; S; room 25

Veal, J S
Denver; 1880 Aug 18; Wednesday; S

Vincent, J T
Denver; 1880 Sept 9; Thursday; S

Vincent, R A
1880 Apr 18; Sunday; D; room 26

Vinton, G A
Denver Tribune; 1880 Sept 16; Thursday; D; room 8
Denver Tribune; 1880 Sept 23; Thursday; B; room 3
Denver Tribune; 1880 Sept 25; Saturday; B; room 3
Denver Tribune; 1880 Sept 26; Sunday; D; room 3

Virgin, H T
Wife & 3 children; City; 1880 Oct 13; Wednesday; L; room 19

Virgin, W (Dr)
Burlington; 1880 July 20; Tuesday; B

Virgin, W T
Burlington, Iowa; 1880 Aug 29; Sunday; S; room 14
Burlington, Iowa; 1880 Sept 18; Saturday; L; room 35
Burlington, Ia; 1880 Sept 22; Wednesday; S

Virgin, W T (Dr)
City; 1880 July 21; Wednesday; D; room 14

Virgin, Wm
Burlington, Iowa; 1880 July 25; Sunday; S; room 14

Vivian, George G
Freeland; 1880 June 8; Tuesday; S; room 6
Freeland; 1880 June 9; Wednesday; S; room 6

Voche, Wm
Chicago; 1880 July 12; Monday; S

Vogel, T J
Denver; 1880 Sept 23; Thursday; D

Volenture, Jas
Denver; 1880 May 15; Saturday; S

von Throsha, C
City; 1880 May 7; Friday; D
City; 1880 May 8; Saturday; D

Vontrotha, Baron
City; 1880 June 18; Friday; S

Vorhies, D (Mrs)
Leadville; 1880 Mar 9; Tuesday; S; room 4

Vosburgh, J
St Louis; 1880 Aug 5; Thursday; L; room 11
St Louis; 1880 May 27; Thursday; S; room 2
St Louis; 1880 Oct 19; Tuesday; D; room 10

W

Wade, Edward C
Washington, D C; 1880 Mar 17;
Wednesday; S; room 17

Wadge, Mrs (see Wedge)
Caribou; 1880 Aug 3; Tuesday; S;
room 8

Waggoner, Chas
Clinton; 1880 Nov 18; Thursday; L;
room 28

Wagman, W A
Ward; 1880 Apr 26; Monday; S; rm 27

Wagner
BC; 1880 July 15; Thursday; B; rm 27

Wagner, G L
Chicago, Ills; 1880 Sept 9; Thursday;
L; room 2

Wagner, H A
Ward; 1880 May 18; Tuesday; S; rm 27
Ward Colorado; 1880 May 22; Satur-
day, room 27
Ward; 1880 June 14; Mon; S; rm 27

Wagner, H C
Ward; 1880 June 3; Thursday; S; rm 27

Wagner, J
BC; 1880 May 18; Tuesday; S

Wagner, T
City; 1880 May 21; Friday; B

Wagner, W A
Ward; 1880 Mar 8; Monday; S; rm 28
Ward; 1880 Mar 18; Thursday; D;
room 27
Ward; 1880 Mar 27; Sat; S; rm 27
Ward; 1880 Apr 5; Monday; S; rm 27
Ward; 1880 Apr 7; Wednesday; S;
room 27
Ward; 1880 Apr 1; Thursday; S; rm 27
Ward; 1880 Apr 12; Monday; S; rm 27

Wagner, W A (cont.)
Ward; 1880 Apr 15; Thur; S; rm 27
Ward, Colorado; 1880 Apr 21;
Wednesday; L; room 27
Ward; 1880 Apr 23; Friday; S; rm 27
Ward, Col; 1880 Apr 29; Thursday; S;
room 29
Ward; 1880 May 2; Sunday; D; rm 27
Ward; 1880 May 11; Tuesday; S; rm 28
Ward, Col; 1880 May 13; Thursday; L;
room 28
Black Hawk; 1880 May 15; Saturday; S
Ward; 1880 May 16; Sunday; S; rm 27
Ward; 1880 May 24; Monday; S; rm 27
Ward; 1880 May 27; Thursday; S;
room 34
Ward; 1880 June 7; Monday; S; rm 27
Ward; 1880 June 11; Friday; S; rm 27
Ward; 1880 June 17; Thursday; S;
room 27
Ward; 1880 June 21; Mon; S; rm 29
Ward; 1880 June 24; Thursday; S
Ward Colorado; 1880 June 28; Mon-
day; L; room 25
Ward; 1880 July 1; Thursday; S; rm 28
Ward; 1880 July 5; Monday; S; rm 27
Ward; 1880 July 15; Thur; S; rm 27
Ward; 1880 July 19; Monday; S; rm 27
Ward; 1880 July 23; Friday; S; rm 27
Ward; 1880 July 26; Monday; L; rm 27
Ward; 1880 July 29; Thur; S; rm 27
Ward; 1880 Aug 2; Monday; S; rm 27
Ward; 1880 Aug 5; Thursday; L; rm 27
Ward; 1880 Aug 12; Thursday; S;
room 27
Ward; 1880 Aug 16; Monday; S; rm 27
Ward, Col; 1880 Aug 20; Friday; S;
room 27
Ward; 1880 Aug 24; Tuesday; S; rm 27
Ward; 1880 Aug 27; Friday; S; rm 27
Ward; 1880 Aug 30; Monday; S; rm 24
Ward; 1880 Sept 3; Friday; S; room 28
Ward; 1880 Sept 6; Monday; S; rm 27

Wagner, W A (cont.)
Ward; 1880 Sept 8; Wednesday; L; room 27
Ward; 1880 Sept 11; Sat; S; rm 27
Ward; 1880 Sept 14; Tuesday; L; rm 24
Ward; 1880 Sept 15; Wednesday; D; room 27
Ward; 1880 Sept 17; Friday; L; rm 27
Ward; 1880 Sept 20; Monday; S; rm 27
Ward; 1880 Sept 23; Thursday; L; room 6
Ward; 1880 Sept 27; Mon; L; rm 27
Ward; 1880 Oct 4; Monday; S; rm 27
Ward; 1880 Oct 7; Thursday; S; rm 28
Sunshine; 1880 Oct 11; Monday; S; room 26
Ward; 1880 Oct 14; Thur; S; rm 21
Ward; 1880 Oct 18; Monday; S; rm 27
Ward; 1880 Oct 21; Thursday; L; room 27
Ward; 1880 Oct 25; Monday; S; rm 27
Ward; 1880 Oct 28; Thur; S; rm 27
Ward, Col; 1880 Oct 29; Friday; S; room 28
Ward; 1880 Nov 8; Monday; S; rm 27
Ward; 1880 Nov 12; Friday; S; rm 27
Ward; 1880 Nov 15; Monday; S; rm 27
Ward; 1880 Nov 2; Tuesday; S; rm 27
Ward; 1880 Nov 20; Sat; L; rm 26
Ward; 1880 Nov 24; Wednesday; S; room 27
Ward; 1880 Nov 29; Monday; S; rm 24
Ward; 1880 Sept 30; Thursday; S; room 28
Ward; 1880 Dec 3; Friday; S; room 28
Ward, Col; 1880 Dec 12; Sunday; S; room 27
Ward; 1880 Dec 16; Thursday; D; room 27

Wagoner, H A (see Wagner)
Ward; 1880 Mar 11; Thursday; S; room 27

Wagoner, T F (see Wagner)
City; 1880 Aug 5; Thursday; S

Wainwright, J W
Chicago; 1880 May 6; Thursday; D; room 15

Wakefield, John
Denver; 1880 Sept 20; Monday; L; room 1

Walinski, Albert
San Francisco; 1880 Aug 18; Wednesday; L; room 1

Walker, E S
City; 1880 June 15; Tuesday

Walker, J B
Racine, WI; 1880 Mar 31; Wednesday; S; room 6

Walker, Thos D
Salt Lake; 1880 July 10; Saturday; D; room 34
Caribou; 1880 July 14; Wednesday; S; room 35

Walker, W C
Salina; 1880 Aug 18; Wednesday; L; room 18

Walker, W H H
Salina; 1880 Sept 9; Thursday; D
Salina; 1880 Sept 25; Saturday; D
Salina; 1880 Oct 23; Saturday; D
Salina; 1880 Nov 3; Wednesday; L; room 12
Salina; 1880 Dec 7; Tuesday; L; rm 35
Salina; 1880 Dec 8; Wednesday; S; room 35

Walker, W M
Salina; 1880 Dec 18; Saturday; D

Walkins, Fred
St Louis; 1880 July 8; Thursday; S

Walkins, L A
Denver; 1880 Aug 2; Monday; S

Walkins, L K
Denver; 1880 July 8; Thursday; S

Wall, L J W
St Louis; 1880 Sept 23; Thursday; S;
room 11

Wallace, F
Ward; 1880 Aug 3; Tuesday; L

Wallace, J M
Leadville; 1880 Aug 4; Wednesday; S

Walling, W B
City; 1880 Mar 12; Friday; L; room 26
Denver, Col; 1880 Mar 13; Saturday;
L; room 15
1880 Mar 14; Sunday; L; room 35
Denver; 1880 Apr 28; Wednesday; B

Walt, T N
Ward; 1880 Nov 12; Friday; L; rm 26

Wandemoer, John
Denver; 1880 May 13; Thursday; D

Wangelin, O H
& Wife; Boulder, Colo; 1880 May 25;
Tuesday; D

Wangelin, Otto H
& Wife; Boulder; 1880 June 27; Sunday; D

Wantly, H A
Salina, Kan; 1880 Sept 6; Monday; D

Ward, H
Denver; 1880 June 15; Tuesday; D
Denver; 1880 June 25; Fri; S; rm 11

Ward, Henry
Denver; 1880 July 6; Tuesday; D

Ward, S D
& Wife; Chicago; 1880 Aug 24; Tuesday; D; room 6

Ward, S G
Nederland; 1880 July 5; Monday; L;
room 33
Nederland; 1880 Aug 15; Sunday; S

Ward, S G (cont.)
Nederland; 1880 Aug 17; Tuesday; D
Nederland; 1880 Oct 18; Monday; S;
room 34
Nederland; 1880 Nov 6; Saturday; D
Nederland; 1880 Nov 8; Monday
Nederland; 1880 Nov 17; Wednesday;
S; room 26
Nederland; 1880 Nov 22; Monday; S;
room 28
Nederland; 1880 Nov 30; Tuesday; D;
room 34
Nederland; 1880 Dec 14; Tuesday; L;
room 13

Ward, Wm H
Caribou; 1880 May 21; Friday; D;
room 17

Warden, E E
& Wife; 1880 Aug 21; Saturday; D

Warner, Arthur
Hannibal, MO; 1880 Mar 12; Fri

Warner, J B
Denver; 1880 Oct 5; Tuesday; D;
room 20

Warner, J M
Port Jeroed; 1880 Aug 17; Tuesday; S;
room 12

Warner, N M
Salina; 1880 Aug 3; Tuesday; D

Warner, W H
Syracuse, NY; 1880 Aug 17; Tuesday;
S; room 12

Warren, James B
Boulder; 1880 Nov 2; Tuesday; D

Washburn, H E
Waverly, Ohio; 1880 June 29; Tues; D
City; 1880 May 3; Monday; S
City; 1880 Aug 7; Saturday; L

Washington, L W
1880 Aug 21; Saturday
Chicago; 1880 Aug 24; Tuesday; S;
room 11

Washington, R J
Va; 1880 Aug 21; Saturday
Va; 1880 Aug 24; Tuesday; S; room 10

Waterman & Farini
1880 Aug 3; Tuesday; B

Waters, C H
& Daughter; Benton, Mass; 1880 June
14; Monday; S; room 4

Waters, W B (Mrs)
Cor 'Journal' Ranford, Ill; 1880 June
14; Monday; S; room 11

Waters, W C
Denver; 1880 Sept 29; Wednesday; D
Ward; 1880 Dec 16; Thursday; S;
room 14

Watkins, E S
Chicago; 1880 Oct 12; Tuesday; S

Watkins, Henry B
Cleveland, O; 1880 Nov 2; Tuesday; D

Watkins, James M
Gallien Age; 1880 Sept 23; Thur; L
Gold____; 1880 Oct 11; Monday; S
Erie; 1880 Oct 15; Friday; L; room 32
Erie; 1880 Oct 16; Saturday; L; rm 14
1880 Oct 24; Sunday; D; room 14
Denver City; 1880 Nov 2; Tuesday; S;
room 34
Golden Agr; 1880 Nov 3; Wednesday;
S; room 34

Watkins, Jas M
Denver City; 1880 Oct 22; Friday; D;
room 13

Watkins, L H
Denver; 1880 Oct 18; Monday; S;
room 20

Watson & Levanion
Dan Castello & Co Circus; 1880 May
23; Sunday; L; room 26

Watson, H H (Mrs)
Golden; 1880 Oct 16; Saturday; D

Watson, Hattie (Miss)
Golden; 1880 July 30; Fri; D; rm 16

Watson, Mrs
Golden; 1880 Aug 31; Tuesday; D;
room 10

Watson, R E
Chicago; 1880 May 20; Thursday; S
Chicago; 1880 July 29; Thursday; S
Denver; 1880 June 15; Tuesday; S
Denver; 1880 Aug 17; Tuesday; D;
room 3
Denver; 1880 Aug 18; Wednesday; L;
room 3
Denver; 1880 Aug 24; Tuesday; S
Denver; 1880 Sept 2; Thursday; S
Chicago; 1880 Sept 14; Tuesday; D;
room 12
Chicago; 1880 Oct 12; Tuesday; S
Denver; 1880 Oct 18; Monday; S;
room 10

Way, R C
& Lady; Longm; 1880 July 5; Mon; D
& Lady; Longmont; 1880 July 5;
Monday; S
& Lady; Left Hand; 1880 Aug 3; Tues-
day; S; room 30

Wayber, N N N
Denver; 1880 Aug 14; Saturday; D

Weaver, Leonard
Pittsburg, Penna; 1880 June 13;
Sunday

Weaver, W C
Denver, Colo; 1880 Apr 19; Monday;
S; room 17

Webb, A E
Golden; 1880 July 29; Thursday; S
Golden, Colo; 1880 Aug 14; Sat; D
Golden, Colo; 1880 Oct 23; Sat; D

Webb, T (Miss)
Golden; 1880 July 24; Saturday; D

Webb, Wm
La Port; 1880 July 25; Sunday; S; rm 5
La Port; 1880 July 29; Thursday; D;
room 29

Webber, John A
Longmont; 1880 Nov 9; Tuesday; L;
room 27

Webber. C S
St Louis; 1880 Aug 24; Tuesday; S;
room 1

Weber, A H
St Louis; 1880 Aug 23; Monday; D;
room 3

Webster, B N
New York; 1880 June 28; Monday; D

Webster, C B
St Louis; 1880 Nov 1; Monday; S;
room 1

Webster, C S
St Louis; 1880 Apr 29; Thursday; D

Webster, Frank
Colo; 1880 Aug 1; Sunday; L; room 4

Wedge, Mrs (see Wadge)
Caribou; 1880 Aug 4; Wednesday; D;
room 29

Week, C R
left after; 1880 Aug 21; Saturday; D

Weekes, E B
Ticket Agt, Breakfast only; 1880 Aug
3; Tuesday; B

Wehsin, Frank
Colo; 1880 July 21; Wednesday; S;
room 4

Weil, G W
Miss; 1880 June 21; Monday; S; rm 11

Weinser, Herman
Cleveland, O; 1880 Nov 21; Sunday; D

Weirnale, J G
Absent after B; 1880 Mar 17; Wednesday; B

Welch, A L
Boulder; 1880 Mar 8; Monday; D
Gone away after S; 1880 Mar 22;
Monday; S
Boulder; 1880 Mar 26; Friday; D
Absent after S; 1880 Apr 28; Wednes-
day; S
City; 1880 May 2; Sunday; D
City returned; 1880 June 22; Tues; D
Absent after S; 1880 June 24; Thur; S
City; 1880 July 1; Thursday; D
Absent after S; 1880 July 2; Friday
Returned; 1880 July 4; Sunday; D
Boulder; 1880 July 10; Saturday; S;
room 84
City; 1880 July 17; Saturday; S
Absent after S; 1880 July 18; Sunday
City; 1880 July 23; Friday; S
Absent after B; 1880 July 29; Thur; B
City; 1880 July 31; Saturday; S
Boulder; 1880 Aug 9; Monday; L
Boulder; 1880 Aug 12; Thursday; D
Boulder; 1880 Aug 16; Monday; B
Denver; 1880 Nov 7; Sunday; D
Denver; 1880 Nov 22; Monday; B
Denver; 1880 Dec 14; Tuesday; D

Welch, Allen
Boulder; 1880 June 28; Monday; D

Welch, C H
Andayo; 1880 Oct 10; Sunday; L;
room 2

Welch, C R
Leadville; 1880 Apr 8; Thursday; B
Absent after B; 1880 Apr 12; Mon; B

Welch, C R (cont.)

Leadville; 1880 May 11; Tuesday; D

Left after dinner; 1880 Aug 24; Tuesday; S

Returned at supper; 1880 Aug 25; Wednesday; S

Absent after Brkfst; 1880 Aug 30; Monday

Returned; 1880 Aug 31; Tuesday; S

Absent after supper; 1880 Sept 2; Thursday

Returned at ; 1880 Sept 4; Saturday; S

Absent after supper; 1880 Sept 7; Tuesday

Returned at supper; 1880 Sept 9; Thursday

With guest at; 1880 Sept 13; Mon; B

Left after; 1880 Sept 15; Wednesday; S

Returned; 1880 Sept 18; Saturday; S

Left after; 1880 Sept 19; Sunday; S

Returned; 1880 Sept 24; Friday; S

Welch, Chas H

1880 June 12; Saturday; D; room 25

Welch, E F

Chicago; 1880 Oct 12; Tuesday; S; room 1

Chicago; 1880 Nov 26; Friday; S; room 2

Welch, E H

Chicago; 1880 Mar 30; Tuesday; S; room 2

Chicago; 1880 Aug 26; Thursday; L; room 1

Welch, J

Ft Collins; 1880 June 1; Tuesday; S

Ft Collins; 1880 Aug 15; Sunday; S

Ft Collins; 1880 Dec 18; Saturday; S

Welch, Jacob

Collins; 1880 Apr 22; Thursday; S; room 6

Wells, B T

Black Hawk; 1880 June 16; Wednesday; S; room 20

Wells, Chas H

Black Hawk; 1880 June 2; Wednesday; D; room 34

Black Hawk; 1880 July 2; Friday; S; room 14

Black Hawk; 1880 Oct 22; Friday; D

Wells, J L

Longmont; 1880 Sept 24; Friday; S

Welsh, C R (see Welch)

Left after; 1880 Aug 7; Saturday; S

Ret; 1880 Aug 16; Monday; S

Welsh, J

Fort Collins, guest ASW & Co; 1880 Oct 18; Monday; D

Wendorf, H C

Cleveland, O; 1880 Aug 20; Friday; S

Wendorff, F T

Dayton, Ohio; 1880 Dec 1; Wednesday; B

Werley, P J

Leadville; 1880 July 10; Saturday; S; room 14

Caribou; 1880 Sept 22; Wednesday; D; room 25

Caribou; 1880 Oct 24; Sunday; L; room 13

West, Geo

Golden, Colo; 1880 Aug 13; Friday; D

West, I N (Capt)

Deadwood; 1880 Aug 10; Tuesday; S

West, J M (Mrs)

City; 1880 Apr 1; Thursday; D

West, John

Caribou; 1880 Oct 7; Thursday; L; room 25

West, S S
Topeka; 1880 Mar 24; Wednesday; S

Westfall, Bent F
Hanibal, MO; 1880 July 5; Monday; S; room 19

Weston, Miss
City to JJE; 1880 Sept 4; Saturday; D

Westover, H
Cheyenne; 1880 Mar 15; Sunday; S; room 6

Westover, Miss
JJE; 1880 Nov 15; Monday; D
JJE; 1880 Nov 17; Wednesday; D

Wetherly, C S
Hartford; 1880 Apr 21; Wednesday; S; room 4

Weyman, Geo
& Family; Longmont; 1880 Sept 24; Friday; S

Wheeler, B Clark
Leadville; 1880 Mar 11; Thursday; D

Wheeler, Chas F
With Donner; 1880 Oct 20; Wednesday; D

Wheeler, O B Jr
Wife & Child; NY; 1880 May 17; Monday; S; room 3
Wife & Child; NY; 1880 May 19; Wednesday; S; room 3

Whissan, Jas
San Francisco; 1880 June 1; Tuesday; S; room 15

Whitacre, E M
East Liverpool; 1880 June 3; Thursday; D; room 34
East Liverpool; 1880 Oct 12; Tuesday; L; room 3

Whitall, M C (Miss)
Phila; 1880 Aug 14; Saturday; D; room 6

White, A F
Williamsburg; 1880 May 10; Monday; S; room 44
Worthington Av Mine; 1880 May 18; Tuesday; S
Washington Av Mine; 1880 May 28; Friday; S; room 19

White, Andw Y
Albany, NY; 1880 July 18; Sunday; D
Albany, NY; 1880 July 19; Monday; S

White, C
1880 Mar 6; Saturday; L; room 28

White, Eben
Longmont; 1880 Mar 8; Monday; S; room 5
Longmont; 1880 Mar 15; Sunday; D; room 5
Longmont; 1880 Mar 23; Tuesday; D; room 44
Longmont; 1880 Apr 3; Saturday; D
Longmont; 1880 Apr 20; Tuesday; D; room 5
Longmont; 1880 Apr 27; Tuesday; D; room 5
Longmont; 1880 May 3; Monday; D; room 5
Longmont; 1880 May 10; Monday; S; room 5
Longmont; 1880 May 17; Monday; S; room 5
Longmont; 1880 May 24; Monday; D; room 5
Longmont; 1880 June 1; Tuesday; L; room 5
Longmont; 1880 June 7; Monday; S; room 5
Longmont; 1880 June 14; Monday; L; room 5

White, Eben (cont.)
Longmont; 1880 June 21; Monday; L; room 5
Longmont; 1880 June 28; Monday; S; room 5
Longmont; 1880 Aug 21; Saturday; D
Longmont; 1880 July 5; Monday; D; room 5
Longmont; 1880 July 19; Monday; D; room 29
Longmont; 1880 Aug 3; Tuesday; S
Longmont; 1880 Aug 14; Saturday; D
Longmont; 1880 Sept 4; Saturday; D
Longmont; 1880 Sept 24; Friday; S
Longmont; 1880 Nov 9; Tuesday; D

White, Fred
Salina; 1880 Aug 9; Monday; D
Salina; 1880 Aug 16; Monday; D
Salina; 1880 Aug 21; Saturday; D
Salina; 1880 Sept 7; Tuesday; D
Salina; 1880 Sept 11; Saturday; D
Salina; 1880 Sept 20; Monday; D
Salina; 1880 Sept 29; Wednesday; S; room 35
Salina; 1880 Sept 30; Thursday; S
Salina; 1880 Oct 1; Friday; L; rm 5
Salina; 1880 Oct 5; Tuesday; D
Salina; 1880 Oct 8; Friday; S; room 14
Salina; 1880 Oct 8; Friday; B
Salina; 1880 Oct 18; Monday; D
Salina; 1880 Oct 20; Wednesday; D
Salina; 1880 Oct 21; Thursday; D
Salina; 1880 Nov 6; Saturday; D
Salina; 1880 Nov 13; Saturday; D
1880 Nov 22; Monday; D
Salina; 1880 Dec 2; Thursday; D

White, Frederick
Salina; 1880 June 17; Thursday; D
Salina, Kan; 1880 July 14; Wed; D
Salina; 1880 July 28; Wednesday; D
Salina; 1880 Aug 1; Sunday; D

White, Fred'k
Salina; 1880 June 21; Monday; D

White, G B
Denver; 1880 Sept 15; Wednesday; L
Denver; 1880 Sept 22; Wednesday

White, Geo B
Denver; 1880 Sept 16; Thursday; D

White, H C
Nederland; 1880 Aug 18; Wednesday; D; room 28

White, J B
Crossed out; Denver; 1880 Sept 22; Wednesday

White, L A
New York; 1880 July 13; Tuesday; D; room 20

Whitehand, G F
Denver News; 1880 Mar 23; Tues; D
Rocky Mountain News; 1880 Sept 22; Wednesday; D

Whitehead, G L
Rocky Mountain News; 1880 Sept 23; Thursday; D
Denver News; 1880 Sept 25; Sat; D

Whitehead, J W
Frisco; 1880 Nov 4; Thursday; L; rm 2

Whitehind, G F
Denver News; 1880 Mar 23; Tues; D

Whitely, Major
& Wife; 1880 Aug 21; Saturday; D

Whitemor, R G
Denver; 1880 June 23; Wednesday; D; room 21

Whitford, O F
East Plattsmouth, Neb; 1880 Apr 15; Thursday; S; room 5

Whitley, R H, Jr
guest of J C M; 1880 Dec 4; Sat; D

Whitlock, W E
New York; 1880 June 7; Monday; S; room 20

Whitmore, F D
Pittsburg, PA; 1880 May 10; Monday; D; room 1

Whitmore, N R
Quincy, Ill; 1880 June 29; Tuesday; S

Whitner, H K
Phila; 1880 May 10; Monday; S; rm 3

Whitner, H K (Mrs)
Phila; 1880 Dec 9; Thursday; D
Phila, Pa; 1880 Nov 15; Monday; D; room 10

Whitner, W R
Phila; 1880 Dec 9; Thursday; D
Phila, Pa; 1880 Nov 15; Monday; D; room 11

Whitt, I B (Mrs)
El Moro; 1880 Oct 12; Tuesday; S

Whittemore, O A
Denver; 1880 June 20; Sunday; S

Whittey, John
Denver; 1880 June 30; Wednesday; D

Whittier, Wm W (MD)
New York City; 1880 July 14; Wednesday; S; room 16

Whittredge, W W
Denver; 1880 Sept 23; Thursday; S

Wickoff, Walter S (see Wikoff)
Denver; 1880 June 30; Wednesday; S; room 11

Wiggins & Loucinda
Dan Castello & Co Circus; 1880 May 23; Sunday; L; room 27

Wike, Geo
Barry, Ills; 1880 Aug 22; Sunday; D

Wikoff, W S (see Wickoff)
Denver; 1880 July 9; Friday; D
Denver; 1880 June 29; Tuesday; S; room 11

Wikoff, Walter S (see Wickoff)
Sunshine; 1880 July 17; Saturday; B
Denver; 1880 July 21; Wednesday; D
Sunshine; 1880 July 30; Friday; S
Denver; 1880 Sept 7; Tuesday; D
Sunshine; 1880 Sept 10; Friday; D

Wilborn, J F
& Wife; Denver, Colo; 1880 Sept 13; Monday; S; room 6

Wilbur, J F
Denver, Colo; 1880 Oct 8; Friday; S; room 3

Wilbur, M C
Colo Springs; 1880 Sept 22; Wednesday; S; room 12

Wilde, A
Lefthand; 1880 July 5; Monday; D

Wilder, Eugene
With Miss Wilder & Miss Carrie Bryant; 1880 Aug 21; Saturday; D

Wilder, J Frank
Lawrence; 1880 Dec 13; Monday; S; room 15

Wilder, J G
Lawrence, KS; 1880 June 2; Wednesday; S; room 14

Wilder, Miss
1880 Aug 21; Saturday; D

Wildman, Val
New York; 1880 Mar 6; Saturday; S; room 6
New York; 1880 Mar 13; Saturday; S; room 5

Wiley, Wm C
New York City; 1880 July 3; Saturday;
D; room 11

Wilhelm, David (Mrs)
1880 Sept 21; Tuesday; D; room 8

Wilkest, J
Deadwood, DT; 1880 Aug 2; Monday;
S; room 21

Wilkins, J L
1880 Aug 17; Tuesday; L; room 26

Wilkinson, C B
& Wife; Denver; 1880 Aug 21; Saturday; D

Willard, Geo
Ohio; 1880 Sept 17; Friday; S; rm 15

Willard, S R
1880 Oct 23; Saturday; D; room 29

Williams
Dan Castello & Co Circus; 1880 May
23; Sunday; L; room 12

Williams, A J
Hockessin, Del; 1880 Oct 29; Friday; S

Williams, A L
Longmont; 1880 Aug 19; Thursday; S
Longmont Cornet Band; 1880 Sept
23; Thursday; S; room 27

Williams, Benj
& Wife; 1880 Aug 21; Saturday; D

Williams, C M (Mrs)
Denver; 1880 Aug 2; Monday; L;
room 11

Williams, E
& Wife; 1880 Aug 21; Saturday; D

Williams, J T
Erie; 1880 June 2; Wednesday; D

Williams, Mrs
Longmont; 1880 Aug 3; Tuesday; D

Williams, S
Longmont; 1880 Aug 19; Thursday; S
Longmont Cornet Band; 1880 Sept
23; Thursday; S; room 3

Williams, Thos R
Kansas City, Mo; 1880 Sept 20; Monday; D; room 2

Williams, W J
Leadville; 1880 Mar 18; Thursday; D

Williams, W K
Longmont; 1880 July 5; Monday; L;
room 28

Williams, Wm H
Denver; 1880 Oct 5; Tuesday; S; rm 15

Williamson, G B
RCMcA; 1880 May 17; Monday; S;
room 27

Williamson, G R
Yellow Pine Mine; 1880 May 16;
Sunday; D

Willis, Albert
Denver; 1880 July 7; Wednesday; S;
room 27

Wilson
Denver; 1880 Sept 20; Monday; S;
room 24

Wilson, Ada
Denver, Col; 1880 June 11; Friday; D;
room 13

Wilson, Chas F
Denver; 1880 July 21; Wednesday; S

Wilson, Chas L
With Fiske Farrar; Denver; 1880 Apr
6; Tuesday; L; room 6

Wilson, D P
S Cliffe; 1880 Aug 17; Tuesday; S;
room 19

Wilson, D P
S Cliffe; 1880 Aug 30; Monday; S; room 20

Wilson, D P (Judge)
S Cliff; 1880 July 22; Thursday
Denver; 1880 July 29; Thursday; S; room 12

Wilson, F H
Denver; 1880 Dec 7; Tuesday; D; room 12

Wilson, G W
NiWot; 1880 May 22; Saturday; D
Denver; 1880 Oct 17; Sun; S; rm 28

Wilson, Horace H
Del; 1880 Nov 21; Sunday; L; room 57

Wilson, John (Rev)
& Wife; Longmont; 1880 Mar 21; Sunday; D

Wilson, L P
S Cliffe; 1880 Aug 12; Thursday; S; room 3

Wilson, Mr
With J C Cooper; 1880 Aug 15; Sunday; D

Wilson, Thos V
City; 1880 June 25; Friday; S

Wilty, L A (Gov)
Louisiana; 1880 June 8; Tuesday; D

Wimer, M B
1880 June 26; Saturday; L; room 25

Winch, Allen
Rowena, Col; 1880 June 30; Wed; S
Left after breakfast; 1880 July 7; Wednesday; D
Boulder; 1880 July 18; Sunday; D
Left after; 1880 July 20; Tuesday; B
Boulder; 1880 July 28; Wednesday; D
Left after; 1880 July 29; Thursday; B
Boulder, Col; 1880 Aug 3; Tuesday; D

Winch, Allen (cont.)
Left after; 1880 Aug 5; Thursday; B
Boulder; 1880 Aug 9; Monday; D
Left after ; 1880 Sept 3; Friday; B
& Wife; Boulder; 1880 Nov 24; Wednesday; L; room 8

Winch, N
Denver; 1880 Aug 4; Wednesday; S; room 33

Winchester, Thomas
Worcester, Mass; 1880 Nov 21; Sun; S

Wing, S C
Louisville, Ky; 1880 Aug 21; Sat; D

Winslow, Edward L
Kalamazoo, Mich; 1880 June 19; Saturday; S; room 13
Kalamazoo, Mich; 1880 June 21; Monday; S; room 13

Wirth, John G
Ward; 1880 Aug 3; Tuesday; D; rm 28
Ward; 1880 June 17; Thursday; S; room 25

Wise, John L
Kansas City, Mo; 1880 Aug 21; Sat; D

Wiswall, C E
Gold Hill; 1880 Mar 6; Saturday; S; room 21
Absent after B; 1880 Mar 8; Mon
Gold Hill; 1880 Mar 8; Monday; S; room 21
Gold Hill; 1880 Mar 20; Saturday; S; room 27
Gold Hill; 1880 Apr 20; Tuesday; L; room 23
Gold Hill; 1880 May 4; Tuesday; D; room 17
Gold Hill; 1880 July 15; Thursday; D; room 21
Gold Hill; 1880 Aug 3; Tuesday; D; room 19

Wiswall, C E (cont.)
  & Wife; Gold Hill; 1880 Sept 22; Wednesday; D; room 35
  Gold Hill; 1880 Sept 29; Wednesday; S; room 17
  Gold Hill; 1880 Dec 15; Wednesday; L; room 29

Wiswall, C E (Mrs)
  Gold Hill; 1880 Apr 20; Tuesday; D; room 21
  Gold Hill; 1880 May 6; Thursday; S; room 21
  Gold Hill; 1880 July 13; Tuesday; S; room 21

Wiswall, H B
  Longmont Cornet Band; 1880 Sept 23; Thursday; S; room 3

Wiswall, J E
  Gold Hill; 1880 Oct 13; Wednesday; S; room 14

Wiswall, W E
  1880 Sept 28; Tuesday; L; room 17

Witner, H K
  Philada; 1880 May 14; Fri; S; rm 16

Wittig, E
  Cremona Park Brass Band, Denver; 1880 Aug 21; Saturday

Wizinski, Albert
  San Francisco; 1880 Nov 28; Sunday; L; room 10

Wolcott, Edw'd O
  Georgetown; 1880 Oct 9; Saturday; L; room 10

Wolfe, Hank D
  Denver; 1880 Apr 4; Sunday; D

Wood, George W
  Cincinnati; 1880 Dec 11; Saturday; S; room 26

Wood, Thos L
  Sunshine; 1880 Apr 13; Tuesday; D
  Sunshine; 1880 Mar 21; Sunday; D; room 15
  Sunshine; 1880 May 22; Saturday; D
  Sunshine; 1880 May 25; Tuesday; D
  Sunshine; 1880 Sept 28; Tuesday; D
  Sunshine; 1880 Oct 17; Sunday; D

Woodbury, T S
  Denver Times; 1880 July 4; Sunday; S; room 17

Woodruff, Wm
  Cheyenne; 1880 Oct 20; Wednesday; S; room 12

Woods, D S
  Canfield; 1880 Mar 12; Friday; D; room 15
  Canfield; 1880 Mar 27; Saturday; D; room 15
  Canfield; 1880 Apr 30; Friday; S; room 21
  Canfield; 1880 May 17; Monday; S; room 17
  Canfield; 1880 June 7; Monday; S; room 14
  Canfield; 1880 June 9; Wednesday; S; room 20
  Canfield; 1880 June 24; Thursday; D
  Michigan; 1880 June 30; Wednesday; S; room 17
  Canfield; 1880 July 22; Thursday; S; room 2

Woods, Miss
  Cincinnati; 1880 July 31; Saturday; S

Woods, Wm
  Cincinnati; 1880 July 31; Saturday; S

Woods, Wm H
  Caribou; 1880 Apr 17; Saturday; D; room 17
  Caribou; 1880 May 28; Friday; S; room 16

Woods, Wm H (cont.)
Caribou; 1880 July 31; Saturday; S
Caribou; 1880 Aug 2; Monday; S; room 5
Caribou; 1880 Aug 4; Wednesday; D; room 11
Caribou; 1880 Nov 15; Monday; D; room 17

Woolfenden, J M
& Wife; Nederland; 1880 Sept 25; Saturday; S; room 14

Woolley, H F
Salina, Kan; 1880 July 7; Wednesday; D; room 44

Workman, S I
Phila, Pa; 1880 July 28; Wednesday; D; room 35

Worthington, F T
Denver; 1880 Apr 20; Tuesday; S; room 1

Wray, Jas
Golden; 1880 May 15; Saturday; S

Write, G B
Denver; 1880 Sept 21; Tuesday; S; room 28

Wughl, Frank
New York; 1880 Sept 7; Tuesday; D; room 14

Wyman, Geo
1880 May 26; Wednesday; D
Wife & Child; Longmont; 1880 Aug 3; Tuesday; D

Wyman, George
Longmont; 1880 July 10; Saturday; D

Y

Yancy, J W
Leavenworth, Kans; 1880 June 29; Tuesday; D

Yardun, J W
1880 Oct 23; Saturday

Yarl & Lister
1880 Aug 3; Tuesday; B; room 8

Yates, Alfred
County Court Jury
1880 Mar 11; Thursday; S

Yates, Doc
Sugar Loaf; 1880 May 10; Monday; S

Yerkes, Chas S
New York; 1880 Sept 1; Wednesday; S; room 3

Yost, S M (Mrs)
N York; 1880 July 6; Tues; D; rm 11

Young, A E (Mrs)
Battle Creek, Mich; 1880 Sept 13; Monday; S; room 12

Young, D R
Nobles Company, New York; 1880 Oct 23; Saturday; D; room 34

Young, J W
Leavenworth, KS; 1880 Mar 12; Friday; D; room 6

Young, Mrs
Returned; 1880 Sept 4; Saturday; S

Young, O M
Maysville, MO; 1880 Mar 22; Monday; S; room 12

Z

Zang, P
Denver, Col; 1880 Nov 11; Thursday;
S; room 6

Zehring, L A
Toledo; 1880 July 1; Thursday; S;
room 3

Zorgu, James
Chicago; 1880 Oct 21; Thursday; S;
room 2

Index

This index includes the names of businesses and people who were mentioned within another guest's listing.

Order Form

Other books available from Iron Gate Publishing. Our books are available online to institutions through Lightning Source, and to individuals on our website:

www.irongate.com

Set Yourself Up to Self-Publish: A Genealogist's Guide
     ISBN 978-1-879579-99-6 $19.95 + $5.00 S&H

Publish Your Genealogy: A Step-by-Step Guide for Preserving Your Research for the Next Generation
     ISBN 978-1-879579-62-0 $24.95 + $5.00 S&H

Publish Your Family History: A Step-by-Step Guide to Writing the Stories of Your Ancestors
     ISBN 978-1-879579-63-7 $24.95 + $5.00 S&H

Publish a Local History: A Step-by-Step Guide from Finding the Right Project to Finished Book
     ISBN 978-1-879579-64-4 $24.95 + $5.00 S&H

Publish a Memoir: A Step-by-Step Guide to Saving Your Memories for Future Generations
     ISBN 978-1-879579-65-1 $24.95 + $5.00 S&H

Publish a Biography: A Step-by-Step Guide to Capturing the Life and Times of an Ancestor or a Generation
     ISBN 978-1-879579-66-8 $24.95 + $5.00 S&H

Publish a Photo Book: A Step-by-Step Guide for Transforming Your Genealogical Research into a Stunning Family Heirloom
     ISBN 978-1-879579-67-5 $24.95 + $5.00 S&H

Publish a Source Index: A Step-by-Step Guide to Creating a Genealogically Useful Index, Abstract or Transcription
     ISBN 978-1-879579-68-2 $24.95 + $5.00 S&H

Publish Your Specialty: A Step-by-Step Guide for Imparting Your Research Expertise to Others
     ISBN 978-1-879579-76-7 $24.95 + $5.00 S&H

www.ingramcontent.com/pod-product-compliance
Lightning Source LLC
Chambersburg PA
CBHW071225290326
41931CB00037B/1972